RENAISSANCE DRAMA ON THE EDGE

Renaissance Drama on the Edge

LISA HOPKINS
Sheffield Hallam University, UK

Routledge
Taylor & Francis Group

LONDON AND NEW YORK

First published 2014 by Ashgate Publishing

Published 2016 by Routledge
2 Park Square, Milton Park, Abingdon, Oxfordshire OX14 4RN
711 Third Avenue, New York, NY 10017, USA

First issued in paperback 2016

Routledge is an imprint of the Taylor & Francis Group, an informa business

British Library Cataloguing in Publication Data
A catalogue record for this book is available from the British Library

The Library of Congress has cataloged the printed edition as follows:
Hopkins, Lisa, 1962–
  Renaissance Drama on the Edge / by Lisa Hopkins.
    pages cm
  Includes index.
  ISBN 978-1-4094-3819-9 (hardcover : alk. paper)
  1. English drama—Early modern and Elizabethan, 1500–1600—History and criticism.
I. Title.
  PR651.H67 2014
  822'.309—dc23

                                                                            2013043322

ISBN 13: 978-1-138-27143-2 (pbk)
ISBN 13: 978-1-4094-3819-9 (hbk)

Contents

Acknowledgements

With thanks to Adam Hansen for organising the conference on 'Early Modern Dis/Locations' at the University of Northumbria, at which the earliest version of chapter eight was first delivered, and at which I met John Mabbett who in turn was kind enough to give me an introduction to Nick Hodgson of Tyne & Wear Archives & Museums, who gave invaluable help on antiquarian writing on Hadrian's Wall; to Oddvar Holmesland of the University of Agder for inviting me to the first Norwegian National Conference on Early Modern Studies to give a paper which eventually became Chapter 6, and to my colleague the Rev. Dr Richard Walton for help with the rivers of Paradise section of that; to Veronica Popescu, Odette Blomenfeld and Julia Milica of the University of Iasi, Romania for inviting me to the conference on 'Wounded Bodies, Wounded Minds' which prompted me to write Chapter 7; to Rory Loughnane and Edel Semple for their invitation to Dublin to give the paper which eventually turned into Chapter 3; to Laura Gallagher and Victoria Brownlee for their invitation to the Biblical Women conference in Belfast, out of which Chapter 4 grew; to the staff of the Adsetts library; to Jerry Sokol for help with jewels; to my former PhD student Andy Duxfield for an extremely helpful suggestion about *The Tempest*; and to my colleague Matt Steggle, who read the final draft and saved me from myself as far as I would let him, as did Ashgate's anonymous reader. Matt, my other Renaissance colleague Annaliese Connolly and my former colleague Tom Rutter were as always all hugely helpful. Finally, as always, thanks to Chris and Sam.

An earlier version of part of Chapter 4 appeared as 'St Helena of Britain in the Land of the Magdalene: *All's Well That Ends Well*', in *Biblical Women in Early Modern Literary Culture*, edited by Victoria Brownlee and Laura Gallagher (Manchester: Manchester University Press, 2014); an earlier version of chapter seven as 'Beautiful Scars: Jewels in English Renaissance Drama', *Linguaculture* 3.1 (2013); and an earlier version of chapter eight in *Philological Quarterly* 89.4 (Fall 2010). Chapter three shares a common ancestry and a small amount of material with 'Marrying the Dead', in *Staged Transgression in Shakespeare's England*, edited by Edel Semple and Rory Loughnane (Palgrave Macmillan, 2013).

Introduction

What does it mean to be on the edge? It means to be in a state of perilous uncertainty, anxious to know but not sure whether not knowing might be preferable to what you eventually find out. It means to be poised between two distinct and potentially quite different states of knowing or of being, or to be in a liminal position between two different countries, or perhaps two different time periods, in the sense that Twelfth Night is the liminal time between the holiday period of the twelve days of Christmas and the normal world of work. It means to walk on the wall which demarcates the space of the city from that of the territory outside it, which might be merely the surrounding countryside or might be something more savage than that, or to walk on the cliff and know that there is nothing at all beyond. It means the boiling point or melting point or tipping point at which something moves or changes into something else. It means the farthest place on the map, though with the proviso that this world itself may share an edge with another one beyond. And it means the places at which the play ceases to be just a play and leaches out into the playhouse to touch on the experience and concerns of the audience.

In a theatre which probes a number of different issues, the two last of those edges – the edge of the map and the edge of the play – have perhaps the most obvious cutting power, particularly in combination. By this I mean that in a country physically and emotionally scarred by the better part of a century of religious controversy and conflict, any plot, issue or language that bore on the vexed questions of faith, choice of confession and possible routes to salvation was bound to generate an interest that spread beyond the play itself to reverberate in the auditorium, while the fact that Shakespeare and his audiences were themselves on the edge between the reign of the 'Welsh' Elizabeth and the Scottish James inevitably focused attention on the relationship between England and other parts of the British Isles. This concern with the interface between geographical and spiritual edges was my primary focus a few years ago in *Shakespeare on the Edge*, and to a certain extent continues to be so here.[1] Now, however, I also explore the potential of some other edges which may intersect with the edge between the stage and the world beyond it. In *Richard III*, Queen Elizabeth says, 'I see, as in a map, the end of all',[2] as if maps could show not just the physical world but also human destiny. In *Shakespeare on the Edge*, I suggested that there was a profound imagined connection between physical and spiritual edges, and I examined Shakespeare's representations of the borders of England and the extent to which eschatological overtones were implicit in those representations. In this book, I return to that idea but expand its parameters both in terms of looking beyond England and also in terms of the fact that I explore not only geographical borders but also the intersection of the material and the spiritual more generally, tracing the contours of the edge which each inhabits, and I look too at authors other than

Shakespeare. I also suggest that an edge may represent something other than itself, that it may as it were be itself an edge between what it is and what it is analogous to, and that it may well be productive to pay particular attention to an edge's adjacencies, that is the areas with which it shares contiguities and borderlands, because all the edges I consider are, I argue, permeable and hence function less as barriers against those adjacencies than as potential sites of bleed to and from them. Moreover, in line with Sharon Emmerichs's identification of 'an early modern vision of community that recognizes a desire to eliminate certain boundaries while demonstrating the absolute necessity for those boundaries' existence', there is in the texts which I examine both a fear that edges might be unstable, permeable and open to the possibility of cross-border traffic and also a recognition that they need to be so,[3] for their adjacencies are ones which must be acknowledged and there must be at least a possibility of a contact zone.

The eight chapters of this book focus on walls, the relationship between secular and spiritual power, cross-border sexual relations, Shakespeare's representation of the borders of France, the link between this world and the next, jewels and places associated with the idea of the numinous, specifically ruins and high places, such as cliffs. Some of these are easily and obviously readable within the paradigm of the edge: walls clearly demarcate the territory owned by one individual or community from that outside it; cliffs mark the edge between the land and the sea; the divide between this world and the next was at times envisaged in terms of a physical frontier with possible crossing places; and three of the chapters focus on actual national borders. Sometimes identity as an edge may seem less clear, but I suggest that the relationship between secular and spiritual potentates can fruitfully be understood as analogous to that between rulers of two different territories, and in the case of what may seem an even less likely topic for such a book, jewels, I shall argue that to an early modern audience these served not only for ornament but as potential conduit between the inside and the outside of the body, positioning the skin itself as an edge.

The two chapters of Part I, 'What is an Edge?', explore two extremes of the term 'edge' itself. The first chapter looks at walls, the most obvious, visible and concrete demarcators of space and territory, and examines two particular sorts of walls, those around private households and those around cities. The second chapter is on something which is not visible at all, which is the purely conceptual edge between secular and spiritual power, two spheres of influence which I read as emblematised and personified in the figures of St Peter, who represented the supposedly God-given authority of the church, and of St Paul, who had advocated obedience to established secular power. On the face of it, the solid edge of a wall and the intangible edge between two kinds of power are completely different from each other, and push the idea of the edge to the very limits of what it will bear. In fact, there are notable common features in the way in which each of these edges functions, for despite the materiality of the first and the immateriality of the second, neither can actually keep separate the things which they might be supposed to divide. The principal difference between them is the way in which they fail to do this: walls are battered, breached or pierced by gates, while the cross-border traffic between the realm of the spiritual and the realm of the secular is ideological rather than physical, with secular power attempting to bolster itself by invoking and aping the spiritual, and the conception of spiritual power being conditioned by the template afforded by the secular. Taken together, these two chapters reveal the flexibility and scope of the edge as an analytic for probing the energies and concerns of early modern English culture as represented in its drama, not least because to think in terms of the edge requires us to attend not only to what something is but also to what it is *not*, the thing which it attempts to define itself in opposition to but with which by that very token it shares an edge, creating an adjacency which may speak of similarity and of an implicit potential for overlap.

The bulk of the book, which comprises Parts II and II, draws on and develops Part I's division of edges into the more or less material and the more or less immaterial, while continuing to argue that there are strong and suggestive similarities between the two categories which have much to offer to an attempt to trace the contours and edges of the early modern English imaginary. Part II, 'The Edge of the Nation', builds to some extent on my argument in *Shakespeare on the Edge* that the borders of nations carry a spiritual as well as a geographical charge. The first chapter in Part II, 'Sex on the Edge', also revisits *Shakespeare on the Edge* in that it considers the borders of England with Scotland and with Wales, but this time I pay attention specifically to the question of cross-border relationships and show how the prevalence of these destabilises any notion of distinct and securely separate nations. The other two chapters of Part II both focus on plays set on or near the borders of France, with Chapter 4 looking at the southern edge of the country and Chapter 5 at the northern, but suggest that in both cases, edges, however firmly marked on a map, tremble and blur under the pressure of the plays' plots and intertextualities, as the ostensible contours of France insistently point us to consider questions related to England. The edges of France are also called on to figure the idea of personal rather than national boundaries, as the plays suggest subtle interconnections between their characters and their settings, and in particular force an implicit equation between personal control and the sense of strongly defined national borders. All the chapters in Part II thus riddle the distinction between personal and national, so the section as a whole builds on and develops the suggestions in Part II that the edge is a point of contact as much as of demarcation, that ideas may have borders just as countries do and that if we want to understand these ideas we need to look not only at them but also at where those borders are and what they are shared with.

Part III, 'Invisible Edges', examines a group of edges which cannot be seen and might indeed be thought not even necessarily to exist, but which are, I suggest, nevertheless as charged as any more tangible ones and equally able to reveal adjacencies and zones of traffic and exchange. The first chapter in Part III, 'The Edge of Heaven', explores the persistence of the idea that certain places on the map might offer points of access to another world and suggests that Shakespeare in particular draws on this, not so much to sign up to it as to exploit its potential both for activating ideas and associations which were politically difficult to mobilise by more direct means, and also for maximising the emotional and symbolic range of the romance mode in particular. The next chapter, 'Jewels and the Edge of the Skin', focuses on the surprising credence afforded to the possibility of cross-border contact of a different but equally metaphysical sort, in the shape of the belief that jewels had quasi-magical properties which could both act directly on the body and the mind and also be acted upon by them, in ways which posit the skin not as a barrier between that which is inside the body and that which is outside but as a permeable contact zone in which the two can interact. In the same way that the idea of the personal was used to destabilise that of the national in Part II, here the idea of the personal is itself destabilised, and something of the same idea is also present in the last chapter, which examines how ruins, often considered a distinct subgroup of physical spaces which shared an edge with the numinous, lent themselves to a reciprocal trope in which ruined buildings and ruined bodies stand in for each other. Collectively, these three chapters build up an idea of the early modern self which posits it as sharing edges with forces beyond and outside itself and as conditioned by the immaterial as much as by the material.

All these borders and edges, I shall argue, were inherently unstable and permeable, not least because a shared feature of many of them was an origin in or an association with the vanished world of the Roman Empire, so that they inevitably spoke of loss and change over time. Reminders of an implicitly dual time frame are frequent, as in *Cymbeline* in which the daughter of an ancient British king rubs shoulders with the marquis of Siena's brother, or *Coriolanus*, a play about an ancient Roman which has an obviously topical application, and each of the edges which I examine reveals an adjacency with the classical past as well as with contemporary concerns, often in ways which condition our perception of those contemporary adjacencies. From an English perspective, the most famous and iconic wall was that which we now know as Hadrian's, which had been built by the Romans, and the most natural and readily occurring symbols of the twin poles of spiritual and secular power were St Peter, founder of the See of Rome, and St Paul, whose advocacy of acknowledging the power of temporal rule had figured that rule as Caesarian. To evoke the paradigm of Roman authority was also, however, to acknowledge the extent to which it had changed over time: the Pope no longer held unchallenged sway over all the lands of western Christendom, and the question which had once seemed settled by the so-called Donation of Constantine was once again open for debate. A number of my chapters are informed by the changes to classical power and authority. Chapter 3 focuses on a number of traditional demarcations between countries and continents traceable back to classical geography as they are explored in a number of texts including the Roman play *Cymbeline* and some which inhabit the vicinity of Hadrian's Wall, and it argues that such border markers are actually revealed as little more than notional in that they prove no bar to the formation of cross-border sexual relations. France too, which like England had a ruling dynasty that claimed descent from princes of Troy, was haunted by memories of classical geography and might still be understood in terms of the three parts into which Caesar had so famously divided it, and I shall be arguing that in Shakespeare's French-set plays, any discussion of the borders of France fundamentally undoes itself by proving equally susceptible of being read as actually about England. The idea of possible crossing points between this world and the next was even more firmly rooted in classical ideas of geography, and this was the edge which was inevitably liable to prove the most intangible and unstable. Even jewels can usefully be situated within a classically authorised schema: in keeping with the general ethos of the Renaissance, jewellery design aimed to recreate classical originals, yet since no fully intact classical pieces survived, the elaborate pieces beloved of so many Renaissance rulers served to remind them of what they did not have as much as of what they did, and jewels themselves, liminally positioned on the surface of the body and supposedly possessed of power to influence its workings, could be read as indicating lack or aberrance inside it. Finally, ruins which were Roman or understood as being so and outstanding geographical features which often had still-remembered Latin names marked possible points of contact with the numinous but also recalled the religious uncertainty which troubled and destabilised ideas about the world beyond and the possibility of contact with it. All these edges thus trembled and blurred to the view, threatening to disintegrate even as they were looked at and forcing a double perspective in which the image of the present was shadowed and troubled by that other picture of the past constantly flickering at its edge.

Permeability, then, is the keynote of the edges I discuss. The first chapter of the book examines the idea of the wall, the quintessential liminal structure. Militarily, walls had always been both significant and symbolic; domestically, the garden wall was becoming an increasingly important feature of grander houses. In this chapter, I couple instances of both these uses, first by examining the strangely and subversively domesticated walls of Shakespeare's *Coriolanus* and then by turning to Marlowe's more militarised use of walls. Ostensibly these two understandings of walls are quite different from and indeed opposite to each other, but in fact each proves to contain within itself the seeds of the other, revealing walls as liminal not only physically but also ideationally, incorporating and representing antithesis. If walls are the most visible of the edges I look at, in the next chapter I turn to the least so, the intangible and potentially highly mobile interface between secular and spiritual power, as emblematised in the significantly different figures of St Peter and St Paul. In Ford's *'Tis Pity She's a Whore*, as I discuss in the third chapter, this boundary asserts itself like a force field between the terrain of the civic authorities and the terrain of the Cardinal, but Shakespeare, characteristically enough, approaches it very differently and far more ambiguously, so that here too elements of one realm leach and bleed into the other.

In the third chapter, I talk about seven plays, one masque and one poem by six different authors which focus on a variety of edges and borders: Shakespeare's *A Midsummer Night's Dream* and *Cymbeline*, Greene's *James IV*, Ford's *Perkin Warbeck* and *'Tis Pity She's a Whore* and Marlowe's *Edward II* are the plays; Milton's *Comus* is the masque; and Marlowe's *Hero and Leander* is the poem. The edges and borders, meanwhile, include ones as diverse as those between city and surrounding country, between England and Wales, England and Scotland, secular and spiritual jurisdictions, and Europe and Asia, yet despite very significant differences of genre, date, authorship and setting, in all of these texts the edge is similarly marked as more honoured in the breach than the observance, above all in its status as a locus of sexual transgression.

In the fourth and fifth chapters, I focus specifically on France, but not on France as we now know it, for its borders were very different from those which we would now recognise and were continuing to shift. Shakespeare shows great interest in those unstable edges in plays as diverse as *All's Well That Ends Well, As You Like It, Love's Labour's Lost, Henry V*, the three parts of *Henry VI*, and *Edward III*. I argue that across this body of plays, two clear and linked ideas emerge, both of which work to destabilise the idea of the border by troping it as something other than itself: first, that the borders of France offer a way of talking about the borders of England in a way that ultimately softens the blow of England's loss of France by emphasising the 'rightness' and 'naturalness' of being bounded within an island, and second, that national borders provide a powerful mechanism for troping personal ones. In the second of the two chapters I also pay attention to a less material and more eschatologically charged edge, that between this world and the next, which I suggest is evoked by the fact that the story of Helena in *All's Well That Ends Well* may invite us to recall that of St Helena, the mother of Constantine, a figure who in Shakespeare's age was connected to a number of important issues about choice of confession and the relative roles and powers of the spiritual and secular authorities.

Saints more generally are the concern of the sixth chapter, specifically the fact that for Shakespeare saints cluster at the fringes of Britain, primarily the Celtic west. Saints disturb the edge between life and death – Derek Krueger notes that 'The bodies of the saints differed from those of ordinary people, for they maintained a connection to their holy souls, even after death, and in many cases they remained uncorrupted'[4]– and between natural and supernatural, so it is not surprising that their preferred habitat should be the edges of the map. Given that I am claiming that the emphasis on the Celtic fringe is eschatologically charged, it is strangely fitting that Shakespeare's interest in Celtic saints should be a phenomenon primarily observable in his last plays, though it is also found in another play which directly figures the border between life and death as a geographical one, *Hamlet*. Each of these plays, I suggest, has something of the quality of a reliquary: although like a reliquary they contain extraneous and apparently unrelated decorative and allegorical matter, each has at its heart the metaphorical fragment of a saint, albeit in the shape of a narrative echo rather than a physical object, and like a reliquary each carries the suggestion of a potential way to heaven. Finally, I suggest that an additional common element in these plays is a pervasive interest in that ultimate symbol of permeability, water, and that watery borders were often seen as particularly charged and energised ones, to which overtones of the spiritual and the supernatural tended to accrue.

Chapter 7 turns to the question of the objects so often used to adorn reliquaries, jewels. Gemstones were spoken of as originating from one or other of the four rivers of Paradise, and Martina Bagnoli notes that 'one specific aspect of the symbolism of gems that was important in the creation of reliquaries was their association with saints, a common theme in exegetical literature', since 'precious metals were incorruptible, … like the flesh of the saints'.[5] However, implicit in Renaissance ideas of how jewels are formed and what powers they have is a sense that they can function not only as signs of wealth but also as signs of pain and deficiency. Drawing on texts from Marlowe to Ford by way of Shakespeare and Webster, I argue that jewels in English Renaissance drama function not only as adornments, but also as beautiful scars, marking sites of loss and lack, and positioning the skin itself as a permeable edge, a zone of potential contact between what lies inside the body and what lies outside it.

The final chapter discusses two sorts of places which on the English Renaissance stage appear to be associated with the divine, ruins and high places. If jewels mark the scar of loss and lack on the body, ruins mark it on the land. To a certain extent all sacred sites could potentially be a gateway to the world of the dead: in *The Winter's Tale* Mamilius reaches automatically for a churchyard setting for a winter's tale,[6] and in *The Atheist's Tragedy* the appearance of the supposedly dead Charlemont in the vicinity of his grave induces utter panic as he is immediately taken to be a ghost. *Hamlet* is characteristically more subtle in this respect, but here too a graveyard proves a place of heightened memory and emotional alertness as Hamlet both mourns Yorick and is able for the first time in the play to admit his love for Ophelia. In a ruin, though, the door to death gapes even wider than in a graveyard, and so does the door to the past, for ruins in Renaissance drama may also be places where the living meet the dead. This was particularly true of two sorts of ruins, prehistoric megaliths and religious houses which had been dissolved at the Reformation. Megaliths in particular were associated with the earliest inhabitants of Britain, and so too were high places, and the final section of the chapter suggests that both for Shakespeare and also for some other dramatists a particular resonance and aura of the numinous appears to have attached to cliffs and high places too, and that they, like ruins, could be contact zones between this world and the next.

Overall, then, this book traces the idea of the edge as it is manifested in a variety of contexts, locations and texts, and in doing so it is perforce eclectic, touching on elements of cultural geography, of British/archipelagic studies and also having something in common with what has been described as 'the turn to religion' in studies of the period.[7] My fundamental question is what cultural work the plays I discuss are undertaking. This does not entail an indifference to their aesthetic qualities, because plays which engage and enchant their audiences are far more effective in embedding ideas in the cultural imaginary, but cruder works may still reveal the contours and adjacencies of particular fears and concerns, and indeed may sometimes do so in brighter and bolder colours than subtler and more complex ones, so I have ranged across non-canonical works as well as canonical ones. Individually and collectively, what all these plays reveal is the evocative and associative potential of the idea of the edge. Discussing relics, on which I touch in the penultimate chapter, Derek Krueger argues that 'at the center of the practices [involving them] lay a basic confidence that matter – fragments of bodies, oil, water, even bits of stone and dust – could contain and convey spiritual power'.[8] The fact that some royalists preserved relics of Charles I indicates that the concept never really went away and suggests that despite the undoubted impact of successive and substantial advances in knowledge and changes in doctrine, the edge between the material and the spiritual continued to be conceived of as energised at least in metaphorical and at times even in actual terms. It could take many forms, but it was always a place of power, and it could always potentially be crossed, in ways that I shall now go on to explore.

Notes

[1]   See Lisa Hopkins, *Shakespeare on the Edge: Border-crossing in the Tragedies and the Henriad* (Burlington: Ashgate, 2005).

[2]   William Shakespeare, *Richard III*, edited by E.A.J. Honigmann (Harmondsworth: Penguin, 1968), 2.4.54.

[3]   Sharon Emmerichs, 'Shakespeare and the Landscape of Death: Crossing the Boundaries of Life and the Afterlife', *Shakespeare* 8.2 (June 2012), p. 173.

[4]   Derek Krueger, 'The Religion of Relics in Late Antiquity and Byzantium', in *Treasures of Heaven: Saints, Relics, and Devotion in Medieval Europe*, edited by Martina Bagnoli, Holger A. Klein, C. Griffith Mann, and James Robinson (London: The British Museum Press, 2011), p. 5.

[5]   Martina Bagnoli, 'The Stuff of Heaven: Materials and Craftsmanship in Medieval Reliquaries', in *Treasures of Heaven: Saints, Relics, and Devotion in Medieval Europe*, edited by Martina Bagnoli, Holger A. Klein, C. Griffith Mann, and James Robinson (London: The British Museum Press, 2011), pp. 138 and 128.

[6]   William Shakespeare, *The Winter's Tale*, edited by J.H. Pafford (London: Methuen, 1963), 2.1.25–30.

[7]   Ken Jackson and Arthur F. Marotti, 'The Turn to Religion in Early Modern English Studies', Criticism 46.1 (2004), pp. 167–90.

[8]   Krueger, 'The Religion of Relics in Late Antiquity and Byzantium', p. 5.

PART I
What is an Edge?

Chapter 1
Walls:
The Edge of Territory

Walls are quintessentially liminal, both literally, in that they mark the boundary between one sort of territory or property and another, and metaphorically, in that they are themselves inherently susceptible to uncertainty about whether they are keeping things in or keeping things out. Militarily, they had of course always been significant, and also symbolic. The walls of the castle built by Edward I at Caernarfon were designed by his architect Master James of St George to evoke those of Constantinople and thus to speak of imperial power and the transmission of cultural heritage from classical Rome; the wall of Flint Castle from which Richard II descends in the play named after him becomes an emblem of both the rank which he is about to forfeit and the power which is about to be taken from him. Domestically, the garden wall was becoming an increasingly important feature of grander houses, not least because of what Roy Strong calls Inigo Jones's 'most enduring and delightful innovation, the garden gate'.[1] Walls of castles might seem to be built primarily for defence and walls of gardens primarily for reasons of status, but elements of the function of their opposites here bleed into each of them, in ways which serve to make the wall as a category seem oddly permeable. In this chapter, I want to show this first by examining the strangely and subversively domesticated walls of Shakespeare's *Coriolanus* and then by turning to Marlowe's more openly militarised and yet also ultimately psychologised use of the idea of the wall, particularly in two plays which are not Roman but are nevertheless conditioned by and responding to ideas of *Romanitas*, the two parts of *Tamburlaine the Great*.

The pairing of these two ostensibly very different treatments of walls may seem an odd one, not least because the *Tamburlaine* plays, as I have already noted, are not Roman plays. However, I have argued elsewhere that there are a number of intersections between the figure of Tamburlaine and the figure of Julius Caesar,[2] and Tamburlaine and Coriolanus also have much in common: both are dedicated and ruthless killers and both valorise their personal identities at the expense of any national or territorial loyalties, but both also prove surprisingly susceptible to the wishes of a woman, even if it is his mother who influences Coriolanus and his wife who influences Tamburlaine. Most notably, both are associated with the destabilising and undoing of edges and boundaries. This may seem counter-intuitive, because Coriolanus is a hero whose life is defined and structured by two opposing cities and the walls which demarcate them as separate, while Tamburlaine acquires if anything something of an association with the idea of protecting and marking boundaries.[3] Nevertheless, Coriolanus proves to be insistently associated both intradiegetically and, I argue, extradiegetically with systematic inversion of the boundaries marked by walls, and situating the *Tamburlaine* plays within the context of Marlowe's treatment of the topic across his *oeuvre* reveals the associations of fragility and permeability which habitually accrue to his representations of walls. Collectively, these two heroes mount a two-pronged attack on the concept of the wall, with *Coriolanus* riddling the distinction between domestic and military and the *Tamburlaine* plays troubling that between the boundary of the city and the boundary of the self, and by implication that between the physical and the psychological more generally. Coriolanus and Tamburlaine are two heroes who metaphorically erect walls in front of their own psyches in that both strive (with considerable success) to appear invulnerable, but to read them in terms of the ways their respective plays interact with the idea of actual walls paradoxically offers us a way to glimpse behind these psychic walls at the same time as it affords a perspective on the more general dynamics of the demarcation between the relationships of individual to household and of household to state.

Coriolanus: The Walls of Rome and the Walls of Home

The walls of Rome, the building of which had led its founder Romulus to kill his twin brother Remus, were particularly iconic; thus Warren Chernaik notes that 'In Livy and in Plutarch, the story of Coriolanus includes at the beginning an incident omitted by Shakespeare: the physical withdrawal of a large number of plebeians to the Sacred Mount, outside Rome, complaining "that the rich men had driven them out of the cittie"'.[4] The walls divided the living from the dead and what was Roman from what was not Roman; however *Romanitas* was always inherently double, as the myth of the city's foundation by twins attests and as *Coriolanus* itself powerfully registers, and there are, I think, strong reasons why Shakespeare would not want to evoke so clear a demarcation as existed in his sources between Roman and non-Roman space. The walls of Rome are certainly important in *Coriolanus*, but perhaps not in ways we would expect, for *Coriolanus* is an oddity. It is a Roman play, but has no obvious political agenda: as James Kuzner observes, 'Advancing a prorepublican reading of *Coriolanus* … is quite difficult to do',[5] but one that supports the opposite position is equally hard to sustain. Coriolanus himself is a Roman, but also a refuser of Rome: the character of Volumnia means that he personally embodies the myth of mothering by the she-wolf, but his image of the gosling refuses that of the geese who saved the city. The play is a tragedy, but it has no soliloquy. Moreover, some of the speeches its hero does make strike a distinctly odd note. Take for instance his apparently defiant declaration,

> Let them pull all about mine ears, present me
> Death on the wheel or at wild horses' heels,
> Or pile ten hills on the Tarpeian rock,
> That the precipitation might down stretch
> Below the beam of sight, yet will I still
> Be thus to them.[6]

Coriolanus here echoes Hamlet in the reference to piling hills upon each other and the Dover cliff scene of *King Lear* in the idea of something stretching beyond sight, but he prefaces the whole with the ludicrous and transparently petulant 'Let them pull all about mine ears'. Even more striking is his wish that 'All the contagion of the south light on you, / You shames of Rome! You herd of – Boils and plagues / Plaster you o'er' (1.4.30–33), for here he closely anticipates Caliban:

> As wicked dew as ere my mother brushed
> With raven's feather from unwholesome fen
> Drop on you both. A southwest blow on ye
> And blister you all o'er.[7]

'Plaster you o'er', 'blister you all o'er' – there is nothing to choose here between the Roman military machine and the island-bred savage. Later in the same speech, Coriolanus hopes that the Roman soldiers will 'infect one another' (34) and says that they have 'run / From slaves that apes would beat' (36–7); Caliban wishes that 'All the infections that the sun sucks up' (2.2.1) may fall on Prospero and complains that his master's spirits chase him 'Sometime like apes that mow and chatter at me' (2.2.9), so that he is in his own person a slave whom apes beat. Given the extent to which Coriolanus thus anticipates Caliban, it would certainly seem difficult to read this sulky curser as a tragic hero.

A paradigm into which *Coriolanus* may well seem to fit more comfortably is that of the soldier with no war to fight. This is a figure which cuts across generic demarcations: Shakespeare is interested in the disruption caused by men in this category in plays as diverse as *Much Ado About Nothing*, *Othello* and *Titus Andronicus*. Here too though *Coriolanus* is an oddity. In *Much Ado*, *Othello* and *Titus*, the temporary absence of an external threat allows soldiers to remain at home, where their actions cruelly expose and ultimately destroy the fragility of the domestic balance which their military efforts have been dedicated to defending. The situation in *Coriolanus* is different in two crucial respects.

In the first place, it is unclear that Rome at the stage at which Shakespeare depicts it actually faces any consistent or meaningful external threat any more. Certainly there are skirmishes with the Volsces, but all the indications are that they are easily beaten off before Coriolanus joins and strengthens them. Moreover, although the Ralph Fiennes film refers to the tensions between the Romans and the Volsces as an 'ancient border dispute', there is no clear indication of what demarcates or differentiates one territory from the other, and it is in fact abundantly clear that the Volsces are in any case already on the verge of being subsumed into the Roman Empire. This is a play of inversion and destabilisation: Coriolanus may regard himself as being in his own person an edge, but the language in which he expresses this belief undoes itself as he threatens, 'He that retires, I'll take him for a Volsce, / And he shall feel mine edge' (1.4.28–9), suggesting the radical instability of the very distinction between Romans and non-Romans which is crucial to his cause and indeed at this stage to his *raison d'être*. Aufidius may call him 'most absolute sir' (4.3.159), but the more appropriate term for him would in fact be 'relative'; it is only the consuls of the people who may deploy an 'absolute "shall"' (3.1.90) and draw absolute borderlines, as when Brutus says 'It will be dangerous to go on. No further' (3.1.26). Coriolanus himself inhabits a world of dizzying inversion in which nothing is what it seems:

> I would they were barbarians, as they are,
> Though in Rome littered; not Romans, as they are not,
> Though calved i'th'porch o'th'Capitol.
>
> (3.1.237–9)

Here boundaries of both nation and species are called into question as words more normally associated with animals – 'littered', 'calved' – are applied to humans and as location proves to provide no secure guarantee of identity. At the end of his time in Rome, Coriolanus finds indeed that inversion is all he has to fall back on as he seeks to turn the tables on his opponents by declaring, 'I banish you' (3.3.123).

Nor are these the only signs of dislocation and of lack of demarcation and of secure boundaries. Throughout the play, images of reversal and of the monstrous abound. The Third Citizen fears that 'for the multitude to be ingrateful were to make a monster of the multitude' (2.3.9–11), and Coriolanus himself expostulates to the citizens that 'He that trusts to you, / Where he should find you lions, finds you hares; / Where foxes, geese' (1.1.168–70), presumably with reference to the board game Fox and Geese, popular since mediaeval times, in which one player is given only one piece, known as the fox, while the other has seventeen which are the geese, and which would be reduced to an absurdity if the player with the fox tried to make it function as one of the geese. The image of geese recurs when he castigates his soldiers:

>   You souls of geese
>   That bear the shapes of men, how have you run
>   From slaves that apes would beat! Pluto and hell!
>   All hurt behind!
>
> (1.4.34–8)

Here what should be before is behind, but Coriolanus' remedy for this situation also produces inversion as the gate closes behind him and he is shut alone into the city, while Menenius says to Sicinius and Brutus 'You talk of pride. O that you could turn your eyes toward the napes of your necks, and make but an interior survey of your good selves!' (2.1.36–8). This time, what should be inside is outside, but on other occasions, what should be inside extrudes into the outside: Cominius attributes Coriolanus' inability to remember the name of his benefactor in Antium to the fact that 'The blood upon your visage dries, 'tis time / It should be looked to' (2.9.92–3). In a society whose rulers trope its political system through a fable of the proper working of the body, the shedding of blood – the movement of a fluid normally contained inside the body to the space outside the body – must surely equate to disorder, and though Volumnia may rejoice that there will be 'large cicatrices to show the people' (2.1.142) the resulting scars are figured as monstrous when Menenius declares that 'Every gash was an enemy's grave' (2.1.149–50). In all these instances, edges and boundaries thus prove unstable and permeable, and in the process, the paradigm of the soldier-at-home becomes increasingly inappropriate.

Other boundaries are also crossed and recrossed, not least because the play reminds us that where Rome itself began and ended was itself very much a movable feast. As the title of the film shown at the Roman Army Museum in Northumbria reminds us, Hadrian's Wall, to us more likely to evoke the divide between England and Scotland, was to the Romans the edge of the empire – except, that is, for the brief period when that frontier was marked instead by the more northerly Antonine wall, exposing the extent to which the boundaries of Rome were fundamentally arbitrary and subject to radical change through time. In the case of *Coriolanus*, the Romans and the Volsces already talk the same language, worship the same gods and eat the same food, and both have a political structure involving senators; total assimilation can then hardly be far away, and with it the unification of the Italian peninsula which Shakespeare has already represented in *Julius Caesar* and *Antony and Cleopatra*, so that Aufidius, who says 'I would I were a Roman, for I cannot, / Being a Volsce, be that I am' (1.10.4–5), will soon find his wish come true. But *Coriolanus* also diverges from the paradigm of the soldier-at-home in a second respect, for Coriolanus, unlike Othello, does not in fact cause disruption within his own domestic economy; indeed his relationship with his wife is conducted with the utmost placidity and equanimity. What Coriolanus does is something rather different: having returned from combat to the domestic sphere, he then travels back to the place of war, albeit in a quasi-domestic capacity as guest and dependant of Aufidius, and exposes the vulnerability of his home not on an emotional plane but on a military one.

In doing so, he raises a number of complex questions. In the first place there is the question shared by all the plays which acknowledge the soldier-at-home paradigm: what is the rôle for a soldier out of wartime, and is he doomed to be an inevitably disruptive figure? Shakespeare's interest in discussion of this issue seems pretty certain to have been born from personal and vicarious experience of the actual phenomenon of soldiers returning from the conflicts in France and Holland in the 1590s and from Ireland in the years after the respective returns of the Essex and Mountjoy expeditions. Other issues, however, seem more closely tied to the precise historical moment of *Coriolanus* itself, and they can perhaps be summed up as the question of what is the rôle of a militarised society when the *casus belli* has been removed – or is it, in fact, not the case that it has been removed, because it was never really external in the first place?

In the England in which *Coriolanus* was written, peace had apparently broken out all over. Mountjoy's triumphant return from Ireland in 1603 had effectively brought hostilities there to an end. A peace treaty had been signed with Spain in 1604. And immediately on his accession James had declared that the perpetually troubled counties of the Scottish Border were henceforth to be known as the Middle Shires of Britain and that all trouble would cease immediately. The official picture did not quite reflect the reality, however. It took more than the word of a Stuart to stop Border Reivers reiving, and trouble continued to flare up in the so-called Middle Shires: in 1608, just about the time *Coriolanus* was being written, the Duke of Buccleuch was commended for his Border services, and "in July 1609 a mass hanging ... was held at Dumfries", with [the earl of] Dunbar presiding, and the Chancellor Dunfermline was able to report ... that the Earl "has purgit the Borders of all the chiefest malefactors'".[8] This persistent unruliness in the Borders is something to which Cathy Shrank alludes in pursuit of her agenda that 'when analyzing the politics of *Coriolanus*, we also need to consider more localized contexts': she compares the emphasis on civility and incivility in *Coriolanus* with Thomas Wilson's *Arte of Rhetorique*, which offers 'a portrait of incivility' in the shape of 'a murderous soldier, born and brought up among "a denne of theues," who also happen to live in a distinctly rural, noncivic environment, beyond Puttenham's "civill" frontiers of the River Trent, in "Tindale and Ryddesdale," reiving country in Northumberland'.[9] There was also difficulty at the other end of Scotland, in the domains of two troublesome earls of Orkney and Shetland, firstly Robert Stewart, illegitimate son of James V, and then his son Patrick. As Peter D. Anderson notes in his biography of Patrick,

> In fitting out his great houses, Patrick took a particular interest in artillery weapons. He acquired by confiscation from pirates and "uncouth fishers ... sik collectioun of gret gunnis and uther weapons for weare, as no hous, palice, or castell, yea all in Scotland wer not furneist with the lyke".[10]

The Earl's palace at Birsay incongruously combines gun holes meant for genuinely defensive purposes with oriel windows thought to have been the largest in Scotland at the time of their construction (the date 1607 is said to have been once legible above the doorway, putting the house a year or so before the composition of *Coriolanus*), which were of course totally indefensible. The result was inevitable: 'During the rebellion of Patrick's son, Robert Stewart, it was held unsuccessfully against the earl of Caithness from 27 to 31 August 1614, surrendering when a heavy cannon was drawn up and trained on the oriel windows of the new hall and of the Chapel Tower'.[11]

What we see in the history of Birsay is an uneasy accommodation between defence and domesticity. *Coriolanus* too is steeped in language which brings together the familiar (and indeed the familial) and the warlike in tense juxtaposition. A striking early instance of this comes in First Citizen's riposte to Menenius' attempt to mystify political distinctions and spin a tale of civic harmony by his fable of the body:

> The kingly crownèd head, the arm our soldier,
> Our steed the leg, the tongue our trumpeter,
> With other muniments and petty helps
> In this our fabric ...
>
> (1.1.113–17)

Unlike Menenius' own myth-making, the Citizen's imagery, like the palace at Birsay, reveals a state in which it is impossible to distinguish personal space from the zone of defence: the arm, activating the always latent pun on arms in the sense of 'arms and armour', is a soldier, the leg a horse, the tongue the trumpet that sounds the declaration of war, and the body as a whole the equivalent of a munitions depot. At the same time though it remains the distinct, individualised (and hungry) body of a private person with a home in Rome.

Even as it stresses the blurring between the domestic and the defensive (and potentially offensive), *Coriolanus* also goes to some pains to stress its own contemporary rather than ancient Roman feel: Marion Trousdale observes that 'In addition to wearing a Roman kirtle, Coriolanus it would appear has a beard and wears a hat',[12] and Brutus seems to be thinking of Jacobean rather than Roman buildings when he says,

> Stalls, bulks, windows
> Are smothered up, leads filled, and ridges horsed
> In earnestness to see him.
>
> (2.1.202–205)

I would like to read the play in relation to a particular event which took place at a specific early modern building, Hardwick Hall in Nottinghamshire, home of the legendary 'Bess of Hardwick', Elizabeth, Countess of Shrewsbury. In 1600, the Queen's Men seem to have visited Hardwick, probably acting Shakespeare; Bess's biographer affirms that they played 'in the great hall of Hardwick, with Bess watching from the gallery over the screen'.[13] I wonder whether Hardwick Hall in turn fed into the imaginary of Shakespearean drama, for in 1603, Bess's 'bad son' Henry Cavendish appeared at the gates of Hardwick Hall with forty armed horsemen, with the aim of rescuing his cousin Arbella, Bess's granddaughter, and enabling her to marry the Earl of Hertford's grandson – a politically dangerous manoeuvre since both Arbella herself and Hertford's grandson had potential claims to the throne, Arbella through her father Charles Stuart, younger brother of James VI's father Henry Lord Darnley, and Hertford's grandson because his grandmother was Lady Catherine Grey, sister of Lady Jane Grey. As Mary S. Lovell points out, Arbella received the letter from Henry alerting her to the imminent rescue plan on Shrove Tuesday 1603. 'The following day, Ash Wednesday … was a significant date since [the earl of] Essex had been executed on Ash Wednesday two years earlier. Arbella wrote to Sir Henry Brounker reminding him of Essex', an association which is not inapposite in the context of *Coriolanus* since, as Clifford Chalmers Huffman notes, 'In 1601 Bishop William Barlow, preaching a pro-government sermon from St. Paul's Cross, referred to Coriolanus as "a gallant young, but a discontented Romane, who might make a fit parallel for the late Earle, if you read his life"'.[14] Lovell further observes that 'By suppertime on Ash Wednesday, Bess had received a report that her son Henry had been seen acting suspiciously', though he did not actually arrive at the gates of Hardwick until the Thursday.[15] Hardwick, being notoriously 'more glass than wall', was absolutely indefensible, but nevertheless the projected attack failed dismally when neither Henry nor Arbella proved to have strength of will enough to pass the porter's lodge without Bess's agreement.[16]

The impregnability of Hardwick is all the more impressive when one considers not only its lack of fortifications but the resolute femaleness of its architecture – topped with Bess's initials, it was unique amongst English country houses in having an internal layout designed expressly for the convenience of women,[17] including a long gallery in which the women of the house could take their exercise without leaving the private sphere of the house, on the same principle as leads Virgilia to resolve that virtue is synonymous with confinement to the home: 'I'll not over the threshold till my lord return from the wars' (1.3.75–6). It was also bedecked with embroideries celebrating female achievement. Tantalisingly, *Coriolanus* might well seem to glance directly at some of those very embroideries: Valeria says to Virgilia,

> You would be another Penelope. Yet they say all the yarn she spun in Ulysses' absence did but fill Ithaca full of moths. Come, I would your cambric were sensible as your finger, that you might leave pricking it for pity.
> (1.3.83–87)

Penelope was the subject of a hanging at Hardwick which had been stitched by Mary, Queen of Scots, perhaps in conjunction with Bess, and was a figure associated with the needlework-addicted Bess: Mary S. Lovell notes that

> in one famous set of tapestries representing goddesses and their virtues there is a distinct resemblance in the faces of Zenobia and Penelope to a portrait of Bess soon after she became Countess of Shrewsbury.[18]

There are other possible references to needlework and tapestries in the play: Aufidius speaks of Coriolanus 'Breaking his oath and resolution like / A twist of rotten silk' (5.4.95–6), and Volumnia says that honour is 'no better than picture-like to hang by th'wall, if renown made it not stir' (1.3.10–11). Moreover, *Coriolanus*, as Janet Adelman has shown, is full of references to feeding, especially breastfeeding, as part of its pervasive interest in hunger.[19] Hardwick Hall provides us with one of the most arresting of Elizabethan images of feeding, a needlework hanging of a grown woman breastfeeding her imprisoned father through the bars of his gaol in order to keep him alive; it also housed a starving woman, for Arbella's habitual response to the political crises in which she found herself repeatedly involved was to refuse to eat.[20]

Such images are not the only respect in which *Coriolanus* resonates with the history of Hardwick, for as well as suggesting a blurring of the boundary between defence and domesticity, *Coriolanus* can also be seen as troubling the concept of securely separate genders. Bess and Volumnia both repel their invading sons through sheer force of will; conversely, Richard Wilson in a suggestive phrase terms Coriolanus himself a 'Bessy',[21] in the sense of a figure associated with the folk rituals of harvest time, while James Kuzner declares that

Shakespeare shows him standing at one gateway leading outside the state of
exception, directing us toward a specifically sexual 'world elsewhere' ...
Coriolanus – who bears a historical likeness to Goldberg's sodomite and a
theoretical likeness to Bersani's gay outlaw – points the way to a life that is
openly vulnerable but also livable, to a Sodom whose residents would renounce
the constructs of discrete social identity and bodily integrity alike, a place in
which subjects would perish but life would not.[22]

To see Coriolanus in terms of the idea of sodomy posits him as potentially
penetrable as much as penetrating; perhaps, then, we might hear a modern English
pun on the termination of his name, *anus* – an idea made more likely by Menenius'
play on Aufidius' name, 'I would not have been so fidiused for all the chests in
Corioles' (2.1.125–6) – and if so we should remember that he is thus also an *anus*,
the Latin word for an old woman, a 'bessy' indeed. Little wonder that Cominius
should speak of Coriolanus' 'Amazonian chin' (2.2.90) when he opposed 'The
bristled lips before him' (91).

Seven years after the Queen's Men's visit, on 13 February 1608, Bess of
Hardwick died. Shakespeare's own mother also died in the same year, in early
September. Either next year or the year after that, Shakespeare wrote *Coriolanus*,
a play which focuses on feeding imagery, corn shortages, and a powerful mother
who, alone and unarmed, prevents an assault on her home by her warrior son.
René Weis sees the death of Mary Shakespeare as the principal prompt for the
play – '*Coriolanus*, featuring Volumnia, a formidable and destructive mother,
followed almost certainly in the wake of Mary Arden's death and is arguably
Shakespeare's most disturbing tragedy'[23] – but in many ways it is Bess of
Hardwick who seems to provide the closer analogue. Most tellingly, perhaps,
the incident of Henry Cavendish failing to penetrate his mother's indefensible
house crystallises *Coriolanus*'s emphases on sterility, on manipulation, and on
forces of destruction which operate in ways other than the obvious. Childlessly
married, Henry Cavendish confronted a four times widowed woman who had been
involved in one of the most spectacular instances of marital breakdown of her day,
when she parted in acrimony from her fourth husband, the earl of Shrewsbury,
after accusing him of an affair with his prisoner Mary, Queen of Scots; at stake
was the desire of a young woman, Arbella, to be allowed to engineer a marriage
which her political position made impossible. When Henry rode away defeated,
matriarchy had won, but what its victory had ensured was the very opposite of
its own function – sterility. The sack of Rome in *Coriolanus* is much anticipated
but never occurs; what takes its place is a private confrontation between mother
and son. The projected invasion of the mother's territory of Hardwick, similarly,
failed in the face of her son's inability to sustain a confrontation with her, and
Arbella remained unmarried for several years. (When she did eventually marry,
it brought disaster, madness and death in short order, in ways that seem to have
been remembered in a number of plays of the period.)[24] Perhaps the analogue may
alert us to the presence of a similar pattern of sterility in *Coriolanus*, where youth
dies and age is left: Volumnia, unusually among Shakespearean women in plays

of a tragic cast, survives; conversely, as James Kuzner notes, 'A "prattling nurse / Into a rapture lets her baby cry ..."; she abandons her infant charge – that most sensitive material for social reproduction'.[25]

The bleakness of the situation is still further underlined by the stark paralleling between the famine of the workers in the play and the voluntary self-starvation of their emotionally thwarted masters – for Volumnia, 'Anger's my meat' (4.2.50) – and again this is something which finds an echo in the history of Hardwick. Both Bess and her fourth husband the earl of Shrewsbury were notorious for pursuing a policy of ruthless enclosure; Bess even depopulated villages,[26] and Gordon McMullan has recently pointed to how significant 'the language of resistance to enclosure' is in *Coriolanus*.[27] Outside the walls, Bess's hungry villagers protest against the enclosures which have robbed them of farmland while, safely inside Hardwick, Arbella, denied marriage, refuses to eat; the same processes are at work in *Coriolanus* too. The link between *Coriolanus* and the Midland corn revolts of 1607 has been often urged;[28] Steve Hindle, for instance, notes that

> in the opening scene of *Coriolanus* (1608) William Shakespeare (re-)presents a 'company of mutinous citizens" armed "with staves clubs and other weapons' protesting about the hoarding of grain in the early days of Republican Rome.... There is an emerging consensus, therefore, that most of I.1 of *Coriolanus* is devoted to England's 'two troublesome years' of insurrection (1607) and dearth (1608).[29]

Perhaps the parallel is even closer and more specific than has been thought, with the events at Hardwick leaving their trace on Shakespeare's imagination. Equally, though, it stretches beyond that, to a more general sense of an England that, at peace with the wider world, is now turning its aggression on itself. It suggests that walls built for the purposes of domesticity may find themselves pressed into the service of defence, and in so doing, it shows us the edge of the domestic blurring into the edge of the civic.

Marlowe and the Wall of the Self

If Shakespeare's use of walls in *Coriolanus* works towards blurring the edge between domestic territory and civic territory, something of an opposite direction of travel can be seen in the work of Marlowe, for in his plays what seems to be clearly established as the edge of a literal and physical terrain reveals an unexpected adjacency with the psychological. Marlowe was a playwright fascinated by walls. From his childhood in walled Canterbury, perhaps with occasional visits to the heavily fortified Dover where his mother had been born and whose cliffs iconically emblematised the edge of England itself, to a Cambridge college life configured by walls and gates, he moved to London, where the mediaeval system of walls and gates was still marked by names even where not by structures, and we know too that he visited the walled city of Flushing, which Tom Rutter calls 'the frontier between Protestant and Catholic Europe'.[30] Marlowe also quotes from his fellow spy Paul Ive's *The Practise of Fortification*, which he must have read in manuscript, and as Alan Shepard's list of military manuals of the period makes clear, Ive is unusual in concentrating solely on fortification rather than on wider aspects of strategy and military history;[31] the work's full title is *The Practise of Fortification: Wherein is shewed the manner of fortifying in all sorts of scituations, with the considerations to be vsed in delining, and making of royal Frontiers, Skonces, and reinforcing of ould walled Townes*.[32]

It is therefore no surprise that throughout his works Marlowe showed himself well aware of the crucial role of walls in the process of fortification. This concern is apparent even in a play in which we might not expect to find it, *Doctor Faustus*, though in fact Faustus's interest in defence is not as atypical as we might expect. In English Renaissance drama a witch is usually a witch of somewhere, as in *The Witch of Edmonton* or *The Late Lancashire Witches*; wizards, by contrast, tend to be associated not with the local but with the national, and above all with national defence. This tendency can be traced back to Merlin, who aided the icon of national defence, King Arthur. In Geoffrey of Monmouth's seminal account, later to be put on stage in William Rowley's play *The Birth of Merlin*, the first mention of Merlin is associated with defence: when the tower that Vortigern was trying to build kept falling down, his magicians 'told him that he should look for a lad without a father, and that, when he found one, he should kill him, so that the mortar and the stones could be sprinkled with the lad's blood',[33] and the tower could then be built; the lad without a father turns out to be the young Merlin. Faustus is certainly a figure of defence and, true to the pattern, concerns himself not only with Wittenberg but with Germany as a whole. He first recalls the depredations of the Prince of Parma, who had been described by Edward Aggas as 'this great beater downe of walles',[34] and then declares 'I'll have them wall all Germany with brass'.[35] Later, he displays a concern with questions of fortification in general when he asks Mephistopheles 'Hast thou, as erst I did command, / Conducted me within the walls of Rome?' (3.1.21–2), and presumably listens attentively when Mephistopheles assures him that

> Upon the bridge called Ponte Angelo
> Erected is a castle passing strong,
> Within whose walls such store of ordnance are,
> And double cannons framed of carvèd brass,
> As match the days within one complete year.
>   (3.1.37–41)

Although he ultimately allows himself to be distracted from this concern with walls and ordnance (if the play in the textually unstable form in which we have it does indeed represent Marlowe's original design), Faustus in the early part of the play thus shows himself acutely aware of the use and value of fortification.

The Jew of Malta is another play which displays such an interest. All the action takes place on Malta, an island which was heavily fortified: as well as the Forts of

St Angelo and St Elmo built by the knights, which had played so crucial a part in the Great Siege, there were older structures such as the walled citadels of Mdina on Malta and Rabat (modern Victoria) on Gozo, and newer ones in the shape of the capital Valletta, of which the foundation stone was laid in the year after the siege. Marlowe may also have known that the Maltese islands were at one time inhabited by the Phoenicians and that John Twyne's *De Rebus Albionicis* (1590) comments on the Phoenicians' propensity to build fortifications.[36] The Malta of Marlowe's play, besieged by the Turks, is a place where people keep close to walls – Barabas boasts of how 'I walk abroad o'nights. / And kill sick people groaning under walls' (2.3.179–80) – and where walls have important symbolic value, as we see when Ferneze orders, 'For the Jew's body, throw that o'er the walls' (5.1.58), marking his ritual expulsion from civic society. Indeed during the course of the play we see Barabas '*Enter with a hammer above, very busy*',[37] and this vignette in which the tiring house structure takes on the identity of a city wall becomes something of a signature image for Marlowe, being repeated in *Dido, Queen of Carthage* where Aeneas, having arrived asking 'Where am I now? These should be Carthage walls'[38] and then promised 'Never to leave these new-uprearèd walls' (3.4.47), similarly '*Enter[s]…, with a paper in his hand, drawing the platform of the city*' (5.1.1 s.d.). In addition, the legendary walls of Aeneas's home city are remembered when Dido says she never 'sent a thousand ships unto the walls' of Troy (5.1.204).

In *Edward II*, walls are a last defence: Lancaster tells the king

> Look for rebellion; look to be deposed.
> Thy garrisons are beaten out of France,
> And lame and poor lie groaning at the gates.
> The wild O'Neill, with swarms of Irish kerns,
> Lives uncontrolled within the English pale.
> Unto the walls of York the Scots made road,
> And unresisted drave away rich spoils.[39]

The Pale, that most contested and ungeographical of borders, has proved ineffective, but the walls of York, whose strength can still be seen today, have kept the Scots at bay and prevented them from going further. The Governor of Damascus in *Tamburlaine the Great*, Part 1, displays the same faith in stone and mortar when he orders, 'Call up the soldiers to defend these walls'.[40] Indeed so central is the idea of walls to Marlowe's concept of a city that Faustus thinks of Amphion simply as 'he that built the walls of Thebes' (2.3.28), while Tamburlaine imagines even paradise as walled – 'Now walk the angels on the walls of heaven'[41] – and indeed this would not have seemed unreasonable in a period when it was still half-believed that Eden, the earthly paradise, might still be found on the earth but that 'according to most of the legends, those who travelled in search of Eden found their way through the gate of the Garden of Eden blocked',[42] by a physical obstacle.

However, for Marlowe walls are also paradoxically sites of vulnerability. Partly this is because he is very aware of the fact that they may be pierced by gates and that those may offer ingress and egress in deeply dangerous ways. In *Tamburlaine the Great*, Part 1, Cosroe dreams of a time

> When she that rules in Rhamnus' golden gates
> And makes a passage for all prosperous arms
> Shall make me solely Emperor of Asia.
> (2.3.37–9)

Here the image of the gate proves a prelude to the idea of incursion and radical political change. Partly, too, it is because Marlowe knows that walls really can be vulnerable. Faustus's declaration that 'I'll have them wall all Germany with brass' inevitably recalls the story of Friar Bacon, who attempted the same feat, and it is therefore worth noting that in the prose romance version of that story (possibly the only version available to Marlowe at the time of *Doctor Faustus*' composition) Friar Bacon takes a walled French town by building a mount in front of the wall, and we hear that Aristotle showed Alexander how 'the poyson of a Basiliske, being lift vp vpon the wall of a Citie, the poyson was conuayd into the Citie, to the destruction thereof';[43] in both these cases walls signally fail to provide security. The same is true in *Edward II* where the king is confident that

> Do what they can, we'll live in Tynemouth here,
> And, so I walk with him about the walls,
> What care I though the earls begirt us round?
> (2.2.220–22)

His rebel barons, however, make short work of this supposed security, as Lancaster declares,

> Let us with these our followers scale the walls
> And suddenly surprise them unawares.
> (2.3.18–19)

Similarly in *Tamburlaine the Great*, Part 2, Tamburlaine's forces '*scale the walls*' (V.i.63s.d.), and indeed the Tamburlaine plays as a whole, borrowing as they do from Paul Ive's *Practise of Fortification*, offer a sustained lesson in ways of damaging walls. We hear of battering them (1, 3.1.66 and 3.3.110–11), shaking them down with noise (1, 4.1.2–3), shaking them down with cannon (2, 1.1.86–8), undermining them (2, 3.2.59–61), breaching them (2, 3.2.68–83 and 2, 3.3.5–7), burning them (2, 3.2.141), making trenches before them (2, 3.3.20–34), piling earth up in front of them (2, 3.3.41–3), bombarding them directly with artillery (2, 3.3.49–54), and generally besieging them (2, 3.5.8). In *The Jew of Malta*, Ferneze says 'First will we raze the city walls ourselves' (3.5.13) and Barabas declares,

> Now whilst you give assault unto the walls,
> I'll lead five hundred soldiers through the vault,
> And rise with them i'th'middle of the town.
> (5.1.90–92)

And in *Dido, Queen of Carthage*, Venus says of the Trojans 'Epeus' horse, to Etna's hill transformed, / Prepared stands to wreck their wooden walls' (1.1.66–7) and Aeneas tells of how

> Priamus, impatient of delay,
> Enforced a wide breach in that rampired wall,
> Which thousand battering-rams could never pierce.
>   (2.1.173–5)

Walls, then, can be sites of danger as much as if not more than sites of safety. Walls are even less help in Marlowe's version of Lucan: although theirs have been ministered to by 'the sacred priests / That with divine lustration purged the walls' (ll. 592–3), the inhabitants of Ariminum still apostrophise them as 'O walls unfortunate, too near to France, / Predestinate to ruin!' (ll. 250–51), and muse that

> Safer might we dwell
> Under the frosty Bear, or parching East,
> Wagons or tents, than in this frontier town.
>   (ll. 253–5)

In fact the walls do indeed prove vulnerable, for Caesar beats them down (ll. 293–6).

Even more serious than this, though, walls are for Marlowe sites of psychological vulnerability. Walls may seem to offer security, but in *Tamburlaine the Great*, Part 1, Cosroe worries that they may have sapped the valour of the Persians who

> Now living idle in the wallèd towns,
> Wanting both pay and martial discipline,
> Begin in troops to threaten civil war.
>   (1.1.145–8)

Walls, it seems, have an emasculating and endangering effect, recalling the English traveller William Biddulph's declaration that Bedouins 'neuer come into any walled Townes or Cities, for feare of treason',[44] and foreshadowing the First Senator of Corioles' implication that walls and gates are barriers to those inside as much as to those outside: 'We'll break our walls / Rather than they should pound us up' (1.4.16–17). Tamburlaine himself is certainly confident that walls do not pose a serious barrier to his subjugation of city after city:

> Those wallèd garrisons will I subdue,
> And write myself great Lord of Africa.
>   (3.3.244–5)

Later, besieging Damascus, a city which becomes virtually synonymous with its walls as they are mentioned by character after character (1, 4.3.62; 1, 4.4.75; 1, 5.1.2; 1, 5.1.156; 1, 5.1.321), he is scornful of the inhabitants who 'walk quivering on their city walls, / Half dead for fear before they feel my wrath' (1, 4.4.3–4).

Soon afterwards Techelles reports that the horsemen have killed the virgins and 'on Damascus' walls / Have hoisted up their slaughtered carcasses' (1, 5.1.130–31): what should have been a locus of strength becomes instead one of fear and shame as the walls which should be manned by strong, living men are inhabited first by cowards and ultimately by dead women.

The culminating siege of Damascus in Part 1 is echoed by the siege of Babylon in Part 2, where the opening stage direction of act five reads '*Enter the* GOVERNOR OF BABYLON *upon the walls*'; soon this will be hideously literalised when Tamburlaine orders 'Hang him in chains upon the city walls' (2, 5.1.108), upon which Tamburlaine then comments,

> So, now he hangs like Baghdad's Governor,
> Having as many bullets in his flesh
> As there be breaches in her battered wall.
> (2, 5.1.157–9)

The wall and the Governor have become effectively coterminous. It is therefore no wonder that walls are vulnerable if they are in fact mere extensions of the inhabitants inside them, strong only insofar as they are strong and sharing all their weaknesses. Even before the death of the Governor, indeed, Second Citizen has declared that

> I will cast myself from off these walls
> Or die some death of quickest violence
> Before I bide the wrath of Tamburlaine.
> (2, 5.1.40–42)

This suggests the walls as a site of death as much as of security, as their role of interface between the inside and the outside becomes hideously literalised and they damagingly reveal the states of mind of those inside to those besieging them.

For Marlowe, in fact, the best walls are actually not walls at all. In *Tamburlaine the Great*, Part 1, Bajazeth declares,

> Let thousands die, their slaughtered carcasses
> Shall serve for walls and bulwarks to the rest.
> (3.3.138–9)

Bajazeth here imagines human bodies providing a far more effective defence than any walls prove able to do, while in Part 2, the Governor of Damascus asks,

> Have we not hope, for all our battered walls,
> To live secure and keep his forces out,
> When this our famous lake of Limnasphaltis
> Makes walls afresh with every thing that falls
> Into the liquid substance of his stream,
> More strong than are the gates of death or hell?
> (5.1.15–20)

This time it is the natural barrier of the stone-making water in which a character puts his faith. In Marlowe's translation of Lucan, a similar reliance on the natural underpins the sharp contrast with the soft and complacent denizens of the walled towns of the *Tamburlaine* plays when we are told that

> When Romans are besieged by foreign foes,
> With slender trench they escape night stratagems,
> And sudden rampire raised of turf snatched up
> Would make them sleep securely in their tents.
> (ll. 513–6)

Most notable, though, is the crossing of the Rubicon as described in the Lucan:

> In summer time the purple Rubicon,
> Which issues from a small spring, is but shallow,
> And creeps along the vales dividing just
> The bounds of Italy from Cisalpine France;
> But now the winter's wrath, and wat'ry moon
> Being three days old, enforced the flood to swell.
> (ll. 215–20)

This magnificent passage shows Marlowe as master not so much of a mighty line as of a subtle and flexible one, in which word placement is both shaped by and shaping of place itself. Its first, third and fourth lines all lilt along in a succession of long, open syllables until each reaches a point of sharp demarcation at which the full force of difference of location is registered: Rubicon, just, France. Hinge-like, each of these snaps shut the line it closes and brings to bear the full psychological and symbolic force of the sense of the edge, and an edge, moreover, whose potency gains strong reinforcement, in the mental landscape of early modern culture, by the presence of water, of whose fluidity and dangerous difference from land we are reminded when we are told that the Rubicon is different in different seasons. The result is a far greater sense of a barrier than any of Marlowe's imagined walls ever constitutes.

The two test cases I have chosen yield different but complementary results. In *Coriolanus*, I suggested an allusion to an event in which walls which were initially intended to be domestic in character had to do the work of defence, and I argued that this worked to reveal the edge between the civic and the domestic as blurred and permeable. In Marlowe's plays and translations, walls which were originally designed to provide an impregnable defence prove in fact to open windows into human minds and reveal their vulnerabilities: made by humans as artificial edges, as opposed to natural edges such as those which rivers and mountains provide, they inevitably share an adjacency with the human mind, and their joint limitations are mutually constitutive and mutually revealing. In both cases, walls thus function less as barriers between what is inside and what is outside than as a means of traffic between the two. In the next chapter, I turn to a less visible but even more fiercely contested frontier involving not any individual household but in effect bearing upon all – the frontier between the domain of the spiritual and the domain of the secular.

Notes

[1]   Roy Strong, *The Renaissance Garden in England* (London: Thames and Hudson, 1979), p. 171.

[2]   See Lisa Hopkins, *The Cultural Uses of the Caesars on the English Renaissance Stage* (Burlington: Ashgate, 2008), chap. 3.

[3]   Hopkins, *The Cultural Uses of the Caesars*, chap. 3.

[4]   Warren Chernaik, *The Myth of Rome in Shakespeare and his Contemporaries* (Cambridge: Cambridge University Press, 2011), p. 170.

[5]   James Kuzner, 'Unbuilding the City: *Coriolanus* and the Birth of Republican Rome', *Shakespeare Quarterly* 58.2 (2007), p. 174.

[6]   William Shakespeare, *Coriolanus*, edited by G.R. Hibbard (Harmondsworth: Penguin, 1967), 3.2.1–6. All further quotations from the play will be taken from this edition and reference will be given in the text.

[7]   William Shakespeare, *The Tempest*, edited by Virginia Mason Vaughan and Alden T. Vaughan (London: Thomas Nelson & Sons, 1999), 1.2.322–5. I have suggested elsewhere that there is also a possible parallel between Coriolanus and Bottom (Lisa Hopkins, *The Shakespearean Marriage* [Basingstoke: Palgrave Macmillan, 1998], pp. 116–7).

[8]   George MacDonald Fraser, *The Steel Bonnets* (London: HarperCollins, 1995), p. 375.

[9]   Cathy Shrank, 'Civility and the City in *Coriolanus*', *Shakespeare Quarterly* 54.4 (Winter 2003), pp. 406 and 417.

[10]   Peter D. Anderson, *Black Patie: The Life and Times of Patrick Stewart, Earl of Orkney, Lord of Shetland* (Edinburgh: John Donald, 1992), p. 45.

[11]   Denys Pringle, 'The Houses of the Stewart Earls in Orkney and Shetland', *New Orkney Antiquarian Journal* 1 (1999), p. 33 and 36–7.

[12]   Marion Trousdale, '*Coriolanus* and the Playgoer in 1609', in *The Arts of Performance in Elizabethan and Early Stuart Drama: Essays for G. K. Hunter*, edited by Murray Biggs, Philip Edwards, Inga-Stina Ewbank and Eugene M. Waith (Edinburgh: Edinburgh University Press, 1991), p. 132.

[13]   David N. Durant, *Bess of Hardwick: Portrait of an Elizabethan dynast* [1977] (London: The Cromwell Press, 1988), p. 185.

[14]   Clifford Chalmers Huffman, <u>*Coriolanus* in Context</u> (Lewisburg: Bucknell University Press, 1971), p. 25.

[15]   Mary S. Lovell, *Bess of Hardwick* (London: Little, Brown, 2005), pp. 438 and 442.

[16]   For the details of the affair, see Durant, *Bess of Hardwick*, and Elizabeth Eisenberg, *This Costly Countess: Bess of Hardwick* (Derby: J.H. Hall and sons, 1985), p. 38.

[17]   See Durant, *Bess of Hardwick*, p. 180.

[18]   Lovell, *Bess of Hardwick*, p. 221.

[19]   See for instance Stanley Cavell, '"Who Does the Wolf Love?": *Coriolanus* and the Interpretation of Politics', in *Shakespeare and the Question of Theory*, edited by Patricia Parker and Geoffrey Hartman (London: Methuen, 1985), pp. 245–72, p. 248, and Janet Adelman, *Suffocating Mothers* (London: Routledge, 1992), p. 143.

[20]   For Arbella's refusals to eat, see Sara Jayne Steen, ed., *The Letters of Lady Arbella Stuart* (Oxford: Oxford University Press, 1994), pp. 34–5.

[21]   Richard Wilson, *Will Power: Essays on Shakespearean Authority* (Hemel Hempstead: Harvester Wheatsheaf, 1993), p. 114.

[22]   Kuzner, 'Unbuilding the City', p. 175.

[23]   René Weis, *Shakespeare Revealed* (London: John Murray, 2007), p. 329.

[24]   See for instance Sara Jayne Steen, 'The Crime of Marriage: Arbella Stuart and *The Duchess of Malfi*', *Sixteenth Century Journal* 22.1 (1991), pp. 61–76.

[25]   Kuzner, 'Unbuilding the City', p. 193.

[26]   Durant, *Bess of Hardwick*, pp. 16 and 108.

[27]   Gordon McMullan, *The Politics of Unease in the Plays of John Fletcher* (Amherst: University of Massachusetts Press, 1994), p. 54.

[28]   See for instance Adelman, *Suffocating Mothers*, p. 147; Jonathan Dollimore, *Radical Tragedy*, 2nd ed. (London: Harvester Wheatsheaf, 1989); McMullan, *Politics of Unease*, p. 52; Annabel Patterson, *Shakespeare and the Popular Voice* (Oxford: Basil Blackwell,1989), pp. 135–46; and Wilson, *Will Power*.

[29]   Steve Hindle, 'Imagining Insurrection in Seventeenth-Century England: Representations of the Midland Rising of 1607', *History Workshop Journal* 66 (2008), p. 41.

[30]   Tom Rutter, *The Cambridge Introduction to Christopher Marlowe* (Cambridge: Cambridge University Press, 2012), p. 15.

[31]   Alan Shepard, *Marlowe's Soldiers: Rhetorics of Masculinity in the Age of the Armada* (Burlington: Ashgate, 2002), p. 7.

[32]   Paul Ive, *The Practise of Fortification* [1589] (Amsterdam and New York: Da Capo Press, 1986).

[33]   Geoffrey of Monmouth, *The History of the Kings of Britain*, translated by Lewis Thorpe (Harmondsworth: Penguin, 1966), p. 167.

[34]   Edward Aggas, *An answeare to the supplication Against him, who seeming to giue the King counsel to become a Catholike, indeuoureth to stirre vp his good subiectes vnto rebellion*, translated by E.A. (London: John Wolfe, 1591), sig. D3v.

[35]   Christopher Marlowe, *Doctor Faustus*, A text, in *The Complete Plays*, edited by Mark Thornton Burnett (London: J.M. Dent, 1999), 1.1.90. All further quotations from the play will be taken from this edition and reference will be given in the text.

[36]   Thomas Roebuck and Laurie Maguire, '*Pericles* and the Language of National Origins', in *This England, That Shakespeare: New Angles on Englishness and the Bard*, edited by Willy Maley and Margaret Tudeau-Clayton (Burlington: Ashgate, 2010), p. 43.

[37]   Christopher Marlowe, *The Jew of Malta*, in *The Complete Plays*, edited by Mark Thornton Burnett (London: J.M. Dent, 1999), 5.5.1 s.d. All further quotations from the play will be taken from this edition and reference will be given in the text.

[38]   Christopher Marlowe, *Dido, Queen of Carthage*, in *The Complete Plays*, edited by Mark Thornton Burnett (London: J.M. Dent, 1999), 2.1.1. All further quotations from the play will be taken from this edition and reference will be given in the text.

[39]   Christopher Marlowe, *Edward II*, in *The Complete Plays*, edited by Mark Thornton Burnett (London: J.M. Dent, 1999), 2.2.159–66. All further quotations from the play will be taken from this edition and reference will be given in the text.

[40]   Christopher Marlowe, *Tamburlaine the Great*, Part 1, in *The Complete Plays*, edited by Mark Thornton Burnett (London: J.M. Dent, 1999), 5.1.56. All further quotations from the play will be taken from this edition and reference will be given in the text.

[41]   Christopher Marlowe, *Tamburlaine the Great*, Part 2, in *The Complete Plays*, edited by Mark Thornton Burnett (London: J.M. Dent, 1999), 2.4.15. All further quotations from the play will be taken from this edition and reference will be given in the text.

[42]   Alessandro Scafi, *Mapping Paradise: A History of Heaven on Earth* (London: The British Library, 2006), p. 51.

[43]   Anonymous, *The famous history of Fryer Bacon* (London: G. Purslowe for F. Grove, 1627), sigs C3v and C4v.

[44]   William Biddulph, *The trauels of certaine Englishmen into Africa, Asia, Troy, Bithynia, Thracia, and to the Blacke Sea ...* (London: T. Haveland for W. Aspley, 1609), p. 69.

Chapter 2
Peter or Paul?
The Edge of the State

The edge of the terrain of the spiritual could sometimes be marked by very firm physical boundaries. As the discussion of Ophelia's burial rites attests, the concept of consecrated ground was well understood and clearly demarcated, and other structures such as lych gates and altar rails also served as physical, tangible edges between different zones. In this chapter, though, I want to consider an edge which is conceptual rather than tangible, and which is, I shall suggest, emblematised in the figure of St Paul, who is understood in this context as implicitly in opposition to St Peter. In his *The life of the glorious bishop S. Patricke*, a text to which I shall recur in Chapter 6, the mediaeval monk Joscelin says that St Paul visited Britain,[1] and John Clapham in *The historie of Great Britannie* also notes that 'some writers of former ages have constantly affirmed, that the Apostles, Saint Peter and Saint Paul, in their owne persons at severall times, came into Britannie'.[2] Although there is no evidence for this story, there is a sense in which it is undeniably true, for St Paul was a figure who bulked very large in the cultural consciousness of early modern England. The cathedral dedicated to him was the main church in London, housing the acting company Paul's Boys, while the adjacent churchyard was the home of stationers, which fitted well with an Apostle famous above all for his writings. Further afield, Hakluyt cited Paul's call to evangelise in his list of incitements to colonisation,[3] implicitly proposing the much-travelled Apostle as a prototype for the principal navigations, traffics and discoveries of the expansionist English nation. In this chapter, I want to consider some of the uses made of Paul and of what he evokes first by Marlowe and then by Shakespeare, in order to argue that the edge which Paul emblematised, while not outwardly visible, was nevertheless of great importance in early modern English culture, and that Shakespeare in particular presents it as vital to be aware of its adjacency with the opposing but complementary edge emblematised by St Peter.

Paul seems to have been a figure of particular interest to Christopher Marlowe. Kyd told Sir John Puckering that he had intended to write a book about St Paul, but that the atheistical Marlowe had mocked at him and dissuaded him from doing so, and in 1593 Richard Baines claimed that among the many blasphemous, scurrilous and generally shocking remarks made by Marlowe was the allegation 'that all the apostles were fishermen and base fellows, neither of wit nor worth; that Paul only had wit, but he was a timorous fellow in bidding men to be subject to magistrates against his conscience'.[4] William Warner, who may or may not have been the 'Warner' whom Kyd identified as Marlowe's friend, similarly reflected on Paul in his *Albions England*: discussing the supposed Donation of Constantine (a subject to which I shall recur in Chapter 4), Warner notes that some people 'say he made a *Paule* a *Saule* that made a Priest of Prince / And in that grace the Empires grace disgraced euer since'[5] – that is, that Constantine's alleged gifting of temporal as well as spiritual sovereignty over Rome to the Pope, which effectively made a priest a prince, had been a step so retrograde for Christianity as a whole that the magnitude of the error involved can be troped only by figuring it as St Paul turning apostate and reverting to his pre-baptismal name of Saul.

Despite his alleged hostility to Kyd's project of writing a book on him, Marlowe can in fact be seen as musing on Paul in his drama, for Paul had featured prominently in the history of Malta, on which he had been shipwrecked and which subsequently owed much of its fame, some of its place-names, its distinguished Christian ancestry and, legend avers, its freedom from snakes, all to him. This particular Jew of Malta is, however, famous principally for his status as perhaps the most celebrated convert in recorded history from ultra-orthodox Judaism to Christianity. As such, he might well serve as an interesting comparator for the analogous conversion of Abigail; moreover, anyone familiar with accounts of the Great Siege of 1565, upon which Marlowe's play is ostensibly based, would be aware that the final engagement was fought in St Paul's Bay, legendary scene of the saint's shipwreck, where the Turks suffered a decisive defeat and left the beach and waters clogged with their dead. It fits well with the ironic, ambiguous tone of Marlowe's play, in which a Christian borrows some books from a Jew just as Christianity 'borrowed' the Torah from Judaism, to remember this story of a Jew distinguished by adherence to Christianity. Paul's may be a submerged presence, but it is a presence which colours almost every aspect of the play, and it reveals the multifaceted appropriateness of using Paul to reflect on the relationship between spiritual and secular powers.

Paul is a figure of more systematic interest to Shakespeare. It has often been remarked that in *The Comedy of Errors* Shakespeare seems to show a marked interest in the journeys and teachings of St Paul.[6] In *Richard III*, the motif of references to St Paul is continued and significantly developed, perhaps because Paul, an academic, mystical speculator who speaks a complex and figurative language, was strongly associated with the theory underlying the idea of the King's Two Bodies,[7] which in the case of Richard allows him to give lesser prominence to his natural body and thus to gloss over the fact of having a physical handicap – something which would in earlier times, as evidenced by King John's attempted blinding of his nephew Arthur, have prevented him from being considered as a candidate for the crown, since no one who was not physically perfect was eligible to rule. Paul's influence can also be seen in the figures of Falstaff,[8] Bottom,[9] and Paulina,[10] and so many others that Julia Reinhard Lupton creates the conceit of a 'Paul Shakespeare':

> Paul Shakespeare's epistles include two letters to the Venetians concerning circumcision (*Merchant of Venice* and *Othello*), a very early letter to the Ephesians on marriage (*Comedy of Errors*, set in Ephesus), and a pair of later, deeper, and more Corinthian commentaries on marriage, liberty, and the law (*Measure for*

Measure and *All's Well That Ends Well*). The Erasmian discourse of folly takes its bearings from the Paul of 1 Corinthians and pops in the serio-comic visions of Bottom in *A Midsummer Night's Dream*. Our imaginary correspondent does not fail to post a final envoi, modelled on Paul's Maltese shipwreck in the Acts of the Apostles, namely *The Tempest*, which sends Paul's achingly personal agon with universalism into orbit around the fragile singularity of the creature Caliban.[11]

R.W. Desai proposes seeing Paul as a central figure in yet another play, *Hamlet*, not least because of 'the prominence Luther gave to the Pauline epistles in his lectures [at Wittenberg] from 1512–1514, which began the Reformation'. Desai notes,

> There are fourteen letters exchanged between Seneca and St. Paul, and the question of whether these are genuine or apocryphal need not concern us here. More important is the strong likelihood that the two men were in close contact with each other. In fact, their paths ultimately converged at Rome, where St. Paul, by his own demand, was brought for trial before Nero and sentenced to death by execution in AD 67, two years after Seneca's death bv suicide. That St. Paul did *not* choose to make his exit the Senecan way is perhaps distantly on the horizon in Hamlet's early wish 'that the Everlasting had not fix'd / His canon 'gainst self-slaughter' (1.2.131–2).

Desai also suggests that 'Hamlet's providential rescue may have some resonances from the account of the shipwreck which St. Paul experienced as described in the penultimate chapter of the book of Acts'.[12]

Paul certainly does seem to be glanced at in *Hamlet* when Claudius, faced with a furious and vengeful Laertes, orders Gertrude to let Laertes go on the grounds that 'There's such divinity doth hedge a king / That treason can but peep to what it would'.[13] Claudius's words go to the heart of the intersection which was central to Pauline theology and on which I wish to focus in this chapter, which is the edge between political and religious authority. Although the national borders of Denmark and Norway are in question throughout the play, Claudius has no doubt that this more metaphysical border is one which is clearly and securely established: kings rule by divine right and no mere secular power can overthrow them. His words are however charged with irony in that he has himself killed a king, his own brother; moreover, the most famous Claudius of history was the Roman emperor of that name, during whose reign Paul undertook many of his journeys and Christianity as a religion began seriously to establish itself, and to come into conflict with the state. King Claudius of Denmark thus becomes less a proof of a secure boundary between secular and spiritual than a reminder of the intensity of the border warfare over the issue, and on this matter as on others, Paul and his fellow Apostle St Peter, founder of the Church of Rome, were often conceived of as not only opposites but opponents – while at Antioch St Peter 'was reproved by St Paul for temporizing over eating with Gentiles',[14] and Michael Goulder observes that 'The two missions were agreed about the supreme significance of Jesus, but they disagreed about almost everything else – the validity of the Bible, whether the kingdom of God had arrived or not, sex, money, work, tongues, visions, healings, Jesus' divinity, and the resurrection of the dead, for example';[15] thus, as we have already seen, William Warner when he discusses the Donation of Constantine is able to make ready and resonant use of Paul to oppose the Petrine authority of the Pope .

In post-Reformation England, there was of course no doubt that it was St Paul, the Apostle consistently preferred by Protestantism, who had the right of it: thus in *The Image of Ireland*, John Derrick declares

> For Peter needes must silence keepe,
> when Paule steppes forthe in place:
> And knowe we not how Paule withstoode,
> sainct Peter to his face?[16]

I want to argue that Shakespeare was not only acutely aware of this conflict but actively took sides in it, and that, whatever his personal religious beliefs may have been, on this issue at least his sympathies lay with Paul. In thus aligning himself in a way which has no smack of what Coleridge called his wonderful philosophic impartiality but is, for him, unusually visible and decisive, Shakespeare suggests that this apparently most immaterial and intangible of edges is, in fact, more readily identified and secured than any marked by walls, and yet this edge too proves ultimately to be characterised by the potential and indeed arguably the necessity for permeability and bleed.

'Papists and Poets': Shakespeare and *Saint Peter's Complaint*

In a recent article on Shakespeare's two tetralogies, Jean-Christophe Mayer observes that

> in the 1611 edition of *The Theatre of the Empire of Great Britain*, Speed denounces [the Jesuit Robert] Parsons's ... unwarranted accusations against the proto-Protestant martyr Sir John Oldcastle [the original of Falstaff], these being 'taken from the *Stage-plaiers*'. Parsons and Shakespeare – 'this Papist and his Poet' – had in fact a lot in common, according to the historian; they were 'of like conscience for lies, the one euer faining, and the other euer falsifying the truth'. The marginalia sum up these statements laconically; one reads: 'Papists and Poets of like conscience for fictions'.[17]

Although Mayer appears to imply that the phrase 'this Papist and his Poet' refers to Parsons and Shakespeare, the 'Papist' part of the tag was in fact applied originally to the poet and Jesuit Robert Southwell, and Michael Wood amongst others has argued for a significant connection between Southwell and Shakespeare, who were distant cousins (amongst other things, Wood argues that in *A Midsummer Night's Dream* the remark that 'The lunatic, the lover and the poet / Are of imagination all compact ...' is 'a curiously precise echo of Southwell'),[18] an idea supported by Frank Brownlow who suggests that Southwell is echoed not only in *Dream* but also in *Lear*.[19] Specifically, Wood argues for seeing Shakespeare as the target of Southwell's injunction in *Saint Peter's Complaint* to his 'worthy good cousin, Master W. S.' to write sacred verse; Wood and others suggest that the reproach was prompted specifically by the recent publication of *Venus and Adonis*, whose verse form *Saint Peter's Complaint* imitates. This was an injunction which was both deeply felt – Anne Sweeney argues, 'If his poetry is read in the light of his mission, Southwell clearly took his authorship very seriously indeed, even that of his lighter poetry'[20] – and which, if it was indeed directed at Shakespeare, was studiously ignored: indeed Alison Shell argues that 'Shakespeare's work exhibits a high level of silence and evasion where religion is concerned',[21] though I would suggest that silence and evasion can in themselves function as indications of where his sympathies lie, since they are *not* militance and commitment. I want to suggest that whether or not he is responding directly to Southwell, Shakespeare in effect uses his own exploration of St Paul to counter the values and politics that underlie Southwell's Petrine comment.

Richard Wilson has already done a good deal of work exploring the implications of Shakespeare's apparent refusal to obey Southwell's injunction. Wilson introduces his argument by declaring that

> in the days before his arrest in June 1592, the Jesuit poet Robert Southwell responded to one of the manuscripts of *Venus and Adonis* which circulated, we know, in recusant households, with a poem of his own in identical stanzas, entitled *Saint Peter's Complaint*, which he prefaced with a dedication rejecting Shakespeare's image of poetry as a passive distillation of experience and deploring the waste of his artistic gifts.

For Wilson, this is 'the clearest indication of how the "finest wit" and "sweetest vein" of his generation had been expected to produce "Christian works" that "lent his talent" to the Catholic cause'.[22] Alison Shell develops this: noting that 'Simon Hunt, Shakespeare's first schoolmaster, who subsequently became a Jesuit, knew Southwell intimately', she points out that

> The allusion to Shakespeare in the religious poem 'Saint Marie Magdalens conversion', published around 1603–04, was noted long ago by the editors of the *Shakespere allusion-book*. But neither they, nor anyone else to date, has addressed the three most suggestive facts about this poem: that, like several other long religious poems of the late 1590s and early 1600s, it is a very obvious pastiche of 'St Peter's Complaint'; that it was published by a Catholic secret press; and that it is very critical of Shakespeare. The author, designated only by the initials 'I.C.', uses Shakespeare as an example of the secular poet, and argues that instead of writing as profane poets do, one should renounce secular subject-matter in favour of the topics of religious conversion and repentance.

Shell echoes I.C. by herself calling Shakespeare 'a secular writer' and argues, 'Though secularism conceptualises religion in various ways – as a private matter, as a virus or as an irrelevance – these can all be subsumed under one heading: that the public statement of doctrinal conviction is something to be avoided'.[23] Mayer too suggests a holding back from commitment on Shakespeare's part. Despite his suggestion, in the quotation with which I began this part of the discussion, that papists and poets had similar agendas, Mayer implies a difference in this respect, for though he argues for a close relationship between Shakespeare's two tetralogies and Parsons's *Conference about the Next Succession*, which proposed the Infanta of Spain as the most suitable successor to Elizabeth I, he nevertheless thinks that 'Parsons's implicit aim in writing the *Conference* was to oppose the idea of a possible separation between matters of religion and matters of state', while he suggests that Shakespeare by contrast is much more ambiguous and harder to read: 'Shakespeare's view of the collusion between temporal power and a politicized clergy leaves theatre audiences uneasy'.[24] In what remains of this chapter, I want to consider Shakespeare's representation of the edge between the temporal and the spiritual in a number of plays, starting with *Henry V* itself, moving on to *Measure for Measure* and *Julius Caesar*, and concluding with *King John*, in order to argue that although this is an edge which is invested with an exceptional degree of force it, too, is ultimately seen as permeable, in ways which may well have potentially troubling consequences given that, unlike the gaps in the mortar of walls, these points of possible slippage are susceptible to deliberate manipulation in the pursuit of particular agendas. At the same time, though, we are repeatedly made aware of the dangers and shortcomings of subscribing to an exclusively Pauline or an exclusively Petrine position; in the case of this particular edge, therefore, it is always important to be mindful of the adjacency.

Henry V and Holy War

At the opening of *Henry V*, the Archbishop of Canterbury seems to be under the impression that he is manipulating the king by offering him a sum of money of unprecedented size for his campaigns in France. This, the Archbishop thinks, will induce the king to take the side of the clergy in a bill currently being brought before Parliament. As the Archbishop explains to the Bishop of Ely,

> He seems indifferent,
> Or rather swaying more upon our part
> Than cherishing th'exhibiters against us;
> For I have made an offer to his majesty –
> Upon our spiritual Convocation,
> And in regard of causes now in hand,
> Which I have opened to his grace at large
> As touching France – to give a greater sum
> Than ever at one time the clergy yet
> Did to his predecessors part withal.[25]

As the Archbishop sees it, the king is 'swaying', a word implying vacillation and indecisiveness. On the side of those opposed to the interests of the church there is the presence of that emotive word 'cherishing', implying an affective investment on the king's part. However, the Archbishop is confident that he can more than counteract the effects of that by the simple expedient of offering money – lots of it. This would of course immediately mobilise standard anti-clerical discourses about the corruption and excessive wealth of some sections of the clergy through a simple shorthand similar to that which energises any collocation of the two words 'bankers' and 'bonuses' or 'fat' and 'cats' at the historical moment at which I write this. Say no more: you have a ready-made and easily demonised symbol of greed and immorality. The Archbishop, however, is wise to that, and mystifies his offer of cash by dressing it up with the setting of a 'spiritual convocation' and the air of the chivalric and the honourable which would to an early modern English audience inevitably accrue to any suggestion of an expedition against the ancient enemy France. All in all, the Archbishop could be forgiven for supposing that he has performed a very neat bit of manipulation.

However, when the king actually appears, one might well wonder who is manipulating whom, as he says to the Archbishop,

> My learnèd lord, we pray you to proceed,
> And justly and religiously unfold
> Why the law Salic that they have in France
> Or should or should not bar us in our claim.
> And God forbid, my dear and faithful lord,
> That you should fashion, wrest, or bow your reading,
> Or nicely charge your understanding soul
> With opening titles miscreate, whose right
> Suits not in native colours with the truth;
> For God doth know how many now in health
> Shall drop their blood in approbation
> Of what your reverence shall incite us to.
> Therefore take heed how you impawn our person,
> How you awake our sleeping sword of war.
> We charge you in the name of God, take heed;
> For never two such kingdoms did contend
> Without much fall of blood, whose guiltless drops
> Are every one a woe, a sore complaint
> 'Gainst him whose wrongs give edge unto the swords
> That makes such waste in brief mortality.
> Under this conjuration speak, my lord,
> For we will hear, note, and believe in heart
> That what you speak is in your conscience washed
> As pure as sin with baptism.

(1.2.10–32)

When Henry says 'we pray you to proceed', he is effectively giving the Archbishop his cue, ordering him to produce language. This is made particularly clear in the Laurence Olivier film, where we have seen the king readying himself for his part, but it is in fact already implicit in the scene. Henry does not let the Archbishop speak at once, though; instead he first clarifies what *kind* of language is to be produced. It should be unfashioned, unbowed, unwrested – in short, spoken from the soul, but at the same time there can be no doubt of what message will be most welcome: it foreshadows the scene in which Henry woos Katherine and wants her to say she loves him, even though it is abundantly apparent that everything she says and does is already predetermined by pressing political necessities. Here, too, Henry wants to sentimentalise and present as spiritual what are essentially matters of secular power, prestige, and money – effectively he is indulging in a bit of mystification of his own. As he does so, he also repeatedly shifts agency and responsibility for everything he himself may be about to do firmly onto the shoulders of the Archbishop: 'what your reverence shall incite us to', 'take heed how you impawn our person', until, in an even more audacious role reversal, it is actually he who exhorts the Archbishop 'in the name of God', as if he were the spiritual authority and the Archbishop the secular one – something to which the Archbishop's worldly interest in finance has of course left him wholly vulnerable. In the end, then, any complaints made by the souls of the dead must be directed not against the king – as he will later confirm to Williams, 'The King is not bound to answer the particular endings of his soldiers' (4.2.51–2) – but against the Archbishop. What Henry has done here is to seize upon the evidence of bleed between the domains of the secular and the spiritual which he finds in the Archbishop's own speech and to ensure that the slippage works firmly to his own advantage, allowing him, one might say, to sit on the fence and enjoy the greenest of the grass on both sides of it.

Moreover, not only must the Archbishop speak 'under this conjuration', but Henry blandly tells him that he himself 'will hear, note, and believe in heart / That what you speak is in your conscience washed'. The logic here is precisely similar to that of the paradoxical 'I do believe her though I know she lies' in sonnet 138,[26] except that the speaker in this case directs the animus of his words not at himself, as the self-mocking speaker of the sonnet does, but at his hapless auditor, trapped in an inescapable double-bind. Later, Henry goes one better and takes a similarly hectoring tone with God himself:

> O God of battles, steel my soldiers' hearts;
> Possess them not with fear; take from them now
> The sense of reckoning, if th'opposèd numbers
> Pluck their hearts from them. Not today, O Lord,
> O not today, think not upon the fault
> My father made in compassing the crown!
> I Richard's body have interrèd new,
> And on it have bestowed more contrite tears
> Than from it issued forcèd drops of blood.
> Five hundred poor have I in yearly pay,
> Who twice a day their withered hands hold up
> Toward heaven, to pardon blood: and I have built
> Two chantries where the sad and solemn priests

Sing still for Richard's soul. More will I do,
Though all that I can do is nothing worth,
Since that my penitence comes after all,
Imploring pardon.

(4.1.282–298)

By the end of this speech, though, a distinctly less confident tone has crept in. 'Though all that I can do is nothing worth' clearly recalls the controversy over the role of works in Renaissance theology, since Martin Luther had declared that salvation was accomplished *sola fide*, by faith alone, challenging the whole idea of 'buying' grace, which is what Henry is so clearly attempting to do. In hinting at this, this speech raises the very issue which bedevils Claudius in *Hamlet* when he tries and fails to pray, and which troubled so many conscientious Renaissance thinkers: no one, not even a king, could command an access of grace if God decided to withhold it. For one bleak moment, Henry contemplates the existence of a real spiritual power which is far greater than he is and may not do what he wants. There is thus a terrifying possibility that those chantry houses might be built on shifting sands and that the ground of the contested frontier strip between the secular and the spiritual, which he had earlier appeared to negotiate with such ease, may open and swallow him.

Disguising as divinity: *Measure for Measure*

The duke in *Measure for Measure* tries a different approach, one which is in fact the logical development of Henry's moment of discomfort. He recognises that he has been a complete failure as a secular ruler; consequently, he tries his hand as a spiritual figure instead: having failed to exercise the authority of an earthly father, he disguises himself as a holy one, and having failed to wield the instruments of punishment available to secular authority, he will try what the ability to prescribe penance can do. In this he succeeds superbly, as Angelo shows when he says

O my dread lord,
I should be guiltier than my guiltiness
To think I can be undiscernible,
When I perceive your grace, like power divine,
Hath looked upon my passes.[27]

For Angelo, the effectiveness of the duke's disguise and the extent to which his scrutiny of others has allowed him to deflect any scrutiny of his own actions or motives serves as an emblem of the inscrutability and invisibility of God himself. Lucio may be right that '*Cucullus non facit monachum*' (5.1.261), but Shakespeare, for whom a pun was a fatal Cleopatra, might well have been tempted to note that it can, it seems, make a monarch.

Measure for Measure is set in Vienna,[28] and Leah Marcus has argued that we should read the play in terms of the so-called Archdukes, Albert and Isabella, joint rulers of the Netherlands and both descendants of the royal house of Austria,[29] who had both forsaken a religious life for marriage and a political one. One might think too of the prince-bishops of the independent state of Salzburg, which took up a significant part of what was then Bavaria[30] but is now Austria, who combined in their own persons both secular and spiritual power. After all, Machiavelli, with characteristic mischievousness, had said of ecclesiastical principalities that

> here the difficulties which have to be faced occur before the ruler is established, in that such principalities are won by prowess or by fortune but are kept without the help of either. They are maintained, in fact, by religious institutions, of such a powerful kind that, no matter how the ruler acts and lives, they safeguard his government. Ecclesiastical princes alone possess states, and do not defend them; subjects, and do not govern them. And though their states are not defended they are not taken away from them; and their subjects, being without government, do not worry about it and neither can hope to overthrow it in favour of another. So these principalities alone are secure and happy. But as they are sustained by higher powers which the human mind cannot comprehend, I shall not argue about them; they are exalted and maintained by God, and so only a rash and presumptuous man would take it on himself to discuss them.[31]

The fact that Shakespeare stayed out of prison when so many of his fellow playwrights spent time there seems in itself to suggest that he was not a rash and presumptuous man, but nevertheless I wonder whether in *Measure for Measure* he might in fact be glancing obliquely at the question of whether principalities governed by a spiritual power really are 'alone … secure and happy'. Certainly the state at the end of *Measure for Measure* is better ordered than it was at the beginning, but one might think that it is an order rather mechanically achieved and sustained, and that what has been produced is essentially modification of behaviour rather than improvement of character – which is in some sense the exact opposite of what one might hope for from genuine spiritual instruction. However since there is not even the faintest sign of any possible alternative to such a state of affairs it is not surprising that, as Machiavelli predicts, most of the characters seem willing enough to accept it, even if the play does not quite want to resolve the question of whether Isabella will choose to stay in such a society or return to a more purely spiritual one. One thing is clear, though: she cannot have both but must choose between them, for secular and spiritual rule are mutually exclusive, and when a secular ruler borrows spiritual authority the effect is a darkly disturbing one which forces this play to break new ground both generically and tonally in ways which offer a formal echo of the cognitive disorientation produced when this particular edge is blurred.

'Render unto Caesar': *Julius Caesar*

I want to turn now to *Julius Caesar*. The very name of Julius Caesar evokes a divide between the secular and the spiritual, since it evokes the Biblical injunction to render unto Caesar the things that are Caesar's (Mark 12: 17), and Anne

Sweeney titles her discussion of Southwell's poem 'Josephs Amazement' 'Caesar or God's?'.[32] Shakespeare's *Julius Caesar*, however, shows us a state in which the edge between secular and spiritual has lost its sharpness and become blurred. This is apparent from the very outset, when Flavius exclaims 'Hence! home, you idle creatures, get you home: / Is this a holiday?'.[33] The etymology of 'holiday', to which Shakespeare's audience were far closer than we are now, is of course 'holy day', and this raises a crucial question: is Caesar, in whose honour these citizens have assembled, a secular figure or a spiritual one or both? Flavius has no doubt about the answer to that: he says 'Disrobe the images, / If you do find them decked with ceremonies' (1.1.64–5), locating Caesar's power firmly within the realm of the secular, and it is notable that Brutus says 'we are contented Caesar shall / Have all true rites and lawful ceremonies' (3.1.240–41), implying that what he has previously received has exceeded his due. However, Caesar clearly wields spiritual power of some sort. He can issue the command 'Go bid the priests do present sacrifice, / And bring me their opinion of success' (2.2.4–5), and he also seems at home dealing with questions of the numinous when he orders

> Forget not, in your speed, Antonius,
> To touch Calphurnia; for our elders say,
> The barren, touchèd in this holy chase,
> Shake off their sterile curse.
>
> (1.2.6–9)

He is, it seems, even coming to believe his own publicity: Cassius says,

> But it is doubtful yet
> Whether Caesar will come forth today or no;
> For he is superstitious grown of late,
> Quite from the main opinion he held once
> Of fantasy, of dreams, and ceremonies.
>
> (2.1.193–7)

Cassius in his first mention of Caesar calls him 'immortal Caesar' (1.2.60), and though there is clearly satiric intent here, there is in fact a marked will in Rome to believe in a link between the secular state and the spiritual world which undermines the very notion of the purely temporal and gives implicit credibility to the idea of divine right to rule. Even Cassius reads celestial and meteorological phenomena as spiritually charged when he declares that 'heaven hath infused them with these spirits / To make them instruments of fear and warning' (1.3.69–71), while Calphurnia more simply asserts that 'When beggars die, there are no comets seen; / The heavens themselves blaze forth the death of princes' (2.2.30–31). Finally, Cassius concedes defeat entirely:

> You know that I held Epicurus strong,
> And his opinion; now I change my mind,
> And partly credit things that do presage.
>
> (5.1.76–8)

The idea that there is a correspondence between the microcosmic and the macrocosmic is most suggestively explored by Brutus:

> Between the acting of a dreadful thing
> And the first motion, all the interim is
> Like a phantasma or a hideous dream:
> The genius and the mortal instruments
> Are then in council; and the state of man,
> Like to a little kingdom, suffers then
> The nature of an insurrection.
>
> (2.1.63–9)

'The dreadful thing' which Brutus is contemplating is an act which some might term regicide, yet his own language implies that the existence of a kingdom is natural and indeed something inherent in 'the state of man' (a phrase in which the word 'state' is of course itself already weighted on the side of established authority and the *status quo*). Moreover, even as he attempts to rationalise the proposed assassination as a purely political act his own metaphor undoes him, for the word 'genius' inevitably brings with it the idea of the immaterial and intangible, as indeed the implicit distinction between it and 'mortal instruments' confirms. Even as he contemplates the killing of a ruler, then, Brutus provides more impressive testimony to support Claudius' theory of the inherent impossibility of such an act than anything that Claudius himself says or does is able to offer.

In a way, Caesar by the end of the play has indeed moved up into the sky, configuring everything which lies below him. In Roman history, Julius Caesar was deified; in Shakespeare's play, his ghost appears to Brutus (4.3.279–81), who subsequently exclaims,

> O Julius Caesar, thou art mighty yet!
> Thy spirit walks abroad, and turns our swords
> Into our own proper entrails.
>
> (5.3.94–6)

In fact, Brutus says that 'The ghost of Caesar hath appeared to me / Two several times by night' (5.5.17–18). We, however, have only seen it once, perhaps suggesting that Brutus has internalised the vision just as Angelo in *Measure for Measure* has internalised his sense of the duke's omniscience and omnipotence; indeed for Richard Wilson, Shakespeare, writing more or less contemporaneously with the invention of the confessional, anticipates Foucault by tracing the ways in which a culture of state-sponsored surveillance becomes internalised to the point that its actual external trappings are no longer needed.[34] By the end of the play, then, the secular is no longer distinct from the spiritual but is wholly permeated by it.

Seeing Like Paul: *King John*

Of particular interest and urgency in any discussion of religion and politics is *King John*. This was a narrative with very considerable contemporary political resonance which Shakespeare, as John Klause points out, treats in a notably apolitical way:

> So little partial was he … that Colley Cibber, in the eighteenth century, finding Shakespeare too 'cold' on the conflict between John and the papacy, gave the subject more heat by rewriting *King John* from the point of view suggested in the revised title: *Papal Tyranny in the Reign of King John.*

Nevertheless, Klause suggests that 'Shakespeare should at least be seen as giving weight to opposing interpretations of the issues which his play evokes. Among these are the relationship of religious to political authority',[35] which is of course central to my theme. Klause also argues that *King John* has a clear and identifiable debt to the work of Southwell. A number of the echoes he identifies are about eyes. For instance, he traces to *Saint Peter's Complaint* the eye imagery of the following passage:[36]

> I do, my lord; and in her eye I find
> A wonder, or a wondrous miracle,
> The shadow of myself form'd in her eye;
> Which, being but the shadow of your son,
> Becomes a sun and makes your son a shadow:
> I do protest I never lov'd myself
> Till now infixed I beheld myself
> Drawn in the flattering table of her eye.[37]

Eyes often constitute an important motif in writing of this period which reflects on religious controversy, in ways which are perhaps influenced by the story of St Paul on the road to Damascus. In *King Lear*, which clearly reflects on the controversy sparked by the exorcisms at Denham,[38] of which Protestants and Catholics took different views, Gloucester is blinded. In Rowley's *A Shoemaker, A Gentleman*, a play to which I shall recur in Chapter 6, Lutius is temporarily blinded by water from the pool but Winifred restores his sight.[39] In *King John*, the question of who is blind and who can see clearly becomes particularly pressing.

Throughout the play, eye imagery abounds. King John speaks to the citizens of Angers of 'your city's eyes, your winking gates' (2.1.215), and eye imagery occurs in a number of other contexts, inevitably reaching its climax in the story of the attempted blinding of Arthur. John introduces the subject by saying that he could broach the subject of Arthur's death to Hubert 'If that thou couldst see me without eyes, / Hear me without ears' (3.2.58–9); next, he implores, 'Good Hubert, Hubert, Hubert, throw thine eye / On yon young boy' (3.2.69–70).

To Arthur himself, Hubert says,

Hubert ... I must be brief, lest resolution drop
Out at mine eyes in tender womanish tears. –
Can you not read it? Is it not fair writ?

Arthur. Too fairly, Hubert, for so foul effect:
Must you with hot irons burn out both mine eyes?
(4.1.35–9)

Seeking to change Hubert's mind, Arthur plays insistently on the various connotations of eyes:

O heaven, that there were but a mote in yours,
A grain, a dust, a gnat, a wandering hair,
Any annoyance in that precious sense!
Then, feeling what small things are boisterous there,
Your vild intent must needs seem horrible.
(4.1.92–6)

Ostensibly the purpose of this harping on the vulnerability of eyes is to awaken feelings of empathy in Hubert, but an audience who regularly attended church on a Sunday could not fail to hear an echo of the biblical injunction to take the mote out of own's one eye (Matthew 7:5), which clearly refers to metaphorical rather than literal eyesight. Moreover, what Hubert actually says to Arthur when he relents, after all the extended discussion about the possibility of blinding him, is 'Your uncle must not know but you are dead' (4.1.127). This suggests that the play's incessant talk of eyes is actually something of a disguise, a blind or proxy for something else, and one might in fact suggest that the play's sustained attention to eyes is part of a wider interest in Shakespeare's plays as a whole in what it is and is not useful and productive to see. Shakespeare himself, as we have seen, might have been considered open to accusations of selective vision. *King John*, however, sees two things with great clarity: firstly, it registers the suffering of the victims of war, most notably Arthur, Constance and Blanche, and secondly, it acknowledges the force and vigour of John's patriotic affirmation of the superiority of secular over spiritual power: 'from the mouth of England / Add thus much more, that no Italian priest / Shall tithe or toll in our dominions' (3.1.78–80). Simultaneously foreshadowing and echoing Henry VIII's defiance of the Pope and the spirit of the Elizabethan Settlement, John here sets out a statement of intent to which Shakespeare himself might, I think, well have subscribed, and which certainly seems to have been the animating principle underlying the behaviour of the many English Catholics who turned their faces against the attempts of the Spanish to invade England.

Shakespeare's caution is especially clear if we compare *King John* with the anonymous Queen's Men play *The Troublesome Reign of King John*. This is similar to Shakespeare's version in many ways, not least in that Hubert appears here too, and here too spares Arthur's eyes. However, it is wildly and crudely anti-clerical. We hear a great deal about the misbehaviour of nuns and friars, and John is poisoned by a monk, after observing that

> Philip, I tell thee man,
> Since Iohn did yeeld vnto the Priest of Rome,
> Nor he nor his haue prospred on the earth.[40]

Finally it closes with the Bastard saying 'If Englands Peeres and people ioyne in one, / Nor Pope, nor France, nor Spaine can do them wrong' (sig. M1v). Shakespeare's play retains the idea of poisoning but moves it to the metaphorical rather than the literal realm. John himself says

> This fever that hath troubled me so long
> Lies heavy on me. O, my heart is sick!
> (5.3.3–4)

His self-diagnosis is later confirmed by his son:

> It is too late. The life of all his blood
> Is touched corruptibly, and his pure brain,
> Which some suppose the soul's frail dwelling-house,
> Doth by the idle comments that it makes
> Foretell the ending of mortality.
> (5.7.1–5)

It is true that John later says he has been poisoned (5.7.36), but we have already been told that he is rambling and what he goes on to say supports that, so that it is impossible to be certain of what has happened.

It is also worth noting the exchange between Blanche and Constance in III.i:

> *Blanche.*   The Lady Constance speaks not from her faith,
>   But from her need.
>
> *Constance.*   O, if thou grant my need,
>   Which only lives but by the death of faith,
>   That need must needs infer this principle,
>   That faith would live again by death of need.
>   (3.1.136–140)

Perhaps in Shakespeare too, need ultimately takes precedence over faith, as for many English Catholics at the time of the Armada, patriotism in the country's hour of need certainly did, and a quietly ironic appreciation of the absurdities and contradictions of the political system and the official religion it enforced seemed to him preferable to openly challenging it. Both Henry V and the Duke of *Measure for Measure* may be morally suspect, but both, albeit in different ways, show themselves able to deploy and indeed arguably suborn the power of the spiritual and to harness it firmly to the cause of their own temporal power, and the ways in which they do so may well be felt to be necessary for the ultimate security and smooth functioning of the state. Perhaps the most profound articulation of such a philosophy of pragmatism comes in the closing lines of *King John*, which Shakespeare puts into the mouth of the Bastard, arguably the most sympathetic character in the play:

> This England never did, nor never shall,
> Lie at the proud foot of a conqueror,
> But when it first did help to wound itself.
> Now these her princes are come home again
> Come the three corners of the world in arms
> And we shall shock them! Nought shall make us rue
> If England to itself do rest but true!
>
> (5.7.112–18)

If Shakespeare ignored the exhortation of *Saint Peter's Complaint*, if that was indeed addressed to him, that may well have been because he was firmly on the side of St Paul when it came to the question of which side of the edge between secular and spiritual authority he wanted to be on.

At the same time, though, it is characteristic of both Shakespeare and of early modern writing on borders in general that each of the plays which appears to offer a perspective on the question also contains within itself the germ of a precisely opposite position. In the first place, all the plays which I have considered in this chapter make it quite clear that both spiritual and secular spheres of influence are primarily imagined and figured in terms of each other. I have already mentioned how central Pauline theology was to the doctrine of the king's two bodies, and this neatly emblematises the ways in which the discourses of secular and of spiritual repeatedly bleed into each other: God had a kingdom, and kings ruled most effectively if they could present themselves as doing so with divine backing even if not necessarily by divine right. To Marlowe, with whom I began the chapter, this parallel would of course have appeared as compelling evidence of the Machiavellian perspective that man had created God in his own image, but it was equally susceptible of the equal and opposite interpretation, which entailed imagining God as demanding allegiance in the same way as the monarch did, and as potentially responding in the same way if allegiance was withheld.

In the second place, we are consistently made aware of the cost of seeing only the edge and ignoring the adjacency. Henry V may manipulate his Archbishop and feel initial confidence in his own ability to cajole his God, but that confidence does slip. In *Measure for Measure*, Duke Vincentio may find that the hood of a monk gives him greater power than the coronet of a duke, but the audience may well feel that it does so at the cost of the genuine spiritual development of his subjects. In *Julius Caesar*, the regicidal Brutus and his friends offer perhaps the canon's most persuasive evidence for the sanctity of monarchs, but the play does not hesitate to reveal weaknesses in both Caesar and his eventual successor. And in *King John*, the youth, vulnerability and eloquence of Arthur and the sharply poignant grief which made Constance a favourite role for Victorian actresses give us the clearest picture in the canon of the price which may need to be paid for the national security which the Bastard so eloquently hymns at the end. Nevertheless, however loudly St Peter may complain, St Paul always continues to be heard; their voices are in a sustained counterpoint, and what all these plays most fundamentally reveal is that the edges which mark each of these two saints' spheres of power can keep their sharpness only if each is constantly ground by the other.

Notes

[1]   Joscelin, *The life of the glorious bishop S. Patricke …*, translated by Fr B.B. (St Omer: [G Seutin?] for John Heigham, 1625), p. 23.

[2]   John Clapham, *The historie of Great Britannie declaring the successe of times and affaires in that iland, from the Romans first entrance, vntill the raigne of Egbert, the West-Saxon prince; who reduced the severall principalities of the Saxons and English, into a monarchie, and changed the name of Britanie into England* (London: Valentine Simmes, 1606), p. 108.

[3]   Peter C. Mancall, *Hakluyt's Promise: An Elizabethan's Obsession for an English America* (New Haven: Yale University Press, 2000), p. 139.

[4]   Lisa Hopkins, *A Christopher Marlowe Chronology* (Basingstoke: Palgrave, 2005), p. 136).

[5]   William Warner, *Albions England* (London: the Widow Orwin for Joan Broome, 1597), p. 85.

[6]   See for instance my '*The Comedy of Errors* and the Date of Easter', *Ben Jonson Journal* 7 (2000), pp. 55–64.

[7]   Marie Axton, *The Queen's Two Bodies: Drama and the Elizabethan Succession* (London: Royal Historical Society, 1977), p. 80.

[8]   Tom Rutter, *Work and Play on the Shakespearean Stage* (Cambridge: Cambridge University Press, 2008), p. 80.

[9]   See for instance Linda Shenk, *Learned Queen: The Image of Elizabeth I in Politics and Poetry* (Basingstoke: Palgrave Macmillan, 2010), p. 189.

[10]   See for instance Huston Diehl, '"Strike All that Look Upon With Marvel": Theatrical and Theological Wonder in *The Winter's Tale*', in *Rematerializing Shakespeare: Authority and Representation on the Early Modern English Stage*, edited by Bryan Reynolds and William N. West (Basingstoke: Palgrave, 2005), p. 21.

[11]   Julia Reinhard Lupton, 'Paul Shakespeare: Exegetical Exercises', in *Religion and Drama in Early Modern England: The Performance of Religion on the Renaissance Stage*, edited by Jane Hwang Degenhardt and Elizabeth Williamson (Burlington: Ashgate, 2011), p. 209.

[12]   R.W. Desai, 'Seneca, Nero, Claudius I, Democritus, Christ, St. Paul, and Luther in *Hamlet*', in *Shakespeare's Intellectual Background*, edited by Bhim S. Dahiya (New Delhi: Viva Books, 2008), pp. 93, 91 and 100.

[13]   William Shakespeare, *Hamlet*, edited by Harold Jenkins (London: Methuen, 1982), 4.5.123–4. All further quotations from the play will be taken from this edition and reference will be given in the text.

[14] For an account of this episode, see for instance Donald Attwater, *The Penguin Dictionary of Saints*, 2nd edition (Harmondsworth: Penguin, 1983), p. 266.

[15] Michael Goulder, *St. Paul versus St. Peter: A Tale of Two Missions* (London: SCM Press, 1994), introduction, pp. ix–x.

[16] John Derrick, *The Image of Ireland* (London: J. Kingston for John Day, 1581), sigs A3v – A4r.

[17] Jean-Christophe Mayer, '"This Papist and his Poet": Shakespeare's Lancastrian kings and Robert Parsons's *Conference about the Next Succession*', in *Theatre and religion: Lancastrian Shakespeare*, edited by Richard Dutton, Alison Findlay and Richard Wilson (Manchester: Manchester University Press, 2003), p. 116.

[18] Michael Wood, *In Search of Shakespeare* (London: BBC Worldwide, 2003), pp. 153–4 and 162. Scott R. Pilarz also speculates on Southwell's influence on Shakespeare, though without reaching any particular conclusion. (Scott R. Pilarz, S.J., *Robert Southwell, and the Mission of Literature, 1561–1595: Writing Reconciliation* [Burlington: Ashgate, 2004], pp. 255–6).

[19] Frank Brownlow, 'Southwell and Shakespeare', in *KM 80: A birthday album for Kenneth Muir* (Liverpool: Liverpool University Press, 1987), p. 27.

[20] Anne R. Sweeney, *Robert Southwell. Snow in Arcadia: Redrawing the English Lyric Landscape, 1586–95* (Manchester: Manchester University Press, 2006), p. 15.

[21] Alison Shell, 'Why Didn't Shakespeare Write Religious Verse?', in *Shakespeare, Marlowe, Jonson: New Directions in Biography*, edited by Takashi Kozuka and J. R. Mulryne (Burlington: Ashgate, 2006), p. 85.

[22] Richard Wilson, *Secret Shakespeare: Studies in theatre, religion and resistance* (Manchester: Manchester University Press, 2004), p. 126.

[23] Shell, 'Why Didn't Shakespeare Write Religious Verse?', pp. 90, 93 and 105.

[24] Mayer, '"This Papist and his Poet"', pp. 127 and 123.

[25] William Shakespeare, *King Henry V*, edited by T. W. Craik (London: Routledge, 1995), 1.1.73–81. All further quotations from the play will be taken from this edition and reference will be given in the text.

[26] William Shakespeare, 'Sonnet 138', in *Shakespeare's Sonnets*, edited by Stephen Booth (New Haven: Yale University Press, 1977), pp. 118–9.

[27] William Shakespeare, *Measure for Measure*, edited by J.M. Nosworthy (Harmondsworth: Penguin, 1969), 5.1.363–7. All further quotations from the play will be taken from this edition and reference will be given in the text.

[28] I note Gary Taylor's suggestion that prior to revision by Middleton the play was set in Ferrara ('Shakespeare's Mediterranean *Measure for Measure*, in *Shakespeare and the Mediterranean*, edited by Tom Clayton, Susan Brock and Vicente Forés [Newark: University of Delaware Press, 2004], pp. 243–269), but I do not think the evidence is conclusive.

[29] Leah S. Marcus, *Puzzling Shakespeare: Local Reading and its Discontents* (Berkeley: University of California Press, 1988), pp. 190–91.

[30] Joscelin, *The life of the glorious bishop S. Patricke*, p. 47.

[31] Niccolò Machiavelli, *The Prince*, translated by George Bull (Harmondsworth: Penguin, 1961), pp. 73–4.

[32] Sweeney, *Robert Southwell*, p. 129.

[33] William Shakespeare, *Julius Caesar*, edited by Norman Sanders (Harmondsworth: Penguin, 1967), 1.1.1–2. All further quotations from the play will be taken from this edition and reference will be given in the text.

[34] Richard Wilson, *Will Power* (Hemel Hempstead: Harvester Wheatsheaf, 1993), p. 156.

[35] John Klause, 'New Sources for Shakespeare's *King John*: The Writings of Robert Southwell', *Studies in Philology* 98.4 (Fall 2001), p. 402.

[36] Klause, 'New Sources for Shakespeare's *King John*', p. 405.

[37] William Shakespeare, *King John*, edited by E.A.J. Honigmann (London: Routledge, 1967), II.i.496–503. All further quotations from the play will be taken from this edition and reference will be given in the text.

[38] F.W. Brownlow, *Shakespeare, Harsnett, and the Devils of Denham* (Newark: University of Delaware Press, 1993).

[39] William Rowley, *A Shoemaker, A Gentleman*, edited by Trudi L. Darby (London: Nick Hern Books, 2002), 3.1.

[40] *The first and second part of the troublesome raigne of Iohn King of England* (London, 1611), sig. L4r.

PART II
The Edge of the Nation

Chapter 3
Sex on the Edge

In the parish records of the small village of Beaumont, in Cumbria, there are three entries from the 1820s recording the baptisms of the two sons and one daughter of local couple George and Isabella Bainbridge. After the record of each christening, the vicar has made a caustic-seeming comment:

> 26 Feb 1826 Thomas son of George and Isabella Bainbridge of Beaumont, Cordwainer. Parents married in Scotland as they say.

> 4 May 1827 Margaret daughter of George and Isabella Bainbridge of Beaumont, Cordwainer. Parents married in Scotland as they say.

> 5 July 1829 James son of George and Isabella Bainbridge of Beaumont, Shoemaker. Parents married in Scotland as they say.[1]

Beaumont is close to the Solway Firth, so it would not have been beyond the realms of possibility that a couple from the village could have been married in Scotland, but I take the vicar to be implying that he does not believe they were married at all, and I think he was right: there seems to be no record to be found in either England or Scotland of a marriage between George and Isabella. Indeed there is perhaps a note of weary resignation detectable in the vicar's tone: 'married in Scotland as they say' could mean 'they say they were married in Scotland, but I don't believe them', but it might also suggest that this was a well-known euphemism, rather as my grandmother (whose father was George and Isabella's great-grandson) would have said that they were 'living over the brush'. Perhaps, too, the vicar is simply registering a general hopelessness about the difficulty of keeping track of marriages in territory so close to the Border. It is clear from the Cumberland registers during this period that there was a general ecclesiastical push to keep the number of irregular unions and illegitimate births as low as possible, and it is seems clear that the vicar of Beaumont found the proximity of Scotland a pronounced hindrance to this project.

A similar phenomenon is also clearly visible in the early modern period. In 1633 the Scottish author William Lithgow published a long poem called *Scotlands Welcome*. Ostensibly, this was written to congratulate Charles I on the occasion of his journey north for his long-delayed Scottish coronation, but Lithgow interrupts the poem for a long excursus to do something quite different, which is to castigate the border town of Berwick-upon-Tweed for being a city of sin:

> Nay; *Barwick*, jumps with *Rome*, in more then this,
> Slaughter, Adultry, Incest, whats amisse?
> In ciuill Law, or *Church*, it will protect them.[2]

For Lithgow, the iniquity of Berwick-upon-Tweed knows no bounds metaphorically because it is in a liminal position literally. Usually in early modern writing it is the English accusing other people (usually the Irish) of practising sexual deviancy, but in this poem Lithgow's personified Scotland levels that charge against the English:

> There's too of late a new eclipsd miscaryage,
> But rather ane abuse, of honest marryage:
> For now young persons, fauncyeing other loues,
> Without consent of Parents (thus it proues)
> Or of their pastors approbation, neither
> Of Towne nor Parish, nay, of Friend or Father;
> Away they goe to *England*; there they're married,
> And sometymes too, lyke Partyes turne miscaryed
> Where fayling of Church rites, this yoke they draw,
> That lawles Loue, may be made loueles Law.
>   (ll. 763–72)

Like the nineteenth-century vicar of Beaumont, Lithgow deplores the permeability of the Border and its vulnerability to exploitation by couples trying to evade the eagle eyes of the church. He fears, it seems, that degrees of kinship and marital history might be insufficiently understood by priests on the other side of the Border, leading to inappropriate and indeed illegal marriages. Even though he is writing ostensibly to celebrate an occasion which marks the closeness between England and Scotland, what Lithgow throughout the poem seems actually to want to see is a far more marked differentiation between the two; indeed for Lithgow, the spiritual salvation of both countries is imperilled by their geographical closeness, because of the dangerous, disturbing possibility of sex across the Border.

Early modern literature is rich in examples of this tension, and it is some of that literature that I want to turn to now, in order to argue that the Border, for all the emotional and practical investment in it by members of both nations, was nevertheless an edge characterised by radical permeability on a number of levels. First and foremost, it was, as Lithgow suggested, an almost totally ineffective barrier against cross-border marriages and other, less licit sexual relationships. For the secular and spiritual powers on both sides of the Border with an interest in controlling and policing it, this was inconvenient, because it led to the formation of alliances and allegiances which cut across national loyalties and interests and habitually operated in ways which were informal and difficult to keep track of. However, cross-border relationships might not only have a political force. Sex on the edge is sometimes sex on the edge not just of a country, or occasionally a continent; on occasions it can be imagined as being in some sense sex on the edge of the world, a coming together of partners from two fundamentally different orders of being which can have profoundly destabilising and far-reaching effects. Elsewhere I have discussed the possible pertinence in this respect of the Border ballad of 'Tam Lin', which tells of a romance between a mortal and the Fairy Queen, under the rubric of 'marrying the dead',[3] but this is a phenomenon not confined to the Border between England and Scotland; it is also to be found in association with the edges of other nations, and it is not only fairies who may be potential sexual partners, but gods or, sometimes, those who are less than human rather than more so, for sex on the edge allows the very category 'human' to be called into question.

Marlowe: Categorisation on the Edge

I want to start in the late sixteenth century, by looking at Marlowe's poem *Hero and Leander*. This is set on the banks of the Hellespont, one of the points where Europe meets Asia, and involves repeated and increasingly dangerous negotiations of that threatening, liminal space. Marlowe tells us that 'At Sestos Hero dwelt' (l. 5), that is on what is now the Gallipoli peninsula, while Leander lived at Abydos, a city in Asia Minor which was later used by Xerxes as a springboard for the invasion of Greece. The difference between Sestos and Abydos thus marks the difference not only between two cities but between two continents, and while it is possible to cross from one to the other, Leander finds it perilous to do so, and not only in the ways that might be expected, for the crossing of the strait explicitly brings his gender identity into question, or at least appears to, when Leander supposes that Neptune's sexual advances must mean that the god has mistaken him for a woman:

> The god put Helle's bracelet on his arm,
> And swore the sea should never do him harm.
> He clapped his plump cheeks, with his tresses played,
> And smiling wantonly, his love bewrayed.
> He watched his arms, and as they opened wide
> At every stroke, betwtixt them would he slide,
> And steal a kiss, and then run out and dance,
> And as he turned, cast many a lustful glance,
> And threw him gaudy toys to please his eys,
> And dive into the water, and there pry
> Upon his breast, his thighs, and every limb,
> And up again, and close beside him swim,
> And talk of love. Leander made reply,
> 'You are deceived, I am no woman, I'.[4]

Marlowe is of course teasing us here – Neptune is perfectly well aware that Leander is no woman, and that is precisely why he is interested – but from Leander's point of view there seems to be a sense that this location is so liminal that change of almost any kind is possible in it. The poem even offers its twin cities as the locus of a 'myth of origins' for the difference between European and non-European when we are told that

> So lovely fair was Hero, Venus' nun,
> As Nature wept, thinking she was undone,

Because she took more from her than she left,
And of such wondrous beauty her bereft:
Therefore, in sign her treasure suffered wrack,
Since Hero's time hath half the world been black.
                              (Sestiad I, 45–50)

This is, then, a space so liminal that the categories of both gender and race may be rendered fluid and unstable, or at least come under scrutiny, when it is traversed. Leander's quest for sex on the edge has brought him considerably more than he bargained for; in a sort of hideous actualisation of Lithgow's fear that the identities of those on the other side of the Border might not be properly understood, his crossing of the Hellespont in quest of the mortal, female Hero threatens instead to throw him into the clutches of the immortal, male Neptune.

In *Edward II*, Marlowe revisits both the Hero and Leander narrative and the edge between Europe and Asia. Here it is specifically national borders which are seen as permeable, unstable, and sometimes literally fluid, and this is something which the play insistently connects to sexual transgression. As the play opens, Gaveston exclaims,

Sweet prince, I come; these, these thy amorous lines
Might have enforced me to have swum from France
And, like Leander, gasped upon the sand.[5]

Leander came close to an involuntary same-sex encounter; Gaveston seeks a voluntary one, and this inversion of the Leander story heralds inversions of other polarities and norms and a troubling of the edges which mark and circumscribe them. Isabella imaginatively inhabits the edge between Europe and Asia when she vows to Sir John of Hainault,

Ah sweet sir John, even to the utmost verge
Of Europe, or the shore of Tanaïs,
Will we with thee to Hainault, so we will.
                              (4.2.29–31)

John Michael Archer notes that 'Lake Maeotis or the Tanais river (the Don) were often said to demarcate Asia from Europe';[6] Ukraina, the name of one of the territories through which the Don flowed, translates as 'on the edge'.[7] Perhaps Isabella focuses on rivers because this was a border strikingly undifferentiated by any other geographical features – as Jane Pettegree notes, 'without this sense of a boundary, Europe is indistinguishable from the rest of the vast Asian continental mass'[8] – and rivers are often figured in this period as border markers of unusual potency (I will turn later to the power of Sabrina, nymph of the river Severn, in Milton's *Comus*). Perhaps too, though, Isabella is aware that borders in general are under pressure in this scene, because as Pettegree also observes, 'Hainault was in the 1590s firmly part of the Spanish Netherlands, a place of exile and polemical agitation for English Catholics. In 1588, the Spanish army of invasion was to have been mustered on the beaches of Gravelines in the county of Hainault'.[9]

It is not only in Hainault that boundaries are threatened and destabilised, and as in *Hero and Leander*, they are so in ways specifically connected to sex, and to the very categories of sexuality and gender. Within England, Edward is not only outraging his wife and his barons by his sexual preferences but also doing his best to destabilise borders, saying dismissively to his barons,

> If this content you not,
> Make several kingdoms of this monarchy,
> And share it equally amongst you all.
> (1.4.69–71)

Indeed Lancaster, in a passage I have already discussed in the first chapter, warns him that his borders, including the all-important one with Ireland, are already threatened (2.2.160–6), as a result of which

> The northern borderers, seeing their houses burnt,
> Their wives and children slain, run up and down,
> Cursing the name of thee and Gaveston.
> (2.2.178–80)

And Edward is to be proved disastrously wrong when, in answer to Spencer Junior's assurance that Mortimer will certainly be captured if he is still in England, he confidently asserts,

> 'If', dost thou say? Spencer, as true as death,
> He is in England's ground; our port-masters
> Are not so careless of their King's command.
> (4.3.20–23)

In fact, Mortimer is already safe in France. In crossing outside the culturally accepted boundaries of sexual relationships, Edward, it seems, has also weakened and disturbed the boundaries of his kingdom.

Edward II is not the only Marlowe play to focus on the motif of sex on the edge; the idea is also central to *A Massacre at Paris*. It is difficult to focus closely on the verbal texture of this play because the surviving text is so clearly mangled and mutilated, conceivably as a result of censorship: the play might look dangerously like an admittedly belated warning to Elizabeth on the dangers of cross-faith and cross-border marriage with a French prince such as Anjou. It could certainly leave no one in any doubt of the disadvantages of having Anjou's mother Catherine de' Medici as a mother-in-law, and there might well seem to be something pointed in the dying King Henry's injunction 'Agent for England, send thy mistress word / What this detested Jacobin hath done' and Navarre's resolution that he will

> with the Queen of England join my force
> To beat the papal monarch from our lands,
> And keep those relics from our countries' coasts.[10]

More important for my purposes than the possible extradiegetic glance at Anjou, though, is that Navarre's mention of 'coasts' is one of a number of references to edges and borders in the play, and that even in the doubtful state of the text it is possible to see that these are consistently figured as troubled and porous. The Guise dismisses Navarre as 'but a nook of France' (2, 88), reminding us of the uncomfortable contiguity of the two, and the Anjou of the play constitutes Poland too as contested border territory when he tells the two Polish lords that he understands Poland to be the theatre of

> The greatest wars within our Christian bounds,
> I mean our wars against the Muscovites,
> And on the other side against the Turk.
>   (10, 10–12)

Even human relationships are figured in terms of disputes over territory, when the soldier hired by the Guise apostrophises Mugeroun 'whereas he is your landlord, you will take upon you to be his, and till the ground that he himself should occupy, which is his own free land' (19, 6–8). Only one entity in the play is taken to be secure and inviolate, and that is the power of Catherine de' Medici, who says of her son King Henry 'if he grudge or cross his mother's will, / I'll disinherit him and all the rest' (11, 41–2), and ultimately it is she who is able to control the borders of both land and family:

>   When thou wast born,
> I would that I had murdered thee, my son!
> My son? Thou art a changeling, not my son.
> I curse thee, and exclaim thee miscreant,
> Traitor to God and to the realm of France!
>   (21, 148–51)

As Volumnia will later threaten to do to Coriolanus, Catherine here defines her son as both not her son and not French, stripping him of identity on every level.

One of the complaints raised against the Guise himself is precisely that he is a disturber of borders, when King Henry says of him,

> Did he not draw a sort of English priests
> From Douai to the seminary at Rheims,
> To hatch forth treason 'gainst their natural Queen?
>   (21, 105–8)

The *ur*-disturbance, though, has of course been that international, inter-confessional marriage between Henry of Navarre and Marguerite of Valois, so liminal that it could not even be celebrated inside the church but had to take place in the doorway. Because of this particular cross-border union, at least three thousand people died in Paris alone during the St Bartholomew's Day massacre. It is thus not surprising that however murky and garbled the text of this play may be in places, the danger of disturbed borders is one subject on which it speaks loudly and clearly, and it, too, links them to sex.

Identity on the Edge: Incest, Imposture and the Inhuman

As well as the Hainault scene in *Edward II*, there is also one in which Edward's enemy Mortimer himself threatens destabilisation of a border, this time that with Wales, when he storms that 'Wigmore shall fly, to set my uncle free' (2.2.195). The border with Wales, at which Mortimer gestures here, could find itself associated with odd or transgressive relationships almost as readily as the Anglo-Scottish Border, often in ways which have an explicitly supernatural valence, which make the Welsh marches feel like the edge of the world rather than simply the edge of the nation. One of the insults cited in bawdy court cases was 'Welsh jade',[11] and perhaps some such cultural stereotype underlies *Henry IV, Part 1*, in which Mortimer has a Welsh wife. In one sense, she is utterly strange to him, since he cannot understand her language:

> This is the deadly spite that angers me,
> My wife can speak no English, I no Welsh.[12]

In another sense, though, she is readily and easily classifiable and assimilable into a wearily familiar paradigm of the feminine, as we see by Hotspur's reaction to her and his behaviour in her presence. When Glendower asks all those present to be seated and to listen while his daughter plays and sings in Welsh, Hotspur immediately responds 'Come, Kate, thou art perfect in lying down' (3.1.221); when he fidgets and Lady Percy tells him to be still, he says 'Neither, 'tis a woman's fault' (3.1.234); and when Lady Percy replies 'Now, God help thee!' he immediately ripostes 'To the Welsh lady's bed' (3.1.235–6). Perhaps some of this blatant sexualisation of Lady Mortimer is explained by Middleton's *A Chaste Maid in Cheapside*, where the entrance of Tim and the Welsh Gentlewoman after their wedding is greeted by Yellowhammer with 'Look gentlemen, if ever you saw the picture / Of the unfortunate marriage, yonder 'tis';[13] in fact, the suggestion in *A Chaste Maid* as a whole might well seem to be that Welsh gentlewomen fall into much the same category as Scottish marriages seem to have done for the nineteenth-century vicar of Beaumont.

It is in *Cymbeline* that Shakespeare most suggestively explores this particular border, and he does so in ways which invest it with a distinctly otherworldly energy. The story of Snow White, which *Cymbeline* in so many ways resembles,[14] features a bride who apparently comes from the realm of the dead, and *Cymbeline* itself has echoes of the fairy bride motif. Imogen prays, 'From fairies and the tempters of the night / Guard me, beseech ye' (2.2.9–10); Belarius says of Imogen 'But that it eats our victuals, I should think / Here were a fairy' (3.6.40–1); Guiderius declares of the supposed Fidele, 'With female fairies will his tomb be haunted' (4.2.217); and Posthumus when he finds the paper which identifies him as a lion's whelp asks, 'What fairies haunt this ground?' (5.4.133). As Regina Buccola observes, 'Although there are no explicit fairy characters in this story, fairies are in fact referenced at key moments in the experience of some of the play's most provocative characters', and 'the skein of religious association in the play threatens always to unwind, revealing that underneath the page-boy disguise and pagan burial rituals, the initial female heir to England's throne just might be the fairy queen, mistress of pagan rituals and guardian of Catholicism's dead'.[15] Certainly when the play's heroine crosses into Wales, many things are called into question. Although her name usually appears as Imogen, it should almost certainly more properly be Innogen, the name of the wife of Brutus. It was Brutus who had supposedly instantiated the original division between England, Scotland and Wales when he divided the three realms amongst his three sons, Locrine, Albanact and Camber, as recalled in the anonymous sixteenth-century play *Locrine* where Camber is called the 'darling of thy mother Innogen',[16] and it might well be possible to see *Cymbeline* as part of a propaganda drive to persuade James to invest his son Henry with the title Prince of Wales which can be traced back to figures such as George Owen of Henllys who, writing on St David's Day, 1608, defended the title of 'Prince of Wales' in the clear hope of seeing it resurrected, as did eventually occur in 1610.[17] When Imogen finds her long-lost brothers in Wales, though, any sense of a radical difference between the two countries and their peoples collapses. Moreover, the fact that she does not at first recognise the supposed Polydore and Cadwal as her brothers may perhaps hint at the possibility which worried Lithgow and with which two others of Shakespeare's late plays, *The Winter's Tale* and *Pericles*, certainly flirt, which is that the too free crossing of borders may lead to incest, either witting or unwitting. After all, Imogen is in Wales partly to escape marriage with the son of her stepmother, and once there, she manages to confuse his body with that of her own husband: 'I know the shape of's leg: this is his hand: / His foot Mercurial: his Martial thigh' (4.2.309–10). Although she does of course have some excuse for this mistake in that the corpse of Cloten, her unwanted suitor, is both headless and also dressed in her husband's clothes, it might nevertheless serve as a suggestive reminder of what can happen when relatives are parted from each other and then subsequently meet again, as Imogen and her brothers do, for the stage is then set for what has recently been identified as genetic sexual attraction, a problem now well documented amongst reunited adoptees and members of their birth families.[18]

Genetic sexual attraction might also explain what happens in a play which is unquestionably about incest, John Ford's *'Tis Pity She's a Whore*, where Giovanni has been away studying in Bologna and Annabella appears not to recognise him when he returns:

> But see, Putana, see; what blessed shape
> Of some celestial creature now appears?
> What man is he, that with such sad aspect
> Walks careless of himself?

Putana.	Where?

Annabella.	Look below.

Putana. O, 'tis your brother, sweet –

Annabella.	Ha!

Putana.	'Tis your brother.

Annabella. Sure 'tis not he.[19]

'Tis Pity too is interested in borders, as we see when the boundary of civil jurisdiction comes to an abrupt end when the officers of the watch try to pursue the murderer Grimaldi once he has safely passed the threshold of his uncle the Cardinal, and the Cardinal abruptly prevents them (3.9.30–41). What we see in this scene is not a national border, but it does nevertheless clearly mark a boundary of another sort, where civic power and jurisdiction run up slap against that of the church, and in this world of invisible and ill-defined borders, sexual transgression flourishes.

There is also strong interest in borders and edges in another Ford play, *Perkin Warbeck*, in which Edward II's question 'Shall I still be haunted thus?' (2.2.153) is recalled when Henry VII opens the play by lamenting 'Still to be haunted, still to be pursued',[20] and this idea of haunting proves the prelude to a heady mixture of the Border as place of *realpolitik*, of sexual irregularity and of magic. James IV of Scotland, who at the time is supporting Warbeck, threatens the Bishop of Durham at Norham Castle that if he will not surrender,

> Tweed
> Shall overflow his banks with English blood,
> And wash the sand that cements those hard stones
> From their foundation.
> (3.4.7–10)

Here the river Tweed, virtually the only natural marker of the otherwise largely geographically featureless border between England and Scotland, is figured as a site of nightmare. For Ford's original audience, this would evoke powerful memories of conflict on the Border within living memory; indeed the distinctively Border 'bastles', which were designed to withstand attack, were still being built as late as the 1650s.[21] When the Bishop refuses to surrender, James falls back on the classic tactics of warfare and reiving on the Border, ordering 'Forage through / The country; spare no prey of life or goods' (3.4.54–5), upon which Warbeck offers a vivid account of what this will actually entail:

> Had I been
> Born what this clergyman would be defame
> Baffle belief with, I had never sought
> The truth of mine inheritance with rapes

Of women, or of infants murdered, virgins
Deflowered, old men butchered, dwellings fired,
My land depopulated, and my people
Afflicted with a kingdom's devastation.

(3.4.58–65)

This kind of devastation and sexual violence was an all-too-familiar effect of the power of the Border Reivers, but so, paradoxically, was a powerful, quasi-autonomous network of Anglo-Scottish intermarriages and alliances which entirely disregarded the geography of the Border and reduced successive English and Scottish Border wardens to frustration and despair. Ford's play echoes this blurring of national lines by staging one international marriage and prefiguring another. One of these, that between Katherine and Perkin, technically effects disparagement of the semi-royal Katherine by marrying her to someone who is almost certainly a low-born impostor; the other, that between James IV of Scotland and Margaret Tudor, which we see arranged during the course of the play, was the ultimate source of the Stuart claim to the throne of England, returning us to the source of Lithgow's concern about the subsequent weakening and attempted abolition of the Border. Alongside this political text, however, runs one rather more fantastic: Perkin and Katherine are ironically acclaimed by Huntley as 'King Oberon and Queen Mab' (3.2.11), and the Duchess of Burgundy is imagined as a witch who has conjured a ghost of the House of York. As in *Cymbeline*, where the idea of sex on the edge of Wales is bound up with images of fairies, sex on the Border between England and Scotland has the potential to activate disturbance of other edges too and mobilises ideas of violation of hierarchical structure and of contact with the unnatural and the taboo.

A work of the same year as *Perkin Warbeck*, Milton's *Comus*,[22] has often been read in the context of the sexual scandal surrounding the Earl of Castlehaven, who was related to the Bridgewater family, for whom Milton wrote the masque,[23] and I have argued elsewhere that this context might also be relevant for *Perkin Warbeck*.[24] In 1631 the Earl was found guilty of sodomising one of his servants, of physically assisting another servant to bugger the Countess, and of pandering his daughter-in-law to yet another servant;[25] *Comus*, it has been suggested, with its insistence on the sexual purity of its participants, was a conscious attempt to improve the reputation of the family, vicariously tainted by association with their notorious relative. There were links between Ford's play and Milton's masque in the shape of Francis Bacon, author of one of Ford's principal sources for the play, who was Castlehaven's brother-in-law, and also of a shared connection with the Lawes brothers: Henry Lawes took the role of the Attendant Spirit in *Comus*, while William seems to have composed the music for the two songs in Ford's last play, *The Lady's Trial*, and to have been employed by the Earl of Newcastle, to whom Ford dedicated *Perkin Warbeck*[26] (and whose daughter, Lady Elizabeth Cavendish, was later to marry Viscount Brackley, who had played the elder brother in *Comus*). Moreover, *Perkin Warbeck* refers overtly to the personal history of the Castlehaven family. The family name of the Castlehavens was Touchet, and the original title of the head of the family, before the creation of the earldom, had been Audley: the name of the renegade peer was, in full, Mervyn Touchet, Lord Audley, Earl of Castlehaven. It was an earlier bearer of that title, James Touchet, Lord Audley, whose story is prominently featured in *Perkin Warbeck* as one of the principal leaders of the Cornish revolt and who is mentioned by name four times.[27]

Comus, like *Perkin Warbeck*, is also concerned with borders and edges and again associates them with transgressive sexual relationships and with the supernatural. At the outset of the masque, the Attendant Spirit details the liminal nature of the location, saying of Neptune that

> this isle,
> The greatest and the best of all the main,
> He quarters to his blue-haired deities;
> And all this tract that fronts the falling sun
> A noble Peer of mickle trust and power
> Has in his charge, with tempered awe to guide
> An old and haughty nation proud in arms;
> Where his fair offspring, nursed in princely lore,
> Are coming to attend their father's state
> And new-entrusted scepter; but their way
> Lies through the perplexed paths of this drear wood.[28]

This proves to be not only a geographical border but one that marks change in other ways too, for all travellers in the wood are offered a drink by Comus, and

> Soon as the potion works, their human countenance,
> The express resemblance of the gods, is changed
> Into some brutish form of wolf, or bear,
> Or ounce, or tiger, hog, or bearded goat,
> All other parts remaining as they were.
> (ll. 68–72)

In this wood which gives entrance to the west, the very nature of the human is destabilised. Later, we meet Sabrina, nymph of the Severn, marker of another part of the border between England and Wales, and we are reminded of her significance in the traditional internal demarcation of the two by the Attendant Spirit's evocation of the Locrine narrative:

> There is a gentle Nymph not far from hence,
> That with moist curb sways the smooth Severn stream;
> Sabrina is her name, a virgin pure;
> Whilom she was the daughter of Locrine,
> That had the scepter from his father Brute.
> (ll. 824–8)

The Severn, like the Hellespont, is also established as a locus of metamorphosis as well as of boundary marking, for when Sabrina originally plunged into the river 'she underwent a quick immortal change' (l. 841), and her story in fact inscribes a transgressive sexuality at the heart of England's narrative of its own borders, for she was driven into the river by her furious stepmother Guendoline, the legitimate wife of Locrine, who had taken Sabrina's foreign-born mother as his mistress. The potential of borders for effecting quasi-magical change is further underlined when the Attendant Spirit says of the magical plant haemony that

> The leaf was darkish, and had prickles on it,
> But in another country, as he said,
> Bore a bright golden flower, but not in this soil.
> (ll. 631–3)

There does seem to be some evidence that, in the north, the border territory of Hadrian's Wall was associated with strange and powerful plants: a document from 1574, often but almost certainly erroneously attributed to Sampson Erdeswicke, declares that 'The Skotts lyches or surgeons, do yerely repayr to the sayd Roman wall next to thes, to gether sundry herbes for surgery, for that it is thought that the Romaynes there by had planted most nedefull herbes for sundry purposes, but howsoever it was, these herbes are fownd very wholesome'.[29] Certainly the idea in the Spirit's description of Haemony seems to be that national borders mark not just political identities but changes in the very character of the land and the vegetation it bears, and indeed the name haemony, which is a change from the moly of the original legend, is etymologically related to blood, and thus figures the plant as sharing a biology with the human and presumably therefore being subject to similar vulnerabilities, which may be conditioned by nationality, as humours and complexions were thought to be in geohumoral theory. Finally, *Comus* shows us the actual seat of government of the Marches when '*The scene changes, presenting Ludlow Town, and the President's Castle*' (l. 957 s.d.), underlying still further the extent to which we are on an edge.

In this liminal place, sexual danger occurs. The wicked Comus forms designs on the virgin Lady, and the Second Brother has no hope that

> Danger will wink on opportunity,
> And let a single helpless maiden pass
> Uninjured in this wild surrounding waste.
> (ll. 401–3)

If liminal locations seem to be conducive to sensuality, unbridled sex seems in turn to have the potential to affect borders, even that between life and death, when the Elder Brother declares that lust so acts on the soul that it

>   grows clotted by contagion,
> Imbodies and imbrutes, till she quite lose
> The divine property of her first being.
> Such are those thick and gloomy shadows damp
> Oft seen in charnel vaults and sepulchres,

Lingering, and sitting by a new-made grave,
As loth to leave the body that it loved.
                              (ll. 466–73)

In the Elder Brother's mind, the effect of lust on the soul is to anchor it so firmly to earth that, dying, it cannot break away from the body to cross the border into the spiritual world. It is therefore not surprising that the Attendant Spirit should thank Sabrina for her rescue of the Lady by expressing a wish that the form and power of the edge she marks should remain unimpaired:

May thy brimmed waves for this
Their full tribute never miss
From a thousand petty rills,
That tumble down the snowy hills.
                              (ll. 924–7)

Just as both William Lithgow and the nineteenth-century vicar of Beaumont worried that a permeable border would lead to sexual impropriety, so the Attendant Spirit associates a strongly marked border with the preservation of chastity.

In many respects, *Comus* obviously and deliberately recalls an earlier play about magic and transgressive sexual desires, *A Midsummer Night's Dream*. That too is a play which is interested in edges and borders, as we see when Lysander tells Hermia,

I have a widow aunt, a dowager
Of great revenue, and she hath no child –
From Athens is her house remote seven leagues –
And she respects me as her only son.
There, gentle Hermia, may I marry thee,
And to that place the sharp Athenian law
Cannot pursue us.[30]

The wood, then, is established as the edge between what is Athenian territory and what is not, and I have also argued elsewhere that Puck, who seems to be derived from the malign Irish spirit known as the Pooka,[31] perhaps gestures at another border when he describes himself as one who can travel 'Over park, over pale' (2.1.3), since the word 'pale' here seems to point us straight in the direction of the area around Dublin, known as the Pale, while the reference to 'Pensioners', that is the gentlemen pensioners who were Elizabeth's ceremonial guard, takes us out of the fairy world to remind us of the realities of the Elizabethan military machine. In some sense, the wood can certainly be seen as the Other of Athens in much the same way as the dystopic Ireland lay threateningly just offshore from the self-proclaimed orderliness of England, and in that liminal territory plighted faith is forfeited, a man acquires a donkey's head, and a fairy queen who might otherwise have reminded us of the Virgin Queen not only falls in love with a monster but also exchanges tales of adultery with her husband (2.1.64–76) as a border once again becomes a *locus* of sexual transgression and magical transformation.

Another play to couple sex on the border with magic is Greene's *The Scottish History of James the Fourth*, which, like *A Midsummer Night's Dream*, features Oberon and, like *Perkin Warbeck* and *Cymbeline*, provocatively juxtaposes the supernatural with the topical and the implicitly political. As *James the Fourth* opens, the lustful Scottish king has just married the virtuous English princess Dorothea, but already regrets this, because during the wedding ceremony he unfortunately looked round the chapel and fell in love with Ida, a Scottish girl. In order to be rid of Dorothea, who is an impediment to his pursuit of Ida, the king, like Posthumus in *Cymbeline*, tries to have her taken into the woods and murdered. The inevitable result of this is cross-border warfare, as we see when Nano announces that Dorothea's father is bent on revenge:

> The English king hath all the borders spoiled,
> Hath taken Morton prisoner, and hath slain
> Seven thousand Scottish lads not far from Tweed.
> (5.5.3–5)

As we saw in both *Perkin Warbeck* and the Lithgow poem with which I began, the iconic status of Berwick-upon-Tweed as the classic border city could leave no one in any doubt about the force of the Tweed as marker of the Border. Even as that force is registered, however, it is implicitly destabilised. At the start of the Induction, in modern editions, Oberon meets 'Bohan, a Scot, attired like a Redesdale man'.[32] W.L. Renwick's ingenious emendation of the text's 'rid-stall' to 'Redesdale' points us immediately in the direction of the Border Reivers whom James tried so hard to suppress, with mixed success, and draws attention to the changing role of the Border. That we should be thinking of contemporary rather than historical events is also slyly pointed up when Bohan tells us in the Induction, 'In the year 1520 was in Scotland a king, overruled with parasites, misled by lust, and many circumstances too long to trattle on now, much like our own court of Scotland this day' (Induction 106–9). Later, the said king is seen hunting (5.1), creating another obvious parallel with James but also echoing *A Midsummer Night's Dream* in this too, and later, *Comus* too is anticipated when Ateukin promises the king that he will 'gather moly, crocus, and the herbs / That heals the wounds of body and the mind' (1.1.263–4). Greene was writing before the accession of James to the English throne, but at a time when that was looking increasingly like the likeliest scenario, and these insistent glances forward serve to gesture firmly towards a world in which the Border itself will be undone, as James sought to rename Cumberland, Northumberland, Dumfriesshire and Roxburghshire 'the Middle Shires' and to present England and Scotland as a seamless geographical and political unity. Even if the physical force of this particular edge is blunted, though, the metaphysical charge it carries is retained; even as the narrative moves towards a reconciliation of England and Scotland, it keeps its fairies alive and available. Moreover, *Cymbeline*, *Perkin Warbeck*, *Comus* and *James IV* collectively suggest that the more alertly a play registers the extradiegetic world of Stuart politics, which worked so insistently to negate the political force of the Border, the greater that play's investment in the idea that politics itself might be trumped and short-circuited by the very different logic of the magical.

I have talked about seven plays and one poem by six different authors which focus on three different borders, but in some ways they all tell the same story, with strongly marked and insistently recurring elements. In that story, the edge constituted by a border is marked as a place of both danger and magic: in *A Midsummer Night's Dream*, *James IV* and *Comus* fairies or spirits actually appear; in *Perkin Warbeck*, Perkin and Katherine are ironically acclaimed by Huntley as 'King Oberon and Queen Mab' (3.2.11); in *Cymbeline*, Belarius notes that he might mistake Imogen for a fairy (3.7.14–15), and Posthumus sees the ghosts of his dead parents and brothers. Above all, though, the border proves a breeding ground for inappropriate or irregular sexual relations. In *'Tis Pity*, where we see the corrupting force of the border between temporal and ecclesiastical power, a brother impregnates his sister. In *Perkin Warbeck*, where we see warfare on the Anglo-Scottish Border, a princess marries a pretender. In *A Midsummer Night's Dream*, the boundary of Athenian control proves the locus for a fairy queen to dally with a man who has an ass's head. In *Cymbeline*, Imogen's crossing of the border into Wales leads her to kin whom she fails to recognise and misidentification of the body of her stepbrother as that of her husband, and in *Comus*, purity is endangered in the liminal zone of the March. In *Edward II* Marlowe, typically, inverts the pattern in that Edward's 'looseness' precedes the destabilisation of the borders of his kingdom, but the link is there nevertheless. The nineteenth-century vicar of Beaumont was, it seems, right to worry about the effect of a border on the morals of his parishioners, for a national border in all these instances proves to be the most insubstantial and permeable of edges. In the next two chapters, I shall continue to explore national borders, with particular reference to Shakespeare's representation of the borders of France, in order to consider what some of the consequences of that permeability might be.

Notes

[1]   Beaumont baptismal register, PRO 106/8 1820–45 inclusive.

[2]   William Lithgow, *Scotlands Welcome* … (Edinburgh: John Wreittoun, 1633), ll. 795–9.

[3]   Lisa Hopkins, 'Marrying the Dead: *A Midsummer Night's Dream*, *Hamlet*, *Antony and Cleopatra*, *Cymbeline* and *The Tempest*', in *Staged Transgression in Shakespeare's England*, edited by Edel Semple and Rory Loughnane (Palgrave Macmillan, 2013).

[4]   Christopher Marlowe, *Hero and Leander*, in *The Collected Poems of Christopher Marlowe*, edited by Patrick Cheney and Brian J. Striar (Oxford: Oxford University Press, 2006), Sestiad 2, 663–76.

[5]   Christopher Marlowe, *Edward II*, in *Christopher Marlowe: The Complete Plays*, edited by Mark Thornton Burnett (London: Everyman, 1999), 1.1.6–8. All further quotations from the play will be taken from this edition and reference will be given in the text.

[6]   John Michael Archer, *Old Worlds: Egypt, Southwest Asia, India, and Russia in Early Modern English Writing* (Stanford: Stanford University Press, 2001), pp. 102, 105,

and 108. John Gillies notes that 'If for no other reason, Marlowe's familiarity with the ancient boundary discourse may be assumed on the basis of his translation of the first book of Lucan's *Pharsalia*'. John Gillies, 'Marlowe, the *Timur* Myth, and the Motives of Geography', in *Playing the Globe: Genre and Geography in English Renaissance Drama*, edited by John Gillies and Virginia Mason Vaughan (Cranbury, N.J.: Associated University Presses, 1998), p. 210.

[7]   Norman Davies, *Vanished Kingdoms: The History of Half-Forgotten Europe* (London: Allen Lane, 2011), p. 260.

[8]   Jane Pettegree, *Foreign and Native on the English Stage, 1588–1611* (Basinsgstoke: Palgrave, 2011), p. 15.

[9]   Pettegree, *Foreign and Native on the English Stage*, p. 91.

[10]   Christopher Marlowe, *The Massacre at Paris*, in *The Complete Plays*, edited by Mark Thornton Burnett (London: J. M. Dent, 1999), 24.55–6 and 18.15–17. All further quotations from the play will be taken from the edition and reference will be given in the text.

[11]   Jonathan Bate, *Soul of the Age: The Life, Mind and World of William Shakespeare* (London: Viking, 2008), p. 180.

[12]   William Shakespeare, *Henry IV, Part 1*, edited by P.H. Davison (Harmondsworth: Penguin, 1968), 3.1.186–7. All further quotations from the play will be taken from this edition and reference will be given in the text.

[13]   Thomas Middleton, *A Chaste Maid in Cheapside*, edited by Alan Brissenden (London: Ernest Benn, 1968), 5.4.88–9.

[14]   See for instance Ros King, *Cymbeline: Constructions of Britain* (Aldershot: Ashgate, 2005), p. 25.

[15]   Regina Buccola, *Fairies, Fractious Women, and the Old Faith: Fairy Lore in Early Modern British Drama and Culture* (Selinsgrove: Susquehanna University Press, 2006), pp. 135 and 165.

[16]   W.S., *The Lamentable Tragedy of Locrine*, edited by Jane Lytton Gooch (London and New York: Garland, 1981), 1.2.199.

[17]   B.G. Charles, *George Owen of Henllys: A Welsh Elizabethan* (Aberystwyth: National Library of Wales Press, 1973), pp. 29, 60, and 116.

[18]   See for instance http://www.geneticsexualattraction.com.

[19]   John Ford, *'Tis Pity She's a Whore*, edited by Derek Roper (Manchester: Manchester University Press, 1997), 1.2.131–136. All further quotations from the play will be taken from this edition and reference will be given in the text.

[20]   John Ford, *Perkin Warbeck*, edited by Peter Ure (London: Methuen, 1968), I.i.1. All further quotations from the play will be taken from this edition and reference will be given in the text.

[21]   Mike Salter, *The Castles and Tower Houses of Cumbria* (Malvern: Folly Publications, 1998), p. 101; see also T.H. Rowland, *Medieval Castles, Towers, Peles and Bastles of Northumberland* [1987] (Morpeth: Sandhill Press, 1994), p. 12.

[22]   Though *Comus* was not published until 1637, the title page of the first edition states that it was performed at Michaelmas 1634. *Perkin Warbeck* was published in 1634.

[23]   This was first suggested by Barbara Breasted in '*Comus* and the Castlehaven Scandal', *Milton Studies* 3 (1971), pp. 201–204.

[24]   Lisa Hopkins, 'Touching Touchets: *Perkin Warbeck* and the Buggery Statute', *Renaissance Quarterly* 52:2 (summer, 1999), pp. 384–401.

[25]   Frances Dolan, *Dangerous Familiars: Representations of Domestic Crime in England 1550–1700* (Ithaca: Cornell University Press, 1994), p. 80.

[26]   See John P. Cutts, 'British Museum Additional MS. 31342: William Lawes' writing for the theatre and the court', *The Library*, 5th series, 7 (1952), pp. 225–34.

[27]   *Perkin Warbeck*, 1.3.133, 3.1.48, 3.1.75, and 3.1.94–8.

[28]   John Milton, *Comus*, in *The Portable Milton*, edited by Douglas Bush (Harmondsworth: Penguin, 1977), ll. 27–37. All further quotations from the masque will be taken from this edition and reference will be given in the text.

[29]   Eric Birley, *Research on Hadrian's Wall* (Kendal: Titus Wilson and son, 1961), p. 4.

[30]   William Shakespeare, *A Midsummer Night's Dream*, edited by Harold F. Brooks (London: Methuen, 1979), 1.1.157–163.

[31]   See for instance K.M. Briggs, *The Anatomy of Puck* (London: Routledge and Kegan Paul, 1959), p. 44.

[32]   Robert Greene, *James the Fourth*, edited by Norman Sanders (London: Methuen & co., 1970), Induction 1.0. All further quotations will be taken from this edition and reference will be given in the text.

Chapter 4
'Gate of Spain':
The Southern Edge of France

The country that we now refer to simply and unproblematically as 'France' was relatively slow to cohere as a geopolitical unity. For much of the mediaeval period large parts of it, in the form of the Angevin Empire, were held by various kings of England in their capacity first as descendants of William the Conqueror, who had been Duke of Normandy, and subsequently as self-proclaimed heirs to Philippe IV through his daughter Isabella, wife of Edward II and mother of Edward III. Just below Normandy, Brittany too was an independent (and non-French-speaking) duchy until the end of the fifteenth century, when the marriage of the Duchess Anne to two French kings in succession, Charles VIII and Louis XII, finally annexed it to the crown. Moreoever, the cultural, linguistic and religious differences between the Catholic north and the Cathar-favouring south – the *langue d'oc* – were so great that it was at times by no means clear that the two would not ultimately break apart into two essentially separate nations. Even when this possibility had receded and France had more or less cohered, it still was not recognisable as the country we know now, for it had a border running south of Franche-Comté, where the Constable of Castile had been carrying out a successful campaign, and of Alsace-Lorraine, which had been the scene of territorial wars with Charles V, so that John Coke's 1550 *The Debate betwene the Heraldes of Englande and Fraunce* calls Lorraine 'a province of Almayne'[1] and John Wilson's 1608 *The English Martyrology* refers to 'Strasburgh in the higher Germany'.[2] In the south of the country, Nice did not become part of France until 1860, having been previously controlled by the Dukes of Savoy; thus in his *A continuation of the historie of France from the death of Charles the eight where Comines endeth, till the death of Henry the second*, Thomas Danett notes how François I, having met the Emperor Charles in Nice, went 'by Auignion to retourne into Fraunce'.[3]

Over the course of the sixteenth century, the borders of France continued to change. In 1556 the French finally prised back Calais from the hands of the English, who had held it for over two centuries, only for it to be captured by the Spanish in 1596 and held by them until the Treaty of Vervins in 1598. Most notably, in 1589 Henri of Navarre succeeded to the throne of France, and the political landscape of its southernmost territories changed overnight, though it was not a simple matter of moving the border: François Bayrou notes that Henri's original possessions of Béarn and Navarre were

> deux principautés souveraines, qu'Henri IV n'avait pas osé annexer au royaume de France, pratiquant seulement une 'union personelle': par une sorte de 'cumul

des mandats', il était roi de France, par ailleurs roi de Navarre et vicomte souverain de Béarn. Louis XIII ne devait procéder à cette annexation qu'en 1620.[4]

(two sovereign principalities, which Henri IV had not dared annex to the kingdom of France, practising only a 'personal union': by a sort of 'plurality of mandates', he was king of France, and in addition king of Navarre and sovereign viscount of Béarn. Not until 1620 would Louis XIII proceed to annexation).

France also continued to have territorial ambitions in Italy and hoped that the marriage of François II to Mary, Queen of Scots would eventually add Scotland to the holdings of the French crown.

An additional complication was that, as every Elizabethan schoolboy knew from a text to which I shall return, Caesar's *Commentaries on the Gallic War*, it was possible to see France as having internal as well as external boundaries. (*The Gallic Wars* was in a sense also the text that established the borders of England, since Thomas Roebuck and Laurie Maguire note that 'Britain enters surviving recorded classical history with Caesar's *Gallic Wars*, when Caesar first sees the British shoreline and the prehistoric inhabitants of Britain'.)[5] For the Romans, 'Gallia in tres partes divisa est' – 'Gaul is divided into three parts' – and the country was inhabited by three completely separate tribes, the Belgae, the Aquitani and the Gauls, whose territory was separated from each other by boundary markers such as the rivers Garonne and Rhône. It was the external boundaries of France, though, which were under most pressure: in his 1624 translation of a French text written a little earlier by an unknown author, *The Spaniards perpetuall designes to a vniuersall monarchie*, Thomas Scott warned that Spain was pressing so close 'neere to the borders of France … there remaines very little for them to conquer; to encompasse it on all sides' and that

they still continue to make some progresse about the Palatinate, vnder colour of passages or other pretents: and proceede in their secret practises vpon diuers other Imperiall Townes, especially that of Strasbourg, (a great and strong place, and of the ancient patrimony of our first Kings:) and likewise vpon the Towne of Besanson, to establish a Parliament there, or transferre thither that of Dole.

Moreover, 'in Monaco, and the Towne and Castle of Correggio, the Spaniards keepe a strong Garrison',[6] while the writer of a 1592 tract noted that in Provence, the city of Aix had only just broken free of the control of the Duke of Savoy, the king of Spain's son-in-law.[7]

A number of Shakespeare's plays inhabit these shifting and embattled borderlands, and indeed apart from a few scenes set in Paris or before the gates of various cities, it is the edges of France to which Shakespeare generally turns his attention. *All's Well That Ends Well* starts and ends in Roussillon, territory fought over by France and Spain; *As You Like It* is set in the Ardennes, border country between France and what is now Belgium, and also glances imaginatively, in its use of the names Orlando, Oliver and Charles, towards Roncevaux in the

Pyrenees, the 'Gate of Spain' of French romance; and *Love's Labour's Lost* is set in Navarre, which within Shakespeare's lifetime had changed from an independent and separate kingdom to a land ruled, albeit in personal rather political union, by the same king as France, in ways which, I have argued elsewhere, could easily be used to reflect on the relationship between England and Scotland.[8] *Henry V*, the three parts of *Henry VI* and *Edward III*, of which Shakespeare is generally accepted to have written part at least, all take as a central concern the ebb and flow of England's attempts to cling on to the territorial possessions in France which she had inherited from the Angevin Empire. In *1 Henry VI*, which opens with a messenger's announcement that 'Guyenne, Compiègne, Rheims, Rouen, Orléans, / Paris, Gisors, Poitiers, are all quite lost',[9] we see battles before Orléans (1.4), Rouen (3.2) and Bordeaux (4.2) before York laments that 'Maine, Blois, Poitiers, and Tours are won away' (4.2.45) and the Dauphin declares triumphantly 'I am possessed / With more than half the Gallian territories' (5.4.138–9); by *2 Henry VI*, Anjou and Maine have been signed away to the father of Margaret of Anjou as part of the negotiations for her marriage, and since 'These counties were the keys of Normandy', when King Henry asks about France in general, Somerset bluntly tells him that 'all your interest in those territories / Is utterly bereft you: all is lost'.[10]

For Shakespeare, then, France evokes not the rural peace and rich slow lifestyle of 'la France profonde' but a frenetic world of shifting frontiers and clashing cultures, and their history is also intricately bound up with that of Britain. In this chapter, I shall explore the plays set on or near the southernmost of those frontiers, before moving in the next chapter to those set in the north. I shall first discuss *Love's Labour's Lost*, which I shall suggest works to remind its readers of the extent to which disputes about the borders of France were bound up with religious disagreements, and then *All's Well That Ends Well*, where I shall revisit the territory of Chapter 2 by suggesting that the name of the play's heroine activates an association with the stories of St Helena of Britain, her husband Constantius Chlorus and their son Constantine, in ways which both bear directly on the edge between spiritual and secular power and also connect France with Britain. For Shakespeare, I shall argue, the borders of France thus both stand for themselves and also stand in for the borders of England, and also work to suggest an association between the borders of the nation and those of the person. Ultimately I suggest that Shakespeare presses the need for strongly marked and securely identifiable borders and edges for countries and for individuals to recognise the need for limits to their personal freedom of action, in ways which echo his apparent willingness to accept a role for the state in matters of religion.

Navarre: The Edge of Catholicism

In the case of *Love's Labour's Lost*, Felicia Hardison Londré suggests a close and direct correspondence between Shakespeare's imagined court of Navarre and contemporary events:

On 2 October 1578, Marguerite de Valois met with her husband, Henri de Navarre, after a two-year separation. She had travelled to the south of France with her 'flying squadron' (*escadron volant*) of attractive maids-of-honor for the reunion in Nérac, but religious factionalism was so intense at the time that the Protestant husband and his Catholic wife could not safely reside in the same city, a situation echoed in the exclusion of the Princess from Ferdinand of Navarre's court in *Love's Labour's Lost*. Another concern of Henri de Navarre and Marguerite was her unpaid dowry, against which he was holding parts of Aquitaine; this too parallels the business discussed by Ferdinand of Navarre and the Princess in the play. Despite these problems, the encounter was celebrated with various festivities and entertainments, including some held outdoors in the lovely park of the chateau de Nérac. Lefranc notes that textual allusions to the park that is the setting for *Love's Labour's Lost* evoke the milieu just as Marguerite de Valois describes it in her memoirs.... Even the Nine Worthies figure prominently in the gathering at Nérac.

Londré further notes, 'There were ... at the court of Henri IV actual people with the same name as secondary characters in the play: Antoine Boyet, minister of finance; de la Motte, a squire like his namesake Moth; and Marcadé'.[11] One might also detect in the play's resolute refusal to supply the expected ending of affirmed and assured marriage a glance at the childless and unsatisfactory marriage of Henri and the spectacularly unfaithful Marguerite, which eventually ended in divorce in 1599 and might well have done so earlier. (Marguerite seems to have feared that Henri would marry his mistress, Gabrielle d'Estrées, so resisted a divorce until the latter's sudden death.)

Love's Labour's Lost focuses on a moment which might or might not change the territorial contours of both France and Navarre. The Princess is coming 'about surrender up of Aquitaine / To her decrepit, sick, and bedrid father', but Boyet's reference to the fact that 'the plea of no less weight / Than Aquitaine, a dowry for a queen' hints that if the king and the princess marry then the question of Aquitaine might find itself settled anyway,[12] since France and Navarre might effectively unite. There is also an ambiguity about what Navarre actually is: officially it was of course a kingdom, but when Dull asks, 'Which is the Duke's own person?' (1.1.179), meaning the King, it has clearly contracted in his mind into a duchy, and this would resonate strongly at a historical moment when the status of the actual kingdom of Navarre was changing profoundly (and as we now know permanently). We are, though, firmly reminded both of Navarre's separate status and of its geographical position next to Spain when the King first observes that 'Our court, you know, is haunted / With a refinèd traveller of Spain' (1.1.160–61) and then regrets that the Princess cannot immediately 'go well satisfied to France again' (2.1.153), and we are also, and even more immediately for Shakespeare's audience, reminded of the religious turmoil associated with its history. This latter is clearly inscribed in lines such as Berowne's reference to 'Love's Tyburn, that hangs up simplicity' (4.3.52), with its troubling evocation of the torture and death of Catholics, the Princess's talk of a 'civil war of wits' (2.1.212) and her idea that 'my beauty will be saved by merit! / O heresy in fair, fit for these days!' (4.1.21–2). Most strongly of all, the troubles that followed the St Bartholomew's Day massacre are remembered by the three names we first hear at 1.1.15 when the King addresses, 'You three, Berowne, Dumaine, and Longaville', for all three were names fundamentally associated with the Wars of Religion, being garbled forms of the names of the Ducs de Biron, Mayenne and Longueville. Edward Aggas, for instance, repeatedly mentions the Duc de Mayenne as an important figure,[13] and the name Dumaine, which was to be heard again in *All's Well That Ends Well*, where it belongs to one of the captains, was particularly resonant because the historical Duc de Mayenne had been wavering between support for Henri IV and support for the Catholic party. Finally, Navarre's border location is underlined by a stress on liminality of another sort when the King speaks, 'Now, at the latest minute of the hour' (5.2.782) and Berowne doubts it would be possible 'to move wild laughter in the throat of death' (5.2.844), and less obviously by the King's address to his three fellow students as

> brave conquerors – for so you are,
> That war against your own affections
> And the huge army of the world's desires.
>   (1.1.8–10)

The idea of personal control is, I shall be suggesting, one which Shakespeare strongly associates with the idea of physical borders, and it is certainly present here in this play which imaginatively inhabits the southernmost edge of France.

Roussillon: St Helena of Britain and the Edge of Roman Authority

All's Well That Ends Well also takes us to the south, being very unusually set in Roussillon.[14] Roussillon-Cerdagne was classic border territory, something which is revealed by Danett's description of how François I 'sent one armie under the leading of the Dauphin his sonne to besiege Perpignian in the countie of Roussilion in Spaine'[15] and which is testified to today by the huge later seventeenth-century fortifications built by Vauban at places such as Villefranche-de-Conflent and Montlouis. In the world of the play it is clearly subject to the king of France, but historically its affiliations had been strongly Catalan, and 'from the thirteenth century onwards, Roussillon's northernmost border … formed a defence line against the growing power of France'; before that, it had been designated by Charlemagne as a bulwark against the Muslim Emirate of Córdoba,[16] so that it had at different times been on different sides of what we would now call the Franco-Spanish border. I have argued elsewhere that the play also evokes another aspect of the potentially fluid geopolitical face of its own historical moment by its insistent glances at questions pertinent to the differences between the two confessions, over which the Wars of Religion were fought, as when the Clown says that 'young Charbon the puritan and old Poysam the papist, howsome'er their hearts are severed in religion, their heads are both one: they may jowl horns together like any deer i'th'herd' (1.3.51–5) and that 'though honesty be no puritan, yet it will do no hurt. It will wear the surplice of humility over the black gown of a big heart' (1.3.90–92).[17] The play also takes us beyond France's borders to Florence (and gestures too over the Pyrenees to Spain, to Santiago de Compostela), perhaps in ways which evoked yet a further country if Shakespeare's audience remembered that the road which would most conveniently take Helena to Florence was the Via Francigena, the old pilgrimage route which pilgrims from Britain had traditionally taken from Canterbury to Rome – and Shakespeare might in fact have been thinking of Britain, for the name of Helena might, I think, have reminded him of St Helena of Britain. In what remains of this chapter, I want to consider what it might mean to think of *All's Well* in terms of the paradigms afforded by and associated with St Helena of Britain and to argue that St Helena, her son the Emperor Constantine and her husband Constantius Chlorus all suggested ways of thinking about the edge between the self and the state.

The story of St Helena, mother of the Emperor Constantine and supposed finder of the True Cross, was well known in Britain – where, according to many versions of her story, she was born – and people may well have been fairly regularly reminded of it since Camden notes that 'Hellens mony [was] many oftentimes found under the walles' of London.[18] (In his *The life of the glorious bishop S. Patricke*, Joscelin had identified Helena as having 'builded the walles of the Citty of London'.)[19] Shakespeare, who was at one time living in the parish of St Helen's Bishopsgate, is certainly likely to have been aware of the legends associated with her. Antonina Harbus notes that St Helena was being claimed as British as early as the eighth century,[20] and she figured in Jacobus de Voragine's hugely popular *The Golden Legend*, where she was said to be the daughter of King Coel (the old King Cole of the rhyme); in this narrative Helena proves her sanctity when, faced with three crosses which have all been found at Golgotha, she identifies the true one when a dead man is laid on it and returns to life, an episode which might conceivably be glanced at when the Helena of the play effects the quasi-miraculous restoration of the suffering king. Thus it is not surprising that Richard Wilson should observe that 'when Helena states that it were better "I met the ravin lion" than stay at home, "although / The air of paradise did fan the house / And angels officed all" … the narrative expectations she prompts by her quest are those of *The Golden Legend*'.[21] Above all, St Helena's status as the mother of Constantine linked her closely to the debates about the relationship between secular and spiritual powers of which the so-called 'Donation of Constantine' was a prime symbol.

For Laurie Maguire, the name of Shakespeare's Helena is a clear and unequivocal pointer, for 'Helen meant only one Helen – Helen of Troy':

> Other historical or mythological Helens – the virtuous St Helena, mother of the Emperor Constantine, for example, whose church in Bishopsgate made her part of the Elizabethan cultural landscape – never displaced the Lacedemonian or

Spartan (as Helen of Troy was also called), and this despite a pre-Reformation predilection for hagionymy. Camden's glossary of names in his *Remains* (1605) does offer St Helena as the name's primary referent; but his view is unusual and does not seem to be shared by literary texts, even when the association is specifically invited, as in the case of the pilgrim Helen in *All's Well That Ends Well*.... When the Shakespeare canon invokes St Helen, she requires appositive explanation: 'Helen, the mother of great Constantine' (*1 Henry VI* 1.2.142).

Maguire reads *All's Well* firmly within this Graeco-Trojan paradigm, seeing it as resembling Euripides' *Helen*, with the king as a Menelaus figure.[22] However, Richard Wilson argues that

> for a play about 'holy wishes' which starts with Helena's joke: 'I wish well.... That wishing well had not a body in it' (1.1.52; 166–8), [it cannot] be incidental to *All's Well* that the largest number of all well-dedications is to the Yorkshire mother of Emperor Constantine, who united Britain and Rome, the first English pilgrim, Saint Helena herself.[23]

St Helena was certainly associated with wells: for instance, John Leland visited St Helen's Well on the Wharfe, West Yorks in around 1540, and even Maguire notes the presence of well imagery in the play when she suggests that 'the name Diana is a repetition of Fontibell, not a correction. Fontibell means "beautiful fountain"'.[24] (Richard Wilson identifies Fontibell specifically as 'the name of the public fountain in London that featured a statue of Diana').[25] Moreover Winifred Joy Mulligan notes that 'later legends lauded St. Helena as a beautifier of cities, a restorer of walls, the builder of highways in Wales, and the architect of the promontory at Land's End',[26] and the Helena of the play too evokes the idea of Land's End, albeit a different one, since the Compostela pilgrimage customarily ended at Finisterre. St Helena of Britain was also frequently confused with Elen of Caernarfon (Elen of the Ways), wife of Magnus Maximus (the Macsen Wledig of Welsh folklore), because Elen too had had a son named Constantine (it is this confusion which seems to have prompted Edward I's decision to rebuild the walls of Caernarfon Castle on the model of those of Constantinople), and Elen was famous for her supposed making of the Roman road Sarn Helen, which Drayton in *Poly-Olbion* calls 'Saint Hellens wondrous way' and says is 'By Festenog ... and supposed made by that Helen, mother to Constantine';[27] if Shakespeare, as seems likely given his friendship with Drayton, shared this misapprehension, St Helena would seem a particularly appropriate association for a heroine linked to journeys and pilgrim ways. Equally, Helen Wilcox suggests that in *All's Well* 'medical science seems to have been put in its place by supernatural influences, and a new Saint Helen appears to be in the making, with her power to effect miracles and her almost sacral embodiment of a "heavenly effect in an earthly actor" (2.3.33)'.[28] Above all, there is a direct link between the saint and the area in which Shakespeare has set the play: the first capital of Roussillon was Elne, whose original name was Castrum Helenae after St Helena, and though the counts subsequently preferred Perpignan, Elne remained the ecclesiastical city.

St Helena was a figure of widespread interest in the period. Hers is the first story in a manuscript compilation of *The Lives of Women Saints of our Contrie of England*, compiled around. 1610,[29] and her search for the True Cross was also the first story in Hakluyt's *Principal Navigations*; in fact she was surprisingly often associated with the exploration of the New World. The island of St Helena was so named because it was discovered by the Portuguese on St Helena's Day, 21 May, in 1502, but it later figured in English exploration narratives: Thomas Cavendish landed there on 8 June 1588 and Abraham Kendall in 1591 with a crew suffering from scurvy who subsequently recovered, and in 1592 Philip II warned his fleet that English captains were lying in wait for them at St Helena. The first settlement on the American mainland, founded by Cortés in 1519, was Villa Rica de Vera Cruz, better known as Vera Cruz, and the derivation of its name from the True Cross allegedly found by St Helena would have been obvious to all.

Above all, though, the story of St Helena encoded a complex set of associations about class, religion and cultural identity, and the roles these could or could not play in the founding of nations and determining the identities and loyalties of future generations. She suggested these issues because her son Constantine was a figure of such immense importance to the twinned debates about choice of confession and choice of successor to Elizabeth, and consequently also to the question which I touched on in Chapter 2 of the political duties of English Catholics. Christopher Highley notes that Robert Persons in *The King of Spaines receiving* says of Philip II that he 'made me to imagen that I saw present that noble Britishe Emperour Constantine the greate, with his renowmed two Catholique children, Constans, and Constantia'; Highley observes that 'Persons here stakes a claim for Catholics to the powerful figure of Constantine against Protestant writers like John Foxe, who famously opened the first edition of his *Actes and Monuments* (1563) with the word "Constantine" and an extended analogy between the Roman emperor and Elizabeth I', and that

> The Constantine analogy receives a further twist in Persons's *The King of Spaines receiving* when Philip's daughter, the Infanta, is likened to both Constantine's mother, the saintly Helena, and to his daughter, Constantia.[30]

The potentially explosive association between St Helena and the Infanta Isabella might help provide an explanation of the most famously problematic of the many problematic moments of this strange, difficult play, when Helena sends her mother-in-law the countess a letter informing her that '*I am Saint Jaques' pilgrim, thither gone*'.[31] J.C. Maxwell observes that 'the first point which I regard as beyond controversy is that Saint Jaques le Grand must be the famous shrine at Compostella',[32] but if so, the same geographical vagueness that led Shakespeare to endow Bohemia with a sea coast seems to be at work again here: Helena is setting out from her mother-in-law's house in Roussillon, giving her a relatively simple journey through the passes of the Pyrenees from France to Spain, but when we next see her she is in Florence, making it not surprising that 'she writes / Pursuit would be but vain' (3.4.24–5), since no one could have predicted that she would take such a route. For Richard Wilson, however, the explanation is simple: '*All's Well* turns away from the Pyrenees to disavow the ultramontanes',[33] that is, to mark disagreement with the position of those English Catholics who argued that a shared religion with Spain should lead to a shared political agenda. It is certainly worth noting that in the year *All's Well* was written, the anonymous *Northerne poems congratulating the Kings majesties entrance to the crowne* commented censoriously on how

> The foolish Pilgrime oft to Spayne doth post,
> O Sacred *Iames* to worship thy drye scull:
> But he that's wise forhights the Spanish cost,
> Iberus waters now are venim full.
> If though thy conscience seeke or purse to fill,
> Spaine can in neither satisfie thy will.
> England (O Pilgrim) keepes Saint *Iames* aliue,
> Whome thou maiest loue, long may it him preserue.[34]

Spain, in this reading, is simply too politically loaded a destination for Shakespeare to have his heroine actually arrive at and one of the ways in which it so is bound up with the story of Constantine.

The cultural uses of Constantine bore specifically on the relationship between law and personal belief. Michael S. Pucci notes, 'Foxe highlights the events of Constantine's reign which demonstrate the relationship between church and state',[35] and Harbus notes that 'the concept of a British Helena acquired new political resonance when Henry VIII sought a direct imperial connection with ancient Rome through his supposed descent from a British Constantine';[36] thus, there is a statue of St Helena in the Henry VII chapel in Westminster.[37] Indeed Winifred Joy Mulligan, noting that 'in 1533 ... Henry VIII discarded King Arthur in favor of the British Constantine',[38] argues that Constantine and his progeny became distinctively associated with Britishness. Henry VIII's 1533 adoption of Constantine was a direct result of the publication of an argument impugning the veracity of the so-called 'Donation of Constantine', the grant by which Constantine had supposedly ceded ultimate authority over the Roman Emperor to the Pope.[39] As Barbara L. Parker notes, 'Luther had ... declared the pope to be Antichrist because of his quest for world rule, the spurious Donation of Constantine having proved that he sought to despoil and usurp the Roman Empire, overthrow the emperor, and rule in his stead',[40] and Henry for once in his life agreed with Luther on this score. Once it was possible to claim that Constantine did not necessarily emblematise imperial submission to papal authority, he became suddenly attractive to Henry, and Harbus suggests, 'When Henry VIII styled himself as the possessor of the "imperial Crown" of the realm of England in 1533, he was claiming imperial authority for himself as British monarch on the basis of Constantine's legendary dual position as both emperor of Rome and King of Britain', though she observes that 'Henry never claims personal genealogical descent from Constantine, but rather the acquistion of the monarch's status in relation to the Church through

Constantine's position: ecclesiastical sovereignty of the English Church from Rome'. However, she also notes that 'the manifestation of the Constantine legend in the Welsh genealogies ... implicitly linked Brutus and Arthur with the Tudors', and that 'the notion that Constantine had a British mother was deployed within the Protestant discourse of England as an "elect nation" of the late sixteenth century, especially in the writings of the Reformation propagandist John Foxe'.[41] Even the notorious sceptic Polydore Vergil allowed the truth of the Helena story and hence of Constantine's British descent. Winifred Joy Mulligan lists numerous sixteenth-century supporters for a British Constantine including the fact that 'Maurice Kyffin, on the occasion of Elizabeth I's birthday, referred to her imperial descent from Constantine', and observes that the idea was particularly topical in 1604, the probable year of composition of *All's Well That Ends Well*, since that year saw an exchange of letters between Lipsius and Camden on the subject of whether Constantine was really born in Britain,[42] of which Drayton at least was aware, for he declares in *Poly-Olbion* that 'for great Constantines birth in this land you shall haue authority; against which I wonder how Lipsius durst oppose his conceit'.[43]

St Helena was, then, associated with Britishness, with patriotism, and with Protestantism, and in all these respects it should not be surprising to find her being evoked in the work of a dramatist who appears to be on the side of St Paul. However, St Helena was an inherently ambiguous figure. Jeanne Addison Roberts points out that

> Geoffrey of Monmouth called her a queen and identified her as the daughter of King Coel of Britain and wife of Constantius, father of Constantine. Other historians claimed, however, that she was a public courtesan and that Constantine was born of a union consummated without benefit of clergy.[44]

This was a question in which a great number of early modern writers were interested. For some of them, Helena was unquestionably married, royal and virtuous. Richard Hakluyt, for instance, referred to her as 'Helena Flauia Augusta, the heire and onely daughter of Coelus sometime the most excellent king of Britaine, the mother of the emperour Constantine the great'.[45] In the manuscript *Lives of Women Saints of our Contrie of England* she is the daughter of King Cole and the legitimate wife of Constantius, and Polydore Vergil too says that Helena was married to Constantius. John Bridges, the Dean of Sarum, spoke of 'Constantine the great ... beeing the sonne of Constantius Chlorus, by the most noble and Christian Queene Helena',[46] while John Gordon in his *Emotikon or A sermon of the vnion of Great Brittannie, in antiquitie of language, name, religion, and kingdome* declared that 'God did conciliate a marriage, betwixt *Constantius Chlorus*, (who had to his part of the Romane Monarchie, Germanie, France, Spaine, and great Brittaine) and *Helena* daughter to *Coilus* or *Coelus*, who was King ouer that part of Brittaine, that did resist the Romans',[47] and sees their son Constantine as bringing together the two parts of Britain which represented his parents' inheritance; he also tells much the same story in his *England and Scotlands happinesse in being reduced to vnitie of religion, vnder our invincible monarke King Iames*,[48] as too do William Warner in

Albions England,[49] Spenser in *The Faerie Queene*,[50] John Clapham in *The historie of Great Britannie declaring the successes of times and affaires in that iland, from the Romans first entrance, vntill the raigne of Egbert, the West-Saxon prince* ...[51], and Lodowick Lloyd in *The consent of time*.[52] Michael Drayton in *Poly-Olbion*, though, sounds a more cautious note: he speaks of '*Constantius* worthy wife – That is *Helen*, wife to *Constantius* or *Constans Chlorus* the Emperour, and mother to *Constantine* the great, daughter to *Coile* King of *Britaine*, where *Constantine* was by her brought forth', but he also feels the need to add that those who dispute this version of events are wrong.[53]

In the counter-tradition to which Drayton delicately alludes, St Helena was sometimes said to have been an innkeeper's daughter. Mulligan notes that

> the unsympathetic Zosimus branded her 'an ignoble woman who bore Constantine out of wedlock,' and the anonymous Valesianus cited her 'very common origin'. St. Ambrose addressed her as a *stabularia*, or serving wench at an inn, which caused medieval writers much consternation. An even thornier problem for medieval writers was the status *concubina* given her by Eutropius and Orosius.[54]

Though this early version of her history tends not to register much during the Renaissance, a faint whiff of unease still attaches to her: Mulligan records that 'Holinshed observed that "S. Ambrose following a common report, writeth that this Helen was a maid in an inne: and some againe write that she was a concubine to Constantius, and not his wife"',[55] and Harbus notes that Camden 'reacted to the growing doubt in the legend by promulgating and defending it'.[56] (The question is perhaps hinted at in Reginald Scot's *Discovery of Witchcraft*, where one of the superstitions derided is the idea that a child can use the name of St Helena to conjure an angel into a beryl, though this will only work if the child in question was born in wedlock.)[57] Unease of a slightly different sort is detectable in Richard Harvey's *Philadelphus, or a defence of Brutes, and the Brutans history*, where we hear that

> Feare amazed *Coil*, till marriage ioined *Constantius* a Roman Duke with his daughter *Helen*, the fayrest mayd aliue: then Contentment setled them both in the kingdome, and Loue brought them foorth into the world *Constantine* the first, whom Excellency lifted vp to the Roman Empire.

Harvey does not leave it here, however; he goes on to note that '*Helen* the daughter of *Coil* the third married *Constantius*, a Roman by the agreeme[n]t of the *Brutans*, not on her owne head, lesse she should seeme incontinent: she was but a part of hir countrey, not aboue it, or out of it',[58] where the always latent pun on 'cunt' / 'country' may well be active in ways that would inevitably sexualise Harvey's Helena.

If St Helena was a figure readable in different ways, so too was her husband – or lover – Constantius Chlorus, who had associations of his own with *All's Well*'s south of France setting, for although he died at York, for some time he used Gaul as a base, with particular associations with Arles,[59] a location of some significance for the history of Christianity: for Drayton, it was remembered as the hotbed of Arianism,[60] and John Clapham in *The historie of Great Britannie* inscribes Arles at the foundation of English Christianity when he says that St Augustine was consecrated Archbishop by the bishop of Arles.[61] Constantius Chlorus was, like his wife, a figure of considerable interest in the early modern period. This was partly because he too had a role to play in the Tudor myth of ancestry, and in some ways a better established one: Matthew Woodcock points out that in the '*Antiquitee of Faery* lond' Spenser links the realm of Troy, from which the Romans claimed a descent which they had allegedly transmitted to the early kings of Britain, with that of Faerie: 'The actions of the successive elfin kings bear clear similarities to those of several of the individuals found in the preceding "*Briton moniments*", inviting comparison between the two chronicles as a means of decoding each part of Gloriana's genealogy'; the actual equivalences are a matter of dispute, but it has been variously proposed that Elfinan is either Hercules or Brutus, that Elfant represents Aeneas, Lucius or Belinus and Elfar Postumus, Constantius Chlorus, or Constantine the Great (Woodcock provides a very helpful table of proposed identifications).[62] Constantius was, however, also celebrated for rather different reasons, and ones which again bore upon the question of the tensions between the different confessions, for he was closely associated with debates about the relative weight of spiritual and secular powers. Robert Persons, in his *A manifestation of the great folly and bad spirit of certayne in England calling themselues secular priestes ...*, says that Eusebius and Zozemenus

> do recount, that this Constantius being a notable wise man, though a heathen, at the same tyme, when *Dioclesian* and *Maximinian* the Emperors to whome he succeeded afflicted infinitely Christians euery where, he (though misliking that extreme cruelty) yet to seeme also to do somwhat, for that he was declared *Caesar* & successor of the Empyre, made an edict or proclamation, that so many of the Christians about him as would sacrifice to his Gods should not only haue his fauour and enioy honors in his court and common welth, but to be vsed and trusted also by him aboue other men, and such as would not, though he meant not to put them to death, yet would he exclude them from his friendship and familarity, and from all dignityes, &c.

Persons's gloss on this is 'Behold heer a worthy wise example, which our English magistrats cannot but remember and think of', and he specifically invokes 'his Maiestie of *Scotland*',[63] who might presumably like to take note of this as an example of religious toleration potentially applicable to himself if and when he succeeded to the throne of England.

Plenty of writers were prepared to follow Persons's lead by applying the story of Constantius first to Elizabeth and then to James, with particular reference to the issue of the relationship between secular and spiritual authority and the related question of toleration. In *A watch-word to all religious, and true hearted English-men*, Francis Hastings argued for a balance between patriotism and religion:

For if religion flourish, the Queene must needes be safe; and, if the Queene bee safe, religion must needs flourish: and, as I think them to deal vnsoundly, that seeke to settle her safetie, without care of religion; so must I deeme them to deale hypocritically, that speake much of religion, without care of her safetie. For he that shall carrie a right and sound care for Queene *Elizabeths* safetie, must first loue religion, and feare GOD: according to that, which *Constantius* the Emperour sayd, who (grieuing at his peoples reuolt from true religion, vpon triall that he made of them) plainly protested, They that will not be true to God, can neuer bee true to man. And therefore such of them as had any office, he displaced, and freed himselfe from the daunger of such hollow-hearted subiects, and seruants.[64]

There is a presumably unintended but nevertheless suggestive lack of specificity about Hastings' term 'religion', and a perhaps rather more studied neutrality can be observed in John Gordon's *A panegyrique of congratulation for the concord of the realmes of Great Britaine in vnitie of religion, and vnder one king*, which uses the figure of Constantius to assure James that

God the protector of his true Church hath continued his admirable graces ouer your Ilands in the second Period of Christianisme, the which begun with the most happie Empire of *Constantius Chlorus*: for during the last persecution, God raysed vp this wise and warlike Emperour in the westerne parts of Europe, in the which *England, Scotland,* and *Ireland* are conteyned, where the said Emperor tooke to wife *Hellen*, borne in your said realmes, who receiued into his protection all the Christians which fled from other prouinces to auoyde the cruell persecution which was made against them by his other associates in the Empire.[65]

I argued some years ago that *All's Well* seems to be interested in toleration of both confessions rather than in the differences between them;[66] both Hastings' 'religion' and Gordon's 'true church' could similarly be read as collapsing different confessions into one overarching Christianity within which the similarities are more important than the differences, and both would be using the husband of St Helena to do it. It may be no more than a coincidence, but it is certainly a striking one, that when James I made peace with Catholic Spain in 1604 he gave the Spanish ambassador the Royal Gold Cup (now in the British Museum), which features Constantius's sister Constantia and her father Constantine.

So what difference does it make to our understanding of Shakespeare's Helena to read her in terms of these paradigms and with these associations in mind? I want at this point to return to Southwell, whom I discussed in chapter 2, though this time not to *Saint Peter's Complaint* but to *Marie Magdalens funeral teares*. A foreword to this, signed 'Your louing friend. S. W.', declares that 'passions I allow, and loues I approue, onely I would wishe that men would alter their obiect and better their intent.... Loue is but the infancy of true charity, yet sucking natures teate, and swathed in her bandes, which then groweth to perfection, when faith besides naturall motiues proposeth higher and nobler groundes of amitye'.[67] It is, it seems, acceptable to write of secular love insofar as it is stepping stone to a higher and more spiritual emotion. Therefore, the writer suggests,

> shal I thinke my indeours wel apaide, if it may wooe some skilfuller pennes from vnworthy labours, eyther to supply in this matter my want of ability, or in other of like piety, (whereof the scripture is full) to exercise their happier talents … sith the finest wits are now giuen to write passionat discourses, I would wish them to make choise of such passions, as it neither should be shame to vtter, nor sinne to feele. (sigs A5v–A6r)

The remark that such work may 'wooe some skilfuller pennes from vnworthy labours' may perhaps seem to echo the injunction in *St Peter's Complaint* to his 'worthy good cousin, Master W.S.' to write sacred verse, and *All's Well* might conceivably be seen as a miniature version of Shakespeare's apparent refusal of that injunction: the pilgrimage route is not followed to its end, and Bertram chooses conformity rather than to hold by his initial refusal to obey the king's command. In this context the idea of St Helena as a paradigm would become especially interesting, since her husband Constantius Chlorus was so emblematic of the debate about religious and secular authority, a crucial question for contemporary English Catholics.

I think, though, that Southwell's emphasis on love is equally suggestive and may help us to understand some of the ways in which I think *All's Well* may be working. At first sight *All's Well That Ends Well* might seem not to offer any examples of true love, but I think it is possible to see the future marriage of Bertram and Helena as genuinely companionate. What Bertram ultimately promises with respect to Helena, whom he has been trying to get rid of for most of the play, is that 'If she, my liege, can make me know this clearly / I'll love her dearly, ever, ever dearly' (5.3.309–10). Initially, Bertram crudely dismissed Helena on the grounds that he 'know[s] her well', with a clear sexual slur; now, he finds that he does *not* know her, nor indeed very much else. I suggest that he can be seen here as recognising in Helena someone who can teach him the things which he has finally learned that he needs to know. This would certainly be a different kind of love from that found in *Romeo and Juliet* and in the early comedies, but by the same token it is also far less dangerous. St Helena went on a long journey in search of truth and salvation and was also, as we have seen, associated with more contemporary forms of voyaging and exploration. I do not think it is too far-fetched to see Bertram too as having been on a long journey, albeit one of the spirit rather than of the flesh, in the course of which he has at last acquired some of the wisdom he so sadly lacked. Moreover, rather as St Helena of Britain had come to be understood in early modern England as primarily a dynastic figure, so a Bertram who is genuinely prepared to settle down with Helena and resume the reins of his life in Roussillon could be seen as doing so for what are essentially dynastic reasons, to secure the comfort of his mother and guarantee the continuation of his family name. To an early modern mind, these would not be negligible as reasons to marry.

The association with St Helena can also help us with the figure of the play's Helena, who has often struck critics as troublingly knowing and sexual. That the king's dysfunction may be sexual is hinted at in his opening negotiation with Helena:

KING
Upon thy certainty and confidence
What darest thou venture?

HELENA   Tax of impudence,
A strumpet's boldness, a divulgèd shame;
Traduced by odious ballads my maiden's name.
(2.1.169–72)

What has his health got to do with her sexuality? Obviously the two are linked on some deeper level, in a way more reminiscent of the leaps and hidden connections of myth than of logical thought.

KING
Thou knowest she has raised me from my sickly bed.

BERTRAM
But follows it, my lord, to bring me down
Must answer for your raising?
(2.3.110–12)

The language here, with its talk of raising things up and then causing them to go down, is wildly suggestive, and so too is Lafew's remark that

I have seen a medicine
That's able to breathe life into a stone,
Quicken a rock, and make you dance canary
With sprightly fire and motion; whose simple touch
Is powerful to araise King Pippen, nay,
To give great Charlemain a pen in's hand
And write to her a love-line.
(2.1.72–8)

There is clearly innuendo in this talk of pens, stones and raising and in the ease with which we move from the idea of medicine to that of love, but in the case of St Helena similar associations could be safely recuperated into a narrative of sanctity, and so it may well be for the Helena of the play.

The story of St Helena is a narrative which to the early modern mind was always shadowed by lewder and more disgraceful versions of itself, and just as *Love's Labour's Lost* trembles on the edge of a resolution to which it will not ultimately commit, so too this other play in which Shakespeare imaginatively visits the South of France also reveals its own opposite lying dark and implicit within itself. In Shakespeare's depiction of them, the southern edges of France are thus not only prone to destabilisation in political and military terms but are also zones of at least potential ideological disturbance, where the relationship between spiritual and secular powers hangs in the balance, and they also reveal a surprising adjacency not only with Spain, as might be expected, but, symbolically, with England. In the next chapter, I shall pursue the idea of a suggested analogy between France and England and shall also argue that Shakespeare suggests an equally powerful and related analogy between defending the borders of the nation and observing the proper boundaries appropriate to personal behaviours.

Notes

[1]   Richard Hillman, *Shakespeare, Marlowe and the Politics of France* (Basingstoke: Palgrave, 2002), p. 91.

[2]   John Wilson, *The English Martyrology* ... (St Omer: English College Press, 1608), p. 199.

[3]   Thomas Danett, *A continuation of the historie of France from the death of Charles the eight where Comines endeth, till the death of Henry the second* (London: Thomas East for Thomas Charde, 1600), p. 90.

[4]   François Bayrou, *Henri IV: Le roi libre* (Paris: Editions j'ai lu, 1997), p. 350.

[5]   Thomas Roebuck and Laurie Maguire, '*Pericles* and the Language of National Origins', in *This England, That Shakespeare: New Angles on Englishness and the Bard*, edited by Willy Maley and Margaret Tudeau-Clayton (Burlington: Ashgate, 2010), pp. 23–48, p. 27.

[6]   Thomas Scott (trans.), *The Spaniards perpetuall designes to a vniuersall monarchie. Translated according to the French* (London: 1624), pp. [*sic*] 2r, 2v and 4r.

[7]   Anonymous, *A true relation of the French kinge his good successe* ... (London: John Wolfe, 1592), sig. B1r.

[8]   See Lisa Hopkins, *Drama and the Succession to the Crown, 1561–1633* (Burlington: Ashgate, 2011).

[9]   William Shakespeare, *King Henry VI, Part 1*, edited by Michael Hattaway (Cambridge: Cambridge University Press, 1990), 1.1.60–61. All further quotations from the play will be taken from this edition and reference will be given in the text.

[10]   William Shakespeare, *Henry VI, Part 2*, edited by Michael Hattaway (Cambridge: Cambridge University Press, 1991), 1.1.111 Salisbury and 3.1.83–5.

[11]   Felicia Hardison Londré, 'Elizabethan Views of the "Other": French, Spanish, and Russians in *Love's Labour's Lost*', in *Love's Labour's Lost: Critical Essays*, edited by Felicia Hardison Londré (London: Routledge: 1997), pp. 325–41, pp. 328–9.

[12]   William Shakespeare, *Love's Labour's Lost*, edited by John Kerrigan (Harmondsworth: Penguin, 1982), 1.1.135–6 and 2.1.8. All further quotations from the play will be taken from this edition and reference will be given in the text.

[13]   Edward Aggas, *An answeare to the supplication Against him, who seeming to giue the King counsel to become a Catholike, indeuoureth to stirre vp his good subiectes vnto rebellion*, translated by E.A. (London: John Wolfe, 1591).

[14]   I note Richard Hillman's argument that the play's real association is with a seigneurie in Dauphiné, but I think the reference to Marseilles specifically invites us to think of the south. Richard Hillman, *French Reflections in the Shakespearean Tragic* (Manchester: Manchester University Press, 2012), p. 171.

[15]   Danett, *A continuation of the historie of France*, p. 94.

[16]   Norman Davies, *Vanished Kingdoms: The History of Half-Forgotten Europe* (London: Allen Lane, 2011), pp. 158 and 162.

[17]   See Lisa Hopkins, 'Paris is Worth a Mass: *All's Well That Ends Well* and the Wars of Religion', in *Shakespeare and the Culture of Christianity in Early Modern England*, edited by Dennis Taylor (Fordham University Press, 2003), pp. 369–81.

[18]   Richard Hingley, *The Recovery of Roman Britain 1586–1906: A Colony so Fertile* (Oxford: Oxford University Press, 2008), p. 34.

[19]   Joscelin, *The life of the glorious bishop S. Patricke* …, translated by Fr B.B. (St Omer: [G Seutin?] for John Heigham, 1625), p. 226.

[20]   Antonina Harbus, *Helena of Britain in Medieval Legend* (Cambridge: D.S. Brewer, 2002), pp. 3 and 19.

[21]   Richard Wilson, 'To great St Jaques bound: *All's Well That Ends Well* in Shakespeare's Europe', in *Shakespeare et l'Europe de la Renaissance*, edited by Yves Peyré and Pierre Kapitaniak (Paris: Actes du Congrès de la Société Française Shakespeare, 2004), http://www.societefrancaiseshakespeare.org/document.php?id=847.

[22]   Laurie Maguire, *Shakespeare's Names* (Oxford: Oxford University Press, 2007), pp. 75–7.

[23]   Wilson, 'To great St Jaques bound'.

[24]   Maguire, *Shakespeare's Names*, pp. 104–105.

[25]   Wilson, 'To great St Jaques bound'.

[26]   Winifred Joy Mulligan, 'The British Constantine: An English historical myth', *Journal of Medieval and Renaissance Drama* 8 (1978), p. 260.

[27]   Michael Drayton, *Poly-Olbion: A Chorographicall description of tracts, riuers, mountains, forests, and other parts of this renowned isle of Great Britain* (London: 1612), pp. 135 and 244.

[28]   Helen Wilcox, 'Shakespeare's Miracle Play: Religion in *All's Well That Ends Well*', in *All's Well, That Ends Well: New Critical Essays*, edited by Gary Waller (London: Routledge, 2007), p. 144.

[29]   C. Horstmann, *The Early South English Legendary* I, *Early English Texts and Studies*, old series 87 (London, 1887), pp. 30–36.

[30]   Christopher Highley, *Catholics Writing the Nation in Early Modern Britain and Ireland* (Oxford: Oxford University Press, 2008), pp. 173–4.

[31]   William Shakespeare, *All's Well That Ends Well*, edited by G.K. Hunter (London: Cengage Learning, 2007), 3.4.4. All further quotations from the play will be taken from this edition and reference will be given in the text.

[32]   J.C. Maxwell, 'Helena's Pilgrimage', *The Review of English Studies* 20 (May 1969), p. 190.

[33]   Wilson, 'To great St Jaques bound'.

[34]   Anonymous, *Northerne poems congratulating the Kings majesties entrance to the crowne* (London: J. Windet for E. Weaver, 1604), sig. B4r.

[35] Michael S. Pucci, 'Reforming Roman Emperors: John Foxe's Characterization of Constantine in the *Acts and Monuments*', in *John Foxe: An Historical Perspective*, edited by David Loades (Burlington: Ashgate, 1999), p. 44.

[36] Harbus, *Helena of Britain in Medieval Legend*, p. 120.

[37] It is reproduced in Peter C. Mancall, *Hakluyt's Promise: An Elizabethan's Obsession for an English America* (New Haven: Yale University Press, 2000), p. 17.

[38] Mulligan, 'The British Constantine', p. 269.

[39] Richard Koebner, 'The Imperial Crown of this Realm: Henry VIII, Constantine the Great, and Polydore Vergil', *Bulletin of the Institute of Historical Research* 25 (1953), p. 32.

[40] Barbara L. Parker, '"Cursèd Necromancy": Marlowe's *Faustus* as Anti-Catholic Satire', *Marlowe Studies* 1 (2011), p. 67.

[41] Harbus, *Helena of Britain in Medieval Legend*, pp. 121–2 and 125.

[42] Mulligan, 'The British Constantine: an English historical myth', pp. 272 and 275.

[43] Drayton, *Poly-Olbion*, p. 129.

[44] Jeanne Addison Roberts, *The Shakespearean Wild: Geography, Genus, and Gender* (Lincoln: University of Nebraska Press, 1991), p. 145.

[45] Richard Hakluyt, *The principal nauigations, voyages, traffiques and discoueries of the English nation made by sea or ouer-land …* (London: George Bishop, Ralph Newberie, and Robert Barker, 1599–1600), p. 2.

[46] John Bridges, *A defence of the gouernment established in the Church of Englande for ecclesiasticall matters Contayining an aunswere vnto a treatuse called, The learned discourse of eccl. gouernment … and in degence of her Maiestie, and of all other Christian princes supreme gouernment in ecclesiasticall causes* (London: John Windet and T. Orwin for Thomas Chard, 1587), p. 1356.

[47] John Gordon, *Emotikon or A sermon of the vnion of Great Brittannie, in antiquitie of language, name, religion, and kingdome* (London: Elliot's Court Press, 1604), p. 45.

[48] John Gordon, *England and Scotlands happinesse in being reduced to vnitie of religion, vnder our invincible monarke King Iames* (London: V. S[immes] for William Aspley, 1604), p. 24.

[49] William Warner, *Albions England* (London: The Widow Orwin for Joan Broome, 1597), p. 85.

[50] Edmund Spenser, *The faerie queene* (London: Richard Field for William Ponsonbie, 1596), pp. 541–2.

[51] John Clapham, *The historie of Great Britannie declaring the successes of times and affaires in that iland, from the Romans first entrance, vntill the raigne of Egbert, the West-Saxon prince; who reduced the severall principalities of the Saxons and English, into a monarchie, and changed the name of Britannie into England* (London: Valentine Simmes, 1606), p. 135.

[52] Lodowick Lloyd, *The consent of time …* (London: George Bishop and Ralph Newberie, 1590), p. 283.

[53] Michael Drayton, *Poly-Olbion*, p. 129.

[54] Mulligan, 'The British Constantine: An English historical myth', p. 259.

[55] Mulligan, 'The British Constantine: An English historical myth', p. 273.

[56] Harbus, *Helena of Britain in Medieval Legend*, pp. 126–7.

[57] Reginald Scot, *The Discovery of Witchcraft* (London: Henry Denham for William Brome, 1584), p. 147.

[58]   Richard Harvey, *Philadelphus, or a Defence of Brutes* (London: John Wolfe, 1593), pp. 71 and 74.

[59]   Drayton's *Poly-Olbion* moves from St Helena's invention of the cross to discussion of the Arrian sect in Arles (Drayton, *Poly-Olbion*, p. 129), and Ammianus Marcellinus's *The Roman historie*, translated by Philemon Holland, speaks of '*Constantius* keeping his winter at Arles', and even though he means Constantius the son of Constantine rather than his father, it does produce a firm association between the name Constantius and that area. Ammianus Marcellinus, *The Roman historie*, translated by Philemon Holland (London: Adam Islip, 1609), p. 8.

[60]   Drayton, *Poly-Olbion*, p. 119.

[61]   John Clapham, *The historie of Great Britannie*, p. 212.

[62]   Matthew Woodcock, *Fairy in* The Faerie Queen: *Renaissance Elf-Fashioning and Elizabethan Myth-Making* (Burlington: Ashgate, 2004), pp. 132–3.

[63]   Robert Persons, *A manifestation of the great folly and bad spirit of certayne in England calling themselues secular priestes Who set forth dayly most infamous and contumelious libels against worthy men of their owne religion, and diuers of them their lawful superiors, of which libels sundry are heer examined and refuted* (Antwerp: A. Conincx, 1602), pp. 78–9.

[64]   Francis Hastings, *A watch-word to all religious, and true hearted English-men* (London: Felix Kingston for Ralph Jackson, 1598), pp. 108–9. See also p. 64 for a further comparison between Elizabeth and Constantine.

[65]   John Gordon, *A panegyrique of congratulation for the concord of the realmes of Great Britaine in vnitie of religion, and vnder one king* (London: R. Read for Geoffrey Chorlton, 1603), pp. 24–5.

[66]   Hopkins, 'Paris is Worth a Mass'.

[67]   Robert Southwell, *Marie Magdalens funeral teares* (London: John Wolfe for Gabriel Cawood, 1591), sigs A3v – A4r.

Chapter 5
'Pas de Calais':
The Northern Edge of France

There is an old French joke about a Belgian who was trying to cross the channel to England but turned back when he came to a sign saying 'Pas-de-Calais', which to the French mind unerringly denotes 'the countryside round Calais' but which to the literal-minded could also be heard to translate as 'there is no Calais'. For Shakespeare's history plays, it is actually the second meaning, which the joke implicitly derides, which is the more available, for they are to various degrees scarred and configured by the devastating fact of the loss of Calais to the French in 1556, which had led Mary Tudor to die saying that when her body was opened 'Calais' would be found engraved on her heart. Both politically and psychologically, this had been a devastating blow for England. It meant more than just the loss of a town, for Calais as the English understood it was not coterminous with the modern Channel port: the total area of the Pale was about 120 square miles, and it was doubly frontier territory, being around ten miles in one direction from Gravelines, which marked the border of the Empire, and around twelve in the other from Boulogne, which marked the start of French territory. Calais was also doubly liminal, for not only did it represent a piece of England in France, but it blurred the boundaries between water and land:

> The network of water-courses, dykes, and canals which had successfully converted so much the marsh into arable or grazing was … controlled, and by the closing of the sluices the country immediately surrounding the town could be inundated in the event of an enemy attack. What it looked like, when flooded, can be clearly realized from the Field of Cloth of Gold painting.[1]

Despite its relatively small size, the strategic and symbolic importance of Calais was thus enormous and meant among other things that it had to have men of stature as governors, including Lord Berners, the translator of Froissart, and Lord Lisle, an illegitimate son of Edward IV. When it was recaptured by the French, the weight of its loss was felt in proportion to that strategic and symbolic value, not to its size.

What was a disaster for the English, though, had been of great assistance to the French, who found themselves if anything even more embattled in the north than in the south, for there the threat was double: from England just across the Channel and from the Spanish-dominated territories to the north. Paradoxically, this was indeed where the pressure from Spain was fiercest, for to the south the Pyrenees provided a formidable natural obstacle. In the north, by contrast, the flatter and far less defensible frontiers of the Spanish-held Netherlands became the theatre of bitter fighting at places such as Thionville, Saint-Quentin and Brest, as recounted in tracts such as Sir John Norris's *Newes from Brest*[2] or the anonymous *A true relation of the French kinge his good successe*, which tells of how the Duke of Parma, leader of the Spanish forces, penetrated as far as Rouen.[3]

Mapping with the Heart: The Ardennes

When Mary Tudor said that 'Calais' was written on her heart, she reached for a metaphor based on an implied correlation between the geographic and the corporeal to express the emotional anguish these geopolitical upheavals caused her, and for the period in general the vulnerability of northern France to attack and invasion was tellingly registered by the use of an analogous conceit in cartography. Maps have their own borders which are almost always more elaborately depicted and, in design terms, much more important than those between nations; moreover, the cordiform projection favoured by Mercator and adopted by Ortelius, which as its name implied used the shape of the human heart in its quest for a three-dimensional feel on a two-dimensional page, was deliberately intended to live up to the affective connotations of the name. As Mary Tudor's metaphor shows, the language of the heart could speak more loudly than that of the material body, and the same was by implication true for cartography, for here geographical features might in fact take second place to emotional pull. Use of the cordiform projection also threw even greater emphasis on the contours of the map as object in its own right rather than those of the contours of the country or countries the map might depict, and this had concomitant effects. Though a mountain chain such as the Pyrenees will not escape notice on a map, the sea will certainly look more important than any land barrier, not least because maps invariably paid detailed and specific attention to coasts as they could be so crucial to mariners, whereas travellers by land not only faced fewer hazards but were more likely to be able to use the evidence of their eyes – there could be no submerged rocks on land – or to ask directions from local inhabitants. Thus Mercator's map of Flanders renders the distinction between French and Flemish territory entirely arbitrary: there is no natural feature to mark it, and in line with his friend Ortelius' motto that 'Geography is the eye of History', the map actually places more emphasis on history than geography in the shape of 'medallions containing the names of the leading Flemish noble families', which prompt Paul Binding to comment, 'The text reads as a litany of loved names and admirable attributes, natural and human'. An even more striking example of sentiment taking precedence over topographical accuracy is afforded by the famous series of maps known by the generic title of 'Leo Belgicus', the 'Belgian lion', in which the seventeen provinces of the Netherlands are defiantly if unnaturalistically depicted in the form of a lion. Conversely on Ortelius' own map of Europe rivers flow across the border between France and what is labelled 'Germania' but bears little relation to Germany as we now know it, while Holland and Zealand appear to be in France:[4] there is no sense that any of these territorial boundaries are natural, inevitable or easily defensible, as events were indeed constantly demonstrating.

When the plays I shall be discussing in this chapter paid attention to the northern edges of France, then, they spoke of a region characterised by profound changes to both territorial boundaries and to individual senses of national identities; by differences and tensions between natural and political border markers; and by points of crisis where language, religious affiliations, and choice of personal and political allegiance were all at stake. In later centuries, this was a geographical area that would see the erection of a vast fortress at Sedan and the Battle of the Bulge; for Shakespeare's age almost anywhere in northern France or the adjacent Low Counties was, might be or had recently been at least a potential and often an actual theatre of war, and territorial boundaries were liable to change and blur. It is not surprising that this should be something which finds a resonance in many of Shakespeare's English history plays, but in fact it is a phenomenon not confined solely to history plays, for the first play to which I am going to turn, *As You Like It*, belongs to the very different genre of pastoral comedy. However, this as much as the history plays which I shall discuss is a play of edges and boundaries; like them, it works to reveal the marked degree of intersection between personal and geographical boundedness, and like the texts I discussed in chapter 2 but in subtly different ways, it suggests the need for limits and edges for people and their degree of individual freedom as well as for nations.

As You Like It is much concerned with border matters, and that is not surprising given the heavily contested nature of the northern French landscape in which it is set. In its principal source, Thomas Lodge's *Rosalynde*, Rosalynde's father Gerismond is the King of France, and his place of banishment seems to be understood as being outside the kingdom, while his brother Torismond tells Saladyne, the Oliver-figure, that he will 'banish thee for euer from the court and countrey of France'.[5] It is true that a number of critics, most notably Richard Wilson,[6] have suggested that Shakespeare effectively disregards this and that the real area of interest of *As You Like It* itself is not in France at all but much closer to home, in the Warwickshire Forest of Arden from which Shakespeare's own mother Mary Arden took her name. It is also undeniable that an area which very much energises the play is Ireland.[7] Nevertheless, Oliver says of Orlando 'I'll tell thee Charles, it is the stubbornest young fellow of France' (1.1.139–41), and Amiens, the name of a character in the play, is also one of the few place-names to appear on Ortelius' map of northern France, while others of the characters, as we shall see, take their names from legendary French heroes. As in *The Tempest*, the difficulty of pinning down a location both adds to the play's range of resonance and allows us to see something important about the society it depicts, for in fact events in both France and Ireland did indeed have sharply felt effects in England, particularly in 1599, the year of *As You Like It*'s composition, in ways that can be seen as remembered in the play. Planning their flight to Arden, Rosalind proposes to have

> A gallant curtle-axe upon my thigh,
> A boar-spear in my hand, and in my heart,
> Lie there what hidden woman's fear there will,
> We'll have a swashing and a martial outside.
>
> (1.3.113–6)

James Shapiro observes of this that 'Shakespeare's decision to disguise Rosalind as a soldier on her way to Arden must have struck some playgoers as an apt one',[8] for in 1598 Henri IV had signed the Treaty of Vervins (which amongst other things procured the restoration to France of Calais, in Spanish hands since 1596), and thus made peace with Spain, with the result that Englishmen who had been fighting for him returned *en masse* to their home country, often in poor condition and lacking employment. Rosalind's appearance, then, might well prompt audiences to think both of France and of connections between France and England.

There is also an extratextual anchor tying the play to the north of France, for *As You Like It* is I think in dialogue with Thomas Heywood's play *The Four Prentices of London*, in which one of the sons, Guy, is apprenticed to a goldsmith, a profession which is the subject of a joke in *As You Like It*, and another, Charles, at one point becomes an outlaw and comments on the fact that his fellow outlaws have 'not a rogue among you that feares God'.[9] It is fairly obvious that *The Four Prentices* has similarities with *Henry V*, a play of the same year as *As You Like It*, as Annaliese Connolly observes: '*The Four Prentices* ... like Shakespeare's *Henry V*, which appeared in 1599, depicts a successful foreign campaign legitimated by the discourse of a just war'.[10] I want to suggest that there are also connections between *The Four Prentices* and *As You Like It*. Though it is impossible to be certain which was written first – *The Four Prentices* was not printed until 1615, but the preface explains that it was written significantly earlier since 'as Playes were then some fifteene or sixteene yeares agoe it was in the fashion' (sig. A2v), which would make it almost or exactly contemporary with *As You Like It*[11] – the two texts echo and chime with each other at a number of points. The Clown says that Prince Tancred of Italy 'hath vow'd to make Venison of all vs poore Outlawes, and kill vs like Deere' (sig. D4r); the French princess disguises herself as a page; all four brothers nearly recognise each other and comment that Bella Franca looks just like their sister (as in fact she is); a knight refrains from killing an enemy sleeping under a tree who is in fact his brother, and another knight recalls how he killed a lion in a forest; Bella Franca and the French Princess steal away from court together with one disguised as a boy and with the Clown following them, though with evil intent; and Bella Franca's words at the end foreshadow Rosalind's:

> Father, I giue a daughter to your hand:
> Brothers, behold, here doth your sister stand.
> Tancred behold the Lady you once ceas'd,
> Onely I leaue Prince Robert here displeas'd.
> (sig. L2r)

Just so does Rosalind offer satisfaction and recognition of kinship to Orlando and her father respectively before acknowledging that she cannot give Phoebe what she wants.

In the course of Heywood's play, we also see a fight between some Spaniards and some citizens of Boulogne. Boulogne is a location with suggestive associations in terms of *As You Like It*'s engagement with borders and edges. Jane Pettegree observes that stories about the French hero Roland (Orlando in Italian) were topical for two reasons, firstly because we should remember the extent to which those of Boiardo and Ariosto in particular were 'deeply invested in the complex politics of contemporary Italy, voicing anxieties not just about the renewed threat of western Islamic expansionism, but also about the growing divisions within Christian Europe' but also because 'the central hero of *Gerusalemme Liberata* – Godfrey of Boulogne – came from a part of France that had, until 1550, been considered by the English to be part of their realm'.[12] In fact the historical Godfrey was Duke of Lower Lorraine and his title was properly Lord of Bouillon, but he may well have been born in Boulogne-sur-Mer and many Renaissance writers certainly referred to him as Godfrey of Boulogne.[13] Another play that connects *As You Like It* to a narrative of Spanish aggression is Kyd's *The tragedye of Solyman and Perseda*, whose principal villain Basilisco is remembered by name in *King John*.[14] Here a chorus of Love, Fortune and Death appears before every act, prefiguring the discussion of Fortune's powers in *As You Like It*; Piston shares the word 'sans' with Jaques when he asks 'Saunce: what languidge is that? / I thinke thou art a worde maker by thine occupation'[15] and another with Corin when he says of a fool 'He weres Ciuet' (sig. B3r); and Perseda, like Rosalind, gives Erastus a chain as token of her affection. It is therefore suggestive that when all the knights are asked to declare their mottoes the Spaniard says that 'Iaques, Iaques, is the Spaniards choice' (sig. A4v), reminding us that the name of Jaques is one which evokes war *in* Spain as much as those of Roland, Oliver and Charles evoke war *against* Spain. For all the apparent lightness of its material, *As You Like It* thus at every turn both textually and intertextually evokes war, banishment, and hostilities in or with Spain.

An association with the contested northern region of France is, I think, particularly significant in terms of the notable hardness of the play's pastoral, because what mainly conditions that hardness is the fact of geographical displacement and its consequences. This is a world where the comparison to 'the old Robin Hood of England' (1.1.116) holds true mainly in respect of the fact that both woodland communities are composed of exiles, outlaws and refugees – the Duke and his men, Celia, Rosalind, Orlando and Adam are all effectively exiles, while Oliver is threatened with exile,[16] and the Duke suggests that they are effectively rendering the deer exiles from and victims in their own natural territory:

> Come, shall we go and kill us venison?
> And yet it irks me the poor dappled fools,
> Being native burghers of this desert city,
> Should in their own confines with forked heads
> Have their round haunches gor'd.
> (2.1.21–5)

It was in fact as a destination for refugees that the Ardennes had been understood by Philippe de Commynes, in a text originally written in the mediaeval period but first translated into English in 1596. Commynes observes of the wars between the King of France and the Duke of Burgundy (ruler of the Low Countries) that 'all the people fled by the bridge ouer the riuer of Maze towards the countrey of Ardennes, and from thence to other places for their more safety', and he goes on to note that

> these miserable soules fled through the countrey of Ardennes with their wiues and children. But a Knight dwelling in those parts who euer to fore had taken part with them, slew now a great number of them, and to recouer the conquerors fauor, sent word thereof to the Duke ... Others fled towards Meziers vpon the Maz being within the realme of Fraunce.[17]

For Commynes, the Ardennes is a place to which people are driven in despair but which ultimately offers them no safety.

As Commynes' reference to the Maz 'being within the realme of Fraunce' implies, the Ardennes was also very much border territory. Evidence from a play some fifteen years later than *As You Like It*, Wentworth Smith's *The Hector of Germany. Or The Palsgrave, Prime Elector*, suggests that there might have been a popular memory of conflict there in the Black Prince's day, for the Bastard in that play remembers 'when the Blacke-Prince, lately my greatest Foe, / Opposde me at Mazieres, and wonne the day'.[18] However, the author who makes clearest the border status and conflict-ridden history of this region is in fact Julius Caesar, on whom Shakespeare wrote a play in the same year as *As You Like It* and whose 'thrasonical brag of I came, saw, and overcome' is mentioned by Rosalind (5.2.30–31; we also hear of 'a Roman conqueror' at IV.ii.3–4). Caesar refers to the area in his *Commentaries on the Gallic War*, a book whose importance I have already touched on in the last chapter; Shakespeare, as Jonathan Bate points out, would have studied it if he stayed at school until the fourth form,[19] and it is mentioned by name in *2 Henry VI, Part 2*, where Lord Say observes that 'Kent, in the *Commentaries* Caesar writ, / Is termed the civil'st place of all this isle'.[20]

In Arthur Golding's 1565 translation, Caesar's expedition to the Ardennes (which Caesar is the first to call by that name) occurs in the context of a general securing of borders. The sequence begins when Caesar 'tooke his iourney into Illyricum, because he harde saye that the marches of the Prouince were wasted by rodes made by the Pirustes'.[21] From these 'marches', which in his eyes constituted the edge of civilisation, he moved on to two more border territories:

> Commending his souldyers and such as had ben the ouersears of the workes he told them what he wold haue done, and wylled them all to assemble at the hauen of Ca[l]lice: from whence he vnderstoode to be the handsomest passage into Britaine, as the which was not distant past a thirtye myles from that place. For yt doing hereof, he left such a number of souldiers as semed suffycient, and him selfe wyth fowre well appoynted Legions and eyght hundred horsemen, went into the country of the Treuires, bicause they neither came to the Parliamentes, nor did him homage, & were reported to rayse ye Germanes on thotherside of the Rhine. (p. 109)

First eyeing a spot on the edge of what is now France because it seems to offer him the easiest way to the edge of what is now England, Caesar next concerns himself with a settlement which he sees as stirring up trouble on the edge of the Rhine, which he is attempting to settle (and where, as Golding's sixteenth-century readers would have been well aware, the Roman legions under Varus would suffer one of their most serious reversals in the reign of Caesar's successor Augustus). This is a passage which very nicely brings out the beleaguered, frontier nature of the territory, with enemies at hand in all directions.

After this initial patrol of borders, Caesar moves to 'the forest of Ardeine which from the Riuer of Rhine kepeth on styl of great wydenesse throughe the middle of the countrye of the Treuires, vnto the entrance of the borders of Rhemes: determyned to laye for warre' (p. 110). During the war that then ensues on yet another edge, 'the borders of Rhemes', Caesar's general Basilius narrowly fails to capture the native leader Ambiorix, who loses many of his followers but is himself able to exploit the distinctive features of the terrain in order to make his escape. The near-miss occurs when Basilius,

> accomplishing his iorney wyth more speede than all men thought it had bene possible for him to do, toke manye tardye in the fieldes, by whose information he went streight toward Ambiorix in a place where he was sayd to soiorne with a fewe horsemen. Fortune beareth a great stroke in al things but specially in war matters. For as it was a great chaunce that he should fall vppon him vnwares and vnprouided, & that they should se him present with their eyes, before they heard any incling at all of hys coming: so was it a great chaunce likewise that he shuld lose all the furniture for the warres that he had about him, and hys horses and wagons bee taken, and yet himselfe escape the death. But thys came to passe, bycause the house being enuironed wyth wood, (as the houses of the Galles for ye most part be, who to eschewe the heate of the weather commonlye do builde nere the woodes and riuers) hys friendes & houshold seruants in that narrow roume endured for a while the brunt of our horsmen, during ye which time, one of hys friendes set him on horsebacke, and the woodes hyd him that he could not be perceyued as he fled. Thus both in fallinge into daunger and in auoydyng the same, fortune greatly auayled. (pp. 164–5)

We have here a clear picture of a strongly marked distinction between a pastoral landscape of fields, in which the workers are vulnerable to capture by the invading force, and a wilder terrain of wood and river which will become Shakespeare's Arden, in which escape and flight are possible and in which the marauding horsemen are harmlessly dispersed just as those of Duke Frederick are, with the help of Fortune.

Having thus escaped Basilius, Ambiorix bids his men to flee, and they disperse in all directions, 'of whom some fled into the forest of Ardeine, and some into the marisses nere hande. Suche as were next the Ocean, hid theym selues in the Ilandes whych the tide was wont to make' (pp. 165–6). Geopolitical uncertainties are echoed here in the uncertain nature of the very land itself, some of which is marshy and some of which consists of possibly temporary islands which may or may not still be there when the tide comes back in. For those of the fugitives who choose the Ardennes as the safest haven, the distinctive nature of the terrain certainly comes to the fore, for

> there was not (as we shewed before) anye hoste of men, nor anye garrison, nor anye towne that was able to defend it self by battell: But the common people being dispersed, wheresoeuer was any blind valley, or any wilde wood, or anye vnhandsome maryshe where they hoped to find any defence or saufgard, conueyed themselues thither. Theis places were knowen to the borderers, and the matter required greate circumspectnes, not so muche for the sauinge of the whole armye, (for there could not happen any peril to the whole power together by men amazed and dyspersed) as for preseruation of euery souldier seuerallye. And yet this thing also in part made to the saufgard of our army. For as the desyer of spoile egged foorth many a great way from the Campe, so the woodes with their blind and vncerteine pathes was a let that they could not come at them in any great companies. (pp. 166–7)

The forest is characterised here as effectively a wilderness, containing no settlement worth the name but abounding in baffling topographical features, difficult to penetrate or map, and rich in places of concealment. In *As You Like It*, we are reminded of the benefits of fortification and urban planning when Touchstone says 'as a walled town is more worthier than a village, so is the forehead of a married man more honourable than the bare brow of a bachelor' (3.3.53–6), but in both the play and Caesar's account the forest itself proves a place of safety simply by virtue of its resistance to either systematic settlement or navigation, as we see in the complexity of Celia's instructions to Oliver on how to find their house:

> West of this place, down in the neighbour bottom,
> The rank of osiers by the murmuring stream
> Left on your right hand, brings you to the place.
> (4.3.79–81)

Caesar's account of the flight of Ambiorix's followers also stresses again the border status of the Ardennes – 'Theis places were knowen to the borderers' – and in *As You Like It* Rosalind reminds us of this when she says that 'an old religious uncle of mine taught me to speak, who was in his youth an inland man' (3.2.335–7): 'inland' in this context seems to imply that the supposed uncle had in the past lived well within the borders of a territory, as opposed to the periphery in which Rosalind and Orlando now find themselves.

Rosalind's 'old religious uncle' may help alert us to a possible reason why this particular play should be so strongly attracted to an area resonant of marginality and exile. A prominent sign of Spanish influence perilously close to the north of France was for some time the presence of the English seminary at Douai in Spanish-ruled Flanders, which lay between Calais and the Ardennes. The swapping of the two dukes' regimes might well recall the toing and froing of the middle part of the sixteenth century when Mary Tudor reversed her brother's Protestantism before having her own policies similarly overturned on the accession of her sister Elizabeth, which had provided the *raison d'être* of the seminary. It is certainly notable that this is a play which makes virtually obsessive reference to Marlowe, who is recalled in Touchstone's musing on how 'When a man's verses cannot be understood ... it strikes a man more dead than a great reckoning in a little room' (3.3.9–12), in Phoebe's quotation from the 'Dead shepherd', 'Who ever lov'd that lov'd not at first sight?' (3.5.81–2), and perhaps too in the evocation of Ovid (3.3.5–6), whom Marlowe had translated. While a student at Cambridge, Marlowe was alleged to have visited what was originally the Douai seminary in its subsequent location in Rheims, a transition which is remembered in his own *Massacre at Paris* where King Henry says of the Guise,

> Did he not draw a sort of English priests
> From Douai to the seminary at Rheims,
> To hatch forth treason 'gainst their natural Queen?[22]

The words in which this accusation was denied on Marlowe's behalf in a letter from the Privy Council are ambiguous:

> Whereas it was reported that Christopher Morley was determined to have gone beyond the seas to Reames and there to remaine; their Lordships thought good to certify that he had no such intent, but that in all his actions he had behaved himself orderly and discreetly, whereby he had done Her Majesty good service and deserved to be rewarded for his faithful dealing.[23]

It is not clear whether the point is that Marlowe had not gone to Rheims at all or that he had gone but had never meant to stay there. What does seem reasonably certain though is that if he had indeed meant to go to Rheims it must have been in connection with intelligence-gathering of some sort, almost certainly to spy on young English Catholics studying there, and Richard Baines, with whom Marlowe was later involved in an incident in Flushing which was probably linked with espionage, was certainly an agent at the seminary. The combination of a known trip to Flushing and a probable one to Rheims meant that Marlowe was unusually closely associated with the religious and territorial conflicts which scarred the debatable territory of northernmost France and the troubled regions which constituted its adjacencies, and allusion to him may well be assumed to bring them into play too.

Such a resonance would certainly not be inappropriate, for *As You Like It* is in its own way a play which is energised by border skirmishes between different belief systems, since Shakespeare stages in it the most direct and immediate confrontation in the canon between the ethos and aesthetic of court and country, a contrast sharpened by the fact that what we see is a countryside in the grip of economic hardship and a court marked by treachery and backstabbing. Ostensibly the conflict between the two is sanitised and rendered formulaic rather than topical by the familiar genre of the pastoral, which works to align the play with the conventional rather than the specific and with the abstract type rather than the particular instance. To think of the battle-scarred history and the border status of the Ardennes, however, troubles that sense of remoteness and abstraction and pulls the play back towards its *fin-de-siècle* contexts of poor harvests, rising prices, concern about the succession, England's vexed embroilment in conflicts in Ireland and France, and the lack of any visible solution to the simmering tensions between the two confessions of Protestantism and Catholicism. There is no gainsaying that *As You Like It* is a comedy not a tragedy, but its strongly marked interest, unusual in Shakespearean comedy, in verbal debate rather than in action or even particularly in plot should alert us to the fact that it is a comedy with serious interests in the extent to which behaviour is conditioned by environment and in what it is really like to live in the centre or in the periphery, and the implications of its setting in the Ardennes help make these interests visible.

Although the Ardennes is in the north of France, *As You Like It* does also remember the south, and in doing so it generates an intertextuality with not only *Julius Caesar* but also the third play Shakespeare wrote that year, *Henry V*. Its principal source, Thomas Lodge's *Rosalynde*, has a distinctly southern feel: Rosalynde's father lives in Bordeaux, most of the characters who pass through the forest are trying to get to Lyon, there are lemon trees in Arden, and the Oliver figure is called Saladyne, a name obviously evocative of the forays of the Moors into southern France. In *As You Like It* itself, the names of Orlando, Oliver and a big man called Charles all point to Roncevaux, which had been mentioned in both *Huon of Bordeaux* and Jean de Serres' *A General Inventory of the History of France*.[24] The battle at Roncevaux – whose liminal location is stressed by the fact that the Song of Roland calls it simply 'Gate of Spain' – was fought in 778, on a pass between France and Spain which formed part of the pilgrimage route to Compostela, by the rearguard of Charlemagne, whom the French chronicler Froissart regarded as the 'heir and successor' of Julius Caesar,[25] and both Charlemagne and his father Pepin were figures in whom Shakespeare was interested. In *Love's Labour's Lost*, Charlemagne, who is scheduled to appear in the aborted pageant of the Nine Worthies alongside his fellow Worthy Godfrey of Bouillon, is presented as a figure comparable to Arthur:

> *Rosaline*. Shall I come upon thee with an old saying that was a man when King Pepin of France was but a little boy, as touching the hit it?

> *Boyet*. So I may answer thee with one as old, that was a woman when Queen Guinevere of Britain was a little wench, as touching the hit it.[26]

In *1 Henry VI*, Alençon again implicitly compares Charlemagne's nephew, albeit not Charlemagne himself, to another iconic figure from English history when he declares that

> Froissart, a countryman of ours, records
> England all Olivers and Rolands bred
> During the time Edward the Third did reign.[27]

In *Henry V*, Charlemagne is remembered as a foundational figure in the history of France: the Archbishop of Canterbury assures the king that

> Hugh Capet also, who usurped the crown
> Of Charles the Duke of Lorraine, sole heir male
> Of the true line and stock of Charles the Great,
> To fine his title with some shows of truth,
> Though in pure truth it was corrupt and naught,
> Conveyed himself as heir to th'Lady Lingard,
> Daughter to Charlemagne, who was the son
> To Louis the Emperor, and Louis the son
> Of Charles the Great.[28]

The mention of Lorraine was both highly topical and also a link to *As You Like It*. In Pierre de Belloy's *A Catholicke apologie against the libels, declarations, aduices, and consultations made, written, and published by those of the League* ..., the complicated affairs of the descendants of Charlemagne are coupled with the Ardennes in an immediately contemporary context. De Belloy first explains that

> Charles of Lorrayn, brother to Lothair King of France the last of Charlemagnes posteritie, of whom the seditious do make so great accompt, left a Sonne named Ottho, who was Duke of Lorrain, and died without issue: so as in him ended the males of Charlemagne. In deed the said aucthor saith, that Godfrey with the beard Earle of Ardenne succeeded his Cosen.

Du Belloy then goes on to add that

> this Male ligne of Godfrey Countie of Arden failed againe, and fel into the person of Ide wife to Eustace Countie of Bolongne on the Sea, the father and mother to Godfrey of Bologne, King of Hierusalem: who in Lorrain succeed his vnkle by the mother Godfrey with the crouch backe: so doe the Males of the house of Bologne are [*sic*] by the same writer continued vntil Lady Isabell, the onely daughter and heire of Charles Duke of Lorrein, who in the yeere. 1418. maried Rene of Aniew, pety sonne to King Iohn of Fraunce. Thus we see by the domesticall testimony of the Princes of Lorrein, the third distaffe in the house of Lorrein since the sayd pretended Ottho Sonne to Charles of France, of which the first had bene sufficient to depriue them of the Succession Royall, not withstanding their auncesters had drawen their Orriginall from the Masculine house of the saide Charlemagne.[29]

This immediately becomes the trigger for an extended discussion of the Salic law and how it disables the claims of both the House of Lorraine and the crown of England, and thus why Henri of Navarre is the true heir to the throne of France.

Charlemagne, then, is a figure of origins, as important to the French as England's own legendary heroes are to the sense of English national identity. However, in what the Archbishop in *Henry V* subsequently goes on to say it proves oddly difficult to pin down the actual borders of Charlemagne's France, or indeed to be sure that it really was France:

> Yet their own authors faithfully affirm
> That the land Salic is in Germany,
> Between the floods of Sala and of Elbe,
> Where Charles the Great, having subdued the Saxons,
> There left behind and settled certain French.
> (1.2.43–7)

This liminal territory, Canterbury declares, did not become identifiably French 'until four hundred one-and-twenty years / After defunction of King Pharamond' (1.2.57–8), while John Coke's 1550 *The Debate betwene the Heraldes of Englande and Fraunce* declares that 'this Charlemayne was a Dowcheman' and talks recklessly of 'Hungariens now called Frenchmen'.[30] Indeed in some respects Charlemagne was as much a figure of division of nations as of national unity, since his realm was divided among his three grandsons after his death, ultimately devolving into separate countries.[31] Charlemagne's nephew Roland and his friend Oliver are thus wholly appropriate figures to evoke for a play set in a troubled and liminal region, serving to remind us both of the marginality of the part of France to which *As You Like It* takes us and also of the fact that a story about one part of the world may well also speak to concerns and agendas primarily associated with quite different and separate places.

Mapping France onto England: The Histories

Henry V, in which Charlemagne is most firmly remembered and which seems to have been written in the same year as *As You Like It*, is of course interested in its own right in the borders of France. The prologue invites us to

> Suppose within the girdle of these walls
> Are now confined two mighty monarchies,
> Whose high upreared and abutting fronts
> The perilous narrow ocean parts asunder. (19–22)

Here the borders of both England and France are effectively reified as they are figured as straining towards each other like the overhanging projecting upper storeys typical of Elizabethan housefronts, with the Channel between them like a street to keep them apart. After Canterbury and the King then discuss the border with Scotland (1.2.140–45), Henry, himself a liminal figure in that he was, as Fluellen reminds us, born at Monmouth (4.7.11), moves from Calais, which is clearly established as a firm base for the English (3.2.45, 3.3.55–6, 3.6.139–40 and 5.0.6–7), first to Harfleur (3.3.8) and then across the Somme (3.5.1), while the French king and the Dauphin fall back on Rouen (3.5.64). In this shifting world it is no wonder that Macmorris should ask, 'What ish my nation?' (3.2.124) or that the disguised Henry's account of Sir Thomas Erpingham's view of their situation should be that they are 'even as men wrecked upon a sand, that look to be washed off the next tide' (4.1.98–9). Nevertheless we end as we began, with the two fixed edges of 'the contending kingdoms / Of France and England, whose very shores look pale / With envy of each other's happiness' (5.2.344–6), and the closing chorus is quick to remind us that all Henry's gains in France will disappear during the reign of his son. The borders of France may be impermanent, but those of England, it seems, are fixed.

The idea of England's borders as fixed occurs even more strongly in *King John*, where attention to where the borders of France lie is clearly primarily a means for interrogating those of England, and those of Shakespeare's own England as much as of its thirteenth-century past, for its anti-papal agenda and motif of repelling foreign invasion give the play an obvious topicality in the years following the Armada and the promulgation of the Papal Bull *Regnans in Excelsis*, which had denied the right of Elizabeth to rule. The main action of the play gets going when the forces of the Archduke of Austria and those of the King of France, with the young English prince Arthur in tow, meet those of King John outside Angers, the capital of Anjou, which despite its location almost at the heart of what is now firmly France thus becomes designated as effectively a frontier town (2.1.0). At the same time as this creates a sense of instability within France, though, it also works to instantiate a sense of England as fixed, for although at this stage, England still had extensive possessions in France, there are repeated reminders that this is going to change. Austria declares to Arthur,

> To my home I will no more return,
> Till Angiers and the right thou hast in France,
> Together with that pale, that white-fac'd shore,
> Whose foot spurns back the ocean's roaring tides
> And coops from other lands her islanders,
> Even till that England, hedg'd in with the main,
> That water-walled bulwark, still secure
> And confident from foreign purposes.
> Even till that utmost corner of the west
> Salute thee for her king.
>
> (2.1.21–30)

This speech starts out by focusing on Arthur's right to France, but it then proceeds to spend seven lines stressing the extent to which England's status as an island sets it apart as self-contained – sometimes, as I shall discuss in chapter 6, referred to as 'a world by itself'[32] – and creates a very strong sense of the English Channel and the White Cliffs of Dover as natural and inevitable markers of a border which would be much more logically situated there than anywhere in France. Perhaps this is why by *3 Henry VI*, Hastings is ready to declare,

> 'Tis better losing France than trusting France.
> Let us be backed with God and with the seas
> Which he hath giv'n for fence impregnable.[33]

King John thus glances forward to a world in which the loss of any English claim to France has been completely accepted, as in *Henry VIII* where warfare between the two nations is either conducted entirely through tournament combat between their two monarchs or resented as a pretext for taxation rather than acclaimed as a national crusade.[34]

The play's emphasis on the importance of 'natural' banks and boundaries is underlined when Hubert says of Lewis and Blanche that

> He is the half part of a blessed man,
> Left to be finished by such as she;
> And she a fair divided excellence,
> Whose fulness of perfection lies in him.
> O, two such silver currents, when they join,
> Do glorify the banks that bound them in;
> And two such shores, to two such streams made one,
> Two such controlling bounds shall you be, kings,
> To these two princes, if you marry them.
> This union shall do more than battery can
> To our fast-closed gates.
>
> (2.1.437–47)

This is a speech energised throughout by the language of borders and of boundedness. Lewis and Blanche are figured as 'silver currents' not for the sake of any sense of freedom or movement that the idea of water may convey but solely so that the force of the trope may be harnessed to the greater glory of 'the banks that bound them in', and the highest achievement to which the two kings can aspire is to be 'such controlling bounds'. Ultimately, the marriage of Lewis and Blanche would create a clearly marked boundary (and I have been suggesting throughout that borders marked by water were considered to be particularly powerful and energised)[35] whose natural, ecological valency has more power than armed might: the united 'stream' the couple will metaphorically constitute will open gates that would otherwise stay shut. It is therefore less surprising than it might seem that John decides that

> Her dowry shall weigh equal with a queen;
> For Anjou, and fair Touraine, Maine, Poictiers,
> And all that we upon this side the sea –
> Except this city now by us besieg'd –
> Find liable to our crown and dignity,
> Shall gild her bridal bed.
>
> (2.1.486–91)

It is true that nothing in the political situation seems to have called for such a wholesale renunciation of territorial claims, but the image structure has pointed clearly towards such an outcome, in which England effectively retreats within the watery boundary that nature has provided for her.

As the play moves towards its conclusion, it becomes no longer a question of whether England should have territory in France, but rather one of whether France should have territory in England. The Bastard says, 'All Kent hath yielded: nothing there holds out / But Dover Castle' (5.1.30–32), and the English Earl of Salisbury is reduced to wishing hopelessly,

> O nation, that thou couldst remove!
> That Neptune's arms, who clippeth thee about,
> Would bear thee from the knowledge of thyself –
> And cripple thee – unto a pagan shore.
>   (5.2.33–6)

This echoes Marlowe's French-born queen Isabella, who wishes, 'O, that mine arms could close this isle about, / That I might pull him to me where I would' (2.4.16–17). But just as Isabella's wish is utterly futile, so the vehicle of Salisbury's image undoes its tenor: England cannot move, and though Salisbury sees this as a weakness in the present situation, it is by the same token a strength, for its status as a fixed island also provides it with a natural defence, and indeed before the end of the play we see the French forced to accept the necessity to flee.

Edward III also looks at the northern borders of France, but in a way which is ultimately more interested in the relation between the borders of nations and those of the self, particularly the self conceived as kernel of virtue and integrity besieged by baser instincts and temptations which must be resisted. Indeed this is, I think, a concern which gives the play itself a greater sense of unity and clarity of outline than has often been supposed. J.P. Conlan observes that 'few scholars are willing to embrace the play wholeheartedly as Shakespeare's own. The problem, they claim, is the play lacks dramatic unity. As they see it, the play appears to be divided into two poorly integrated halves'. For Conlan himself, '*Edward III* is most cohesive as a brilliantly incisive critique of the official propaganda sustaining the persecution of English recusants after the Invincible Armada's defeat', since

> Juxtaposing Edward's lecherous conduct with his greatest victory at sea, this play demonstrated to the queen that while the naval victory may have indeed been the result of the reformation of the monarch's conduct, the reformation of the monarch's conduct in this particular instance had been effected only by his vassal's wife's willingness to resist him to the death in embracing her traditional belief, the belief that the sanctity of wedlock outweighed her obligation to the king.

However Conlan's view that 'This sacramental understanding of marriage, though appropriate in a fourteenth-century context, articulated in Elizabethan times what could have been described as recusant views' is unconvincing; there are plenty of wives in Renaissance drama who refuse to commit adultery without being labelled Catholic for it.[36] I would suggest that a much more coherent thread binding the two parts of the play together is a sense that the boundaries of personal behaviour are analogous to the borders of nations.

Edward III, which opens with a French exile being made Earl of Richmond,[37] goes on to riddle national and territorial identities yet further by taking as one of its central events the fourteenth-century English conquest of Calais after Edward refuses the French king's command to do homage for the duchy of Guyenne, having first settled trouble on England's border with Scotland (1.1.127–30, 1.2.23). In 1.2 (a scene generally accepted as being by Shakespeare) the Countess of Salisbury's house briefly stands in for that border when she is besieged by King David of Scotland before being relieved by English troops, and the scene as a whole is full of talk of edges and liminal spaces: Montague asks the Countess 'We are not Scots, / Why do you shut your gates against your friends?' (1.2.82–3), the Countess begs the king, 'More happy do not make our outward wall / Than thou wilt grace our inner house withal' (1.2.143–4), and King Edward muses, 'As wise as fair; what fond fit can be heard / When wisdom keeps the gate as beauty's guard?' (1.2.162–3). This proliferation of gates and walls is in fact highly appropriate for a scene during which we are pressingly aware that Edward himself might step over a metaphorical edge, leaving the terrain of virtue to pursue the Countess, and our awareness of that possibility underlines the extent to which external borders are in this play insistently associated with the limits and protocols of personal control.

Edward III here triumphs over lust and defends his borders (the play also remembers another figure associated with the enforcement of both chastity and borders, Tamburlaine,[38] when we hear of a 'flint-heart Scythian' in a speech which moves on to talk about poets' pens [2.1.72]). In this he resembles the future Edward I in Greene's *Friar Bacon and Friar Bungay*, who overcomes his unsuitable passion for Margaret of Fressingfield in a narrative in which Friar Bacon's plan to wall England with brass fails but in which natural borders hold strong and firm. In Greene's play, Henry III says,

> Great men of Europe, monarchs of the West,
> Ring'd with the walls of old Oceanus,
> Whose lofty surges like the battlements
> That compass'd high-built Babel in with towers.
> Welcome, my lords, welcome, brave western kings,
> To England's shore, whose promontory-cleeves
> Shows Albion is another little world.[39]

Henry is half right: the Tower of Babel fell, but the English Channel and the Pyrenees are immutable markers of difference, and later the Edward of this play too will acknowledge the importance of bounds and restraint when he resigns Margaret to Lacy.

In *Edward III*, the link between geographical and personal borders is clearly illustrated when the king asks,

> Shall the large limit of fair Bretagne
> By me be overthrown, and shall I not
> Master this little mansion of myself?
>
> (2.2.93–5)

The implication is obvious: if he can conquer a territory, he can and must conquer himself. Later, when he hears that the queen is coming to France, he imaginatively links the idea of commitment to his marriage with that of a firmly marked border when he says 'She shall be welcome, and to wait her coming / I'll pitch my tent near to the sandy shore' (4.2.60–61). Presumably the idea is that he will be ready and waiting to receive her as soon as she lands, but he is also acknowledging the force of a boundary marker beyond which he must not and will not stray. The sense of an affinity between personal transgression and insecurely marked actual borders also underlies the moment when Edward comes nearest to falling into temptation:

> *King Edward.* No more: thy husband and the queen shall die.
> Fairer thou art by far than Hero was,
> Beardless Leander not so strong as I:
> He swum an easy current for his love,
> But I will through a Hellespont of blood
> To arrive at Sestos, where my Hero lies.
> *Countess.* Nay, you'll do more: you'll make the river too
> With their heart bloods that keep our love asunder.
> (2.2.150–58)

As we saw in chapter 3, the strait between Sestos and Abydos marks the difference not only between two cities but between two continents, and while it is possible to cross from one to the other, Leander finds it both disorienting and ultimately fatal to do so: first the crossing of the strait brings his gender identity into question, or at least appears to, when Leander supposes that Neptune's sexual advances must mean that the god has mistaken him for a woman, and finally he drowns. It is, therefore, a profoundly and dangerously liminal space that Edward evokes as he decides on what his own sexual behaviour will be. Conversely, when he finally resolves on the path of virtue, he recurs to the idea of strongly defined, natural borders:

> Arise, true English lady, whom our isle
> May better boast of than ever Roman might
> Of her, whose ransacked treasury hath tasked
> The vain endeavour of so many pens.
> (2.2.192–5)

The idea of the sprawling Roman empire attaches itself to the violated Lucrece, while the Countess is both chaste and the inhabitant of an island, two ideas which were themselves linked in the Renaissance imagination: one origin proposed for the name Elizabeth derived it from 'insulae', proposing an absolute equation between the impenetrable boundaries of the Virgin Queen herself and those of her sea-girt realm.

It is no surprise that immediately after renouncing any idea of the Countess, Edward should turn his mind to literal border areas:

> Warwick, I make thee Warden of the North;
> Thou, Prince of Wales, and Audley, straight to sea,
> Scour to Newhaven: some there stay for me.
> Myself, Artois, and Derby will through Flanders.
>   (2.2.201–204)

When the play, as presaged here, actually moves to northern France, we are made strongly aware of the potentially shifting, unstable nature of borders, which are arbitrary and political rather than created by natural geographical features. The First Frenchman, talking to the First Citizen, says of the English forces,

> Content thee, man, they are far enough from hence,
> And will be met, I warrant ye, to their cost,
> Before they break so far into the realm.
>   (3.2.13–15)

Almost immediately, though, this confidence is shown to be misplaced when King John of France, referring to himself in the third person, tells Edward that he is 'musing thou shouldst encroach upon his land' (3.3.47), and accuses the English king of being 'One that hath ... no abiding place' (3.3.53). On this shifting edge between nations, the physical is directly equated with the symbolic in the ritual arming of the Black Prince before this, his first battle. His father intones,

> Edward Plantagenet, in the name of God,
> As with this armour I impall thy breast,
> So be thy noble unrelenting heart
> Walled in with flint and matchless fortitude,
> That never base affections enter there.
>   (3.3.179–83)

For the king, the breastplate is essentially a metaphor for the heart it walls in, an idea echoed when Derby adds the helmet:

> Edward Plantagenet, Prince of Wales,
> As I do set this helmet on thy head,
> Wherewith the chamber of thy brain is fenced,
> So may thy temples with Bellona's hand
> Be still adorned with laurel victory.
>   (3.3.185–8)

The 'fence' which the helmet provides for the prince's head is here imaginatively connected to the future role envisaged for him as guardian of England's own borders and interests. The 'wall' around the prince's heart and the 'fence' around his head jointly serve to underline the extent to which the personal is intimately connected to the political and to which the edge between nations can stand in for the edge between the self and society.

In all the plays which I have explored both in this chapter and in the last, Shakespeare has turned his attention to the borders of France as he understood them: in *As You Like It* to the Ardennes, where France meets what are now Belgium and Luxembourg, and imaginatively to Roncevaux, where the rearguard of Charlemagne's army had held back the Moors whom his father Pepin had already had to expel from Carcassonne; in *All's Well That Ends Well* to Roussillon, where France marches with Spain; in *Love's Labour's Lost* to Navarre and Béarn, which the accession of Henri IV had bonded to the French crown in an uneasy and theoretically temporary personal union; in *King John* to Normandy and northern France; and in *Edward III* to Calais, where France looks across at England. Across this body of plays two clear and linked ideas emerge: first that the borders of France offer a way of talking about the borders of England, and moreover of doing so in a way that ultimately softens the blow of England's loss of France by emphasising the 'rightness' and 'naturalness' of being bounded within an island, and second that national borders provide a powerful trope for personal ones, so that to be English is to be bounded. I wonder then if it is coincidence that *As You Like It*, *All's Well That Ends Well*, *Love's Labour's Lost*, *King John* and *Edward III* are all susceptible of readings grounded in the religious and perhaps more particularly the political implications of the differences between the two confessions. Shakespeare himself was certainly related to some Catholic conspirators and may perhaps have had some personal sympathy for the old religion, but, as I have argued in chapter 2, if so it did not prevent him from pursuing a resolute quietism and staying out of trouble – being, in fact, bounded, and implicitly adhering to a definition of an appropriate English identity as fundamentally constituted by insularity rather than amenability to influences and fluctuations from the Continent. It is therefore not perhaps surprising that for Shakespeare the borders of France are a favourite place to explore, since they allow him to investigate ideas pertaining to the border between the national, the personal, and the geographical.

Notes

[1] Muriel St Clare Byrne, ed., *The Lisle Letters* (Harmondsworth: Penguin, 1983), p. 60.

[2] Sir John Norris, *Newes from Brest. A diurnal of al that Sir John Norreis hath doone since his last arivall in Britaine: also of the taking in of the forte by Croyzon, and the names of such captaines gentlemen and others that were slaine and hurte in this service* (London: Peter Short for Thomas Millington, 1594).

[3] Anonymous, *A true relation of the French kinge his good successe ...* (London: John Wolfe, 1592), sig. A3r.

[4] Paul Binding, *Imagined Corners: Exploring the World's First Atlas* (London: Headline Books, 2003), pp. 170, 98–9, and 216–7.

[5] Thomas Lodge, *Rosalynde* (London: Abel Jeffes for T. G. and John Bushie, 1592), sig. G2v.

[6]   Richard Wilson, '*As You Like It* and the enclosure riots', in *Will Power: Essays on Shakespearean Authority* (Hemel Hempstead: Harvester Wheatsheaf, 1993).

[7]   See Chris Butler, '"The howling of Irish wolves": *As You Like It* and the Celtic Essex Circle', in *Celtic Shakespeare: The Bard and the Borderers*, edited by Willy Maley and Rory Loughnane (Burlington: Ashgate, 2012).

[8]   James Shapiro, *1599: A Year in the Life of William Shakespeare* (London: Faber and Faber, 2005), p. 264.

[9]   Thomas Heywood, *The Foure Prentises of London* (London: Nicholas Okes for J. Wright, 1615), sig. C3v. All further quotations from the play will be taken from this printing and reference will be given in the text.

[10]   Annaliese F. Connolly, 'Guy of Warwick, Godfrey of Bouillon, and Elizabethan Repertory', in *Early Modern England and Islamic Worlds*, edited by Bernadette Andrea and Linda McJannet (Basingstoke: Palgrave Macmillan, 2011), p. 142.

[11]   On the date of *The Four Prentices* see for instance Tom Rutter, *Work and Play on the Shakespearean Stage* (Cambridge: Cambridge University Press, 2008), p. 177n6; and Mary Ann Weber Gasior, who argues for a likely date of 1594 (*Thomas Heywood's The Four Prentices of London: A Critical, Old-Spelling Edition* [New York: Garland, 1980], p. xiv).

[12]   Jane Pettegree, *Foreign and Native on the English Stage, 1588–1611* (Basinsgstoke: Palgrave, 2011), pp. 125–6.

[13]   See for instance Gilles Corrozet, *Memorable conceits of diuers noble and famous personages of Christendome, of this our moderne time* (London: Richard Field for James Shaw, 1602), sig. A5v.

[14]   William Shakespeare, *King John*, edited by E.A.J. Honigmann (London: Routledge, 1967), 1.1.244.

[15]   Thomas Kyd, *The tragedye of Solyman and Perseda* (London: Edward Allde for Edward White, 1592), sig. B2r.

[16]   William Shakespeare, *As You Like It*, edited by Agnes Latham (London: Methuen, 1975), 3.1.6–8. All quotations from the play will be taken from this edition and reference will be given in the text.

[17]   Philippe de Commynes, *The historie of Philip de Commines Knight, Lord of Argenton*, translated by Thomas Danett (London Ar. Hatfield for J. Norton, 1596), pp. 76–7.

[18]   Wentworth Smith, *The Hector of Germany. Or The Palsgrave, prime Elector* (London: Thomas Creede for Josias Harrison, 1615), sig. A4r.

[19]   Jonathan Bate, *Soul of the Age: The Life, Mind and World of William Shakespeare* (London: Viking, 2008), p. 98.

[20]   William Shakespeare, *Henry VI, Part 2*, edited by Michael Hattaway (Cambridge: Cambridge University Press, 1991), 4.7.49–50.

[21]   Julius Caesar, *The eyght bookes of Caius Iulius Caesar conteyning his martiall exploytes in the realme of Gallia and the countries bordering vppon the same translated oute of latin into English by Arthur Goldinge* (London: William Seres, 1565), p. 108. All further quotations from the text will be taken from this edition and reference will be given in the text.

[22]   Christopher Marlowe, *The Massacre at Paris*, in *The Complete Plays*, edited by Mark Thornton Burnett (London: J.M. Dent, 1999), xxi, 105–8.

23   Quoted in Charles Nicholl, *The Reckoning: The Murder of Christopher Marlowe* (London: Jonathan Cape, 1992), p. 92.

24   John, Lord Berners, *Huon of Bordeaux* (London: Thomas Purfoot for Edward White, 1601), chapter 37; and Jean de Serres, *A General Inventory of the History of France*, translated by Edward Grimeston (London: George Eld, 1607), p. 78.

25   Richard Hillman, *Shakespeare, Marlowe and the Politics of France* (Basingstoke: Palgrave, 2002), p. 6.

26   William Shakespeare, *Love's Labour's Lost*, edited by John Kerrigan (Harmondsworth: Penguin, 1982), 4.1.120–25.

27   William Shakespeare, *King Henry VI, Part 1*, edited by Michael Hattaway (Cambridge: Cambridge University Press, 1990), 1.2.29–31.

28   William Shakespeare, *King Henry V*, edited by T.W. Craik (London: Routledge, 1995), 1.2.69–77. All further quotations from the play will be taken from this edition and reference will be given in the text.

29   Pierre de Belloy, *A Catholicke apologie against the libels, declarations, aduices, and consultations made, written, and published by those of the League* … (London: G. Robinson for Edward Aggas, 1585), pp. 2–3.

30   Hillman, *Shakespeare, Marlowe and the Politics of France*, p. 20.

31   See for instance Norman Davies, *Vanished Kingdoms: The History of Half-Forgotten Europe* (London: Allen Lane, 2011), pp. 104–6.

32   William Shakespeare, *Cymbeline*, edited by J.M. Nosworthy (London: Cengage Learning, 2007), 3.1.13.

33   William Shakespeare, *Henry VI, Part 3*, edited by Michael Hattaway (Cambridge: Cambridge University Press, 1993), 4.1.42–4.

34   William Shakespeare, *Henry VIII*, edited by A.R. Humphreys (Harmondsworth: Penguin, 1971), 1.1.33–8 and 1.2.56–60.

35   See Lisa Hopkins, *Shakespeare on the Edge: Border-crossing in the Tragedies and the* Henriad (Burlington: Ashgate, 2005), chapter 3.

36   J.P. Conlan, 'Shakespeare's *Edward III*: A Consolation for English Recusants', *Comparative Drama* 35.2 (summer 2001), pp. 177–8, 186 and 189.

37   Anonymous, *King Edward III*, edited by Giorgio Melchiori (Cambridge: Cambridge University Press, 1998), 1.1.1–4. All quotations from the play will be taken from this edition and reference will be given in the text.

38   See Lisa Hopkins, *The Cultural Uses of the Caesars on the English Renaissance Stage* (Burlington: Ashgate, 2008), chapter 3.

39   Robert Greene, *Friar Bacon and Friar Bungay*, in *Five Elizabethan Comedies*, edited by A.K. McIlwraith (London: Oxford University Press, 1934), 2.1.1–7.

PART III
Invisible Edges

Chapter 6
The Edge of Heaven

Where is Paradise, and is there a direct route to it? The edge between this world and the next was the most important of all, and yet it was one which remained recalcitrant to definition. In this chapter, I shall be suggesting that this particular edge is one which may be apprehended from a distance, but that for Shakespeare in particular it recedes as it is approached. In mediaeval maps, Paradise is usually to be seen in the East, sometimes in or near modern Sri Lanka, but Renaissance maps take a less literal view. Alessandro Scafi in his comprehensive study of the appearance of Paradise on maps notes, 'It was Martin Luther who initiated a new approach to the problem of pinpointing Eden on a map.... Paradise, he said, had vanished because of the tragedy of human sin': thus the Wittenberg Bible does offer a visual representation of Paradise but does not situate it in relation to any landmarks we could now recognise. In William Biddulph's 1609 *The trauels of certaine Englishmen into Africa, Asia, Troy, Bithynia, Thracia, and to the Blacke Sea* ..., we hear of two possible locations for Paradise. The first is Ankara in Turkey:

> It is but a little village, and called by the Turkes, Anchora, but most vsually by the Christians there dwelling it is called Eden, not the garden of Eden, (which place is vnknowen vnto this day) but because it is a pleasant place, resembling in some sort the garden of Eden (as the simple inhabitants thereof suppose) therefore it is called Eden.

The next is the habitation of the Chelfalines, who live on the border between Persia and Mesopotamia:

> These people perswade themselves, and report vnto others, that they dwell in that place which was called Eden.... But some hold that this pleasant garden Eden did extend ouer all the earth. But by the second chapter of Genesis it appeareth manifestly, that this garden wherein man was placed, which we call Paradise, was a certaine place on earth, but spreading ouer all.

However Biddulph concludes that

> howsoeuer it be somewhat probable, that these Chelphalines dwell now in that Country which was called Eden, yet Plato, and Aristotle, and Lactantius, and others, doe constantly affirme (as they haue receiued of ancient monuments) that Mountaines, and Riuers, and Ilands, and Countries, haue receiued much alteration in this kinde. Sicilia is said to haue beene diuided from Italy, Cyprus from Syria, England from France, by the violence of the Sea, whereas before they were ioined, as Pelooneius is to the rest of Grecia, or as the towne of Rye

(at an high water) seemeth to be to the rest of England: So that no certainty can
be giuen either by reading, or trauelling, of the place where Eden was, because
these Riuers run in other streames.[1]

In a variation of this view, Calvin argued more metaphysically that 'the original
geography of Eden had not been dislocated by the Flood, but that only its delight
had been lost', a view at which Biddulph perhaps gestures when he declares, 'I
resolue my selfe, that no man liuing can demonstrate the place, which God (for
the sinnes of Adam) accursed';[2] following Calvin, Walter Ralegh 'believed that
the Flood had wiped out a highly localized Paradise within the region of Eden and
that, since the rivers were still there, the former site of paradise could be indicated
on a map', though Scafi notes wryly, 'For such an experienced navigator ... it is
perhaps curious that he omitted to provide his map with any mathematical aid'.[3]

Calvin was not the only person who did not think of the question simply
in geographical terms. Early on in Sir Thomas More's *Utopia*, we are told that
Raphael 'had two favourite quotations, "The unburied dead are covered by the
sky" and "You can get to heaven from anywhere"'.[4] Coupled, these appear to
suggest that there is a link of some sort between the fate of the body and the fate
of the soul, and that it is therefore possible to take an optimistic view of the ease
with which one could journey from this world to the next. For Raphael there is no
one fixed frontier post between the two but a border which is both ubiquitous and
permeable, and though More's narrator questions whether all aspects of Utopia
are in fact perfect, here surely is an offer which no one could baulk at: that one
could move easily and from anywhere from this world to a better one. In this
sense, Paradise might be accessible from everywhere, even if its precise location
cannot be pinpointed on a map. Similarly when Mephistopheles says, 'Why this
is hell, nor am I out of it', he clearly suggests that hell is a state of mind rather
than a physical location,[5] and C.A. Patrides notes that 'St. Ambrose had long since
observed that "the real Paradise is no earthly one which can be seen; that is placed
in no spot of the ground, but in the highest part of our nature, which receives
animation and life from the powers of the soul, and from the communication of
the Spirit of God"'.[6] Not everyone agreed, though: in Henry Chettle's *The Tragedy
of Hoffman*, for instance, Hoffman promises his father's skeleton 'hand in hand
/ Wee'le walke to paradise';[7] in the speech which William Falbeck appended to
Thomas Hughes's *The Misfortunes of Arthur* we hear, 'Before the conscience
of Gueneuora / The map of hell shall hang';[8] in Kyd's *The tragedye of Solyman
and Perseda*, Piston explains that he is rifling the pockets of a corpse because
'Seeing he was going towards heauen, / I thought to see, if he had a pasport to S.
Nicholas or no';[9] and Sharon Emmerichs argues that in *Hamlet*, 'Laertes' claim to
the priest that "A minist'ring angel shall my sister be / When thou liest howling"
(5.1.236) demonstrates his belief that the grave itself is Ophelia's primary avenue
into Paradise, rather than the state of her soul upon her death'.[10] This more
physicalised view of the transition between worlds was echoed in the fact that
while the Renaissance saw a decline in the traditional association of Paradise

with the East and India, some other traditions remained surprisingly vibrant. In a survey of the field, Clayton MacKenzie lists a number of possible locations suggested for a geographically real Paradise which include the Low Countries, Newfoundland and Bermuda; the sixteenth-century Jesuit Guillaume Postel even very unusually postulated that Paradise was at the North Pole.[11] The most popular choice, however, was England,[12] and perhaps there are some traces of this idea in Shakespeare, for MacKenzie points out that John of Gaunt's speech in *Richard II* which identifies England as 'This other Eden – demi-paradise'[13] has much in common with traditional representations of Paradise,[14] and it has been suggested by a number of critics that Shakespeare was actually recalling in that passage an image specifically associated with saints and angels, the Wilton Diptych.[15] Certainly in Greene's *Friar Bacon and Friar Bungay*, Henry III refers to England as 'like that wealthy isle / Circled with Gihon and swift Euphrates',[16] so the idea that England might be the location of Paradise is by no means alien to the English Renaissance stage.

The association of the British Isles with the other world can be traced back to classical times. Josephine Waters Bennett, discussing a longstanding tradition 'which identified Britain with the Otherworld not merely in a geographical or mythological sense, but with the Otherworld as the abode of the spirits of the dead', tells a particularly evocative story from classical times which a number of Elizabethan historians and chorographers repeated:

> Procopius of Caesarea … recounts a third-century legend that the souls of the dead are actually ferried across to Britain from the continent. He says that 'countless persons' report that the fishermen in the ports opposite to Britain make nightly trips to the island in boats not their own, carrying invisible cargoes. These ferrymen hear voices and the calling of a roll of names when they reach Britain, but they see no one. They make the trip in miraculous time, returning before morning, with their boats very light.[17]

This idea could be seen as related to 'the Celtic custom of ferrying bodies across to islands for interment, a practice that contributed to an ideas of an Isle of the Dead where departed souls lingered',[18] and the suggestion that Britain itself is in effect the other world is not far distant from the Virgilian tag 'penitus toto divisos orbe Britannos', (Britons totally divided from the whole world'), which James echoed when a Royal Proclamation of October 1604, announcing him King of Great Britain, referred to it as 'a little world within it selfe'[19] and which Shakespeare translates in *Cymbeline* as 'Britain's a world by itself'. The presence of that phrase in *Cymbeline* should alert us to the fact that for Shakespeare suggestions of access to the other world cluster more at the fringes of Britain than in England itself, and that unlike earlier figurings of Paradise, they are associated specifically with the west, which was for Renaissance authors a general site of evocative and quasi-magical potential, as when Samuel Daniel notes, 'We see all the west world (lately discouered) to bee … in their first and natural free nakedness' and that Arthur 'fled into the mountaines, and remote desarts of the west parts of the Isle, and left all to the inuadors, daily growing more and more vpon them', so that to go west is in effect to find your earlier self.[20] I want to suggest that this is not something surprising but is a phenomenon we ought to be able to understand if, as I have been arguing, physical borders shared an imaginative space with spiritual ones, meaning that in border territories we might potentially be in direct contiguity with the supernatural. In this chapter, I want to examine Shakespeare's representation of the eschatological charge which may accrue to the edges of Britain, and I want to do so particularly through the lens of what later adaptations and appropriations of some of his plays can show us both about what Shakespeare does and also, and perhaps even more suggestively, about what he does *not* do.

Saints on the Edge

In Shakespeare's case, what we often find at the edge of the map are memories of saints and images of journeys with spiritual as well as literal ends, and given that I am claiming that these physical locations carry an inherent eschatological charge, I want to suggest that it is equally not surprising that this should be a phenomenon primarily observable in his last plays, although it is also present, albeit to a rather lesser extent, in another play which directly figures the border between life and death as geographical one, *Hamlet*, which talks openly of death as 'the undiscover'd country, from whose bourn / No traveller returns' (3.1.79–80) and where Gertrude's name evokes St Gertrude, who in Danish culture was the patron saint of both literal and figurative journeys who 'would be of help, not only on any journey in this life, but also on the final one after death'.[21] Ophelia, whose name is a transliteration of the Greek word for help, is similarly associated with both journeys and spiritual aid when she sings a song whose words and music are both based on a popular ballad about the former pilgrimage site of Walsingham.[22] The phenomenon is, though, most marked in the last plays. A remarkable feature of all these is that the heroines of all four are emblematically named. Unlike the Rosalinds and Violas of earlier plays, Perdita, Miranda, Marina and Imogen are names which openly invite us to think in specifically allegorical terms: Perdita represents loss, Miranda what is to be admired or wondered at, Marina the ebb and flow of the sea, and Imogen the buried British past. Moreover, that which has been lost, that which is to be wondered at and that which is Britain's past could all be read as charged with memories and resonances of Catholicism, and the Blessed Virgin Mary was often figured as Stella Maris, the star of the sea. Watery borders were often seen as particularly charged and significant ones, to which overtones of the spiritual and the supernatural often accrue, not least because water both provided the entry to the classical underworld, in the shape of the river Styx, and also played a crucial role in the Christian paradise, where 'the river of the water of life, bright as crystal' is to be found 'flowing from the throne of God and of the Lamb through the middle of the street of the city' (*Revelation* 22.1), doubly identified as topological feature and soteriological agent; indeed Augustine saw

Paradise and Earth as physically connected by 'the four rivers, which flowed from a single source in the middle of the Garden and emerged into the known regions of the earth having travelled a considerable distance underground', the Gihon of the Bible becoming the Nile on Earth and the Pishon the Ganges, while the Tigris and the Euphrates had retained their original names.[23]

In *Pericles*, the story is introduced by Gower's observation that 'it hath been sung at festivals, / On ember eves and holy ales',[24] and Lorraine Helms compares it to 'romances and saints' lives' in the way it is 'theatrically representing a valiant virgin whose eloquence and courage are rightly rewarded'.[25] Although the play's framework is ostensibly pagan, and Diana appears to Pericles in a vision and tells him to go to Ephesus (5.1.227–9), Cerimon's restoration of Thaisa has the feel of a miracle, as does Marina's remark that 'there is something glows upon my cheek / And whispers in mine ear, "Go not till he speak"' (5.1.86–7). Marina herself is certainly like a saint: her own account of herself is:

> I never spake bad word, nor did ill turn
> To any living creature. Believe me, la,
> I never killed a mouse nor hurt a fly.
> I trod upon a worm against my will,
> But I wept for't.

> (4.1.72–6)

This is confirmed when the First Gentleman observes that the effect of her presence in the brothel is 'to have divinity preached there' (4.5.4). There is also an insistent but low-key evocation of St Paul in the fact that the play opens in Antioch and Pericles' next visit is to Tarsus, an echo underlined by Gower when he speaks of how when Pericles goes to Tarsus 'each man / Thinks all is writ he speken can' (2.0.12–13), where 'writ' may evoke Holy Writ. There is language with religious associations elsewhere in the play too, as the unsuccessful suitors are termed 'martyrs' (1.1.39). *The Winter's Tale* is also eminently susceptible of a saint-centred reading, as we see when Julia Reinhard Lupton speaks of 'signs of Catholicism' in its last act; she argues, 'The return to Sicily converts the Old Testament profile of the play's sublimely rageful Leontes into a living emblem of saintly penance.... The "sainted spirit" of the dead Hermione, on the other hand, epitomizes the tradition of the virtuous martyr'.[26] One might, too, note the intriguing reference in a text of the same year as *The Winter's Tale*, William Barlow's *An answer to a Catholike English-man ...*, to an accusation that 'at Dover, some Catholikes were put in Beares skinnes, and so baited to death by Dogges', which could provide a potentially intriguing context for a play whose second half sees a bear turn on humans and an audience told, 'It is requir'd / You do awake your faith' (5.3.94–5).[27] In a sense the edge of the map is the natural and indeed the only place to find such stories as these. Both saints and metaphorical journey stories disturb the borders between life and death, natural and supernatural, so it is not surprising that their preferred habitat should be the edges of the map, in the skirts of the Mediterranean, on the imagined sea-coast of Bohemia where reality blurs into fantasy and in the territories of the Celtic fringe.

One might also note a remarkable facet of the early seventeenth-century afterlife of all the last plays, which is the number of times they find themselves mined and revisited for uses connected with interest in saints, often in ways which intersect with what early modernists would now term the British question by focusing on the Celtic fringe. As Richard Wilson observes, at Candlemas 1610 Sir John Yorke of Gowthwaite Hall in Nidderdale hosted a performance for an audience including his relatives, the five children of the Gunpowder conspirator Robert Wintour and, rumour had it, the Jesuit Father John Gerard. We do not know what the play was, but we do know that the company's repertory included *Pericles* and *King Lear*,[28] and *Pericles* recurs again in a 1619 booklist from the English Jesuit mission at Saint-Omer. *The Tempest*, too, is reused in a surprisingly religious context. In 1638, a play entitled *The Seven Champions of Christendom* was published with an ascription to John Kirke and a note on the title page that it was 'acted at the Red-Bull in St. Iohns Streete, with a generall liking'. This tells the stories of St George, St Anthony, St James, St Andrew, St Patrick and St David, though St George is securely at its centre. The play opens with him as a young orphan in the care of the witch Calib, who has killed his parents, the earl and countess of Coventry. She intended to kill George too but instead has grown fond of him and brought him up with her own son, the clownish Suckabus, whose father is the devil Tarpax. The ghosts of George's parents reveal his true identity, and he turns on Calib, who is taken down to hell by Tarpax. George liberates the other six champions, whom Calib has taken prisoner, and accompanied by Suckabus heads off in quest of adventures, including the killing of a dragon and a lion by Andrew and Anthony, an encounter with the giant Ormandine and his enchanted garden for David, and various chivalric encounters for James, Denis and Patrick, while George himself saves a princess from a dragon and finally rescues all the rest when they have been trapped by the villainous Brandron, who has also turned the daughters of the king of Macedon into swans. When the king converts to Christianity the daughters are restored to their proper shapes, and George gives them as wives to Anthony, David and Patrick before departing in quest of further adventures.

Accepting the ascription to Kirke, W.J. Lawrence noted in 1924 that the *Dictionary of National Biography* suggested that Kirke might have been the grandson of Spenser's friend Edward Kirke,[29] which might account for the play's repeated reminders of the association between St George and the red cross, but in 1969 John Freehafer argued first for a date of 1613 or 1614, on the basis of various contemporary allusions, and second that the likely author was actually Wentworth Smith and that this is in fact the same play as the *St George for England* 'by Will. Smithe' recorded by Warburton. Freehafer also contended that the play was 'in subtantial part a … burlesque of Shakespeare's *Tempest*' and argues too for significant debts to *The Winter's Tale* and *The Two Noble Kinsmen*. Principally, though, he sees the influence of *The Tempest*, suggesting that Tarpax and Suckabus are based on Ariel and Caliban and Ormandine on Prospero.[30]

There certainly are echoes of *The Tempest* in the play, not least the fact that the witch is called Calib, but it is worth noting that the chivalric contest involving the Emperor's daughter is much more like *Pericles* and that there are also suggestive parallels with *Cymbeline*, that classic Celtic fringe play in which Cloten actually quotes the Virgilian mantra that 'Britain's a world by itself' (3.1.13). The ghosts of George's parents appear to him to reveal his parentage, of which Calib has kept him ignorant, just as the ghosts of Posthumus's parents appear to him in *Cymbeline*; as in *Cymbeline*, we are reminded of the importance of Wales, this time by the presence of St David; and again as in *Cymbeline*, where Imogen's name should more properly be Innogen, echoing that of the wife of Brutus, the Brutus myth is prominent in *The Seven Champions*, since Ormandine stresses that both George and David are descended from Brutus.[31] Finally, many modern readings of *Cymbeline* have stressed its place within seventeenth-century jostlings for pre-eminence amongst the various constituent parts of James's fledgling entity of Great Britain, and this is something also strongly marked in *The Seven Champions*, where national identity is stressed from the outset, as Calib introduces the other six champions to George:

> This is, my *George*, the fiery youth of *Spain*,
> Cal'd by the name of *Iames*: this *Anthony* of *Italy*:
> This the brave Northerne Knight, brave *Andrew*:
> This *Irelands Patricke*: *Britaines David* this:
> And this the lively briske crosse capring French man *Denis*.
> (sig. B4v)

George himself, meanwhile, is firmly English, being in fact the heir to the earl of Coventry and being told by the ghost of his father that '*Englands* Red Crosse shall *George*, then *St. George* wear' (sig. C1v), and in due course both St David and St Andrew acknowledge his pre-eminence. Indeed towards the end of the play George says first, 'For England, and the Brittaines doe I fight', though it has been David who has previously been identified as British, and then, 'I stand for Scotland now', to which Andrew meekly replies, 'You have wonne it fairely; take it as your owne' (sig. L1r). George is also an essentially folkloric, chthonic figure rather than a specifically religious one: Calib compares him to 'an April tender bud' (sig. B4v), and his own language is rich in allusion to flowers and spring, as when he says, 'How soone fresh flowers fall, which now did grow' (sig. C1v) or talks of 'the pride and glory of the youthfull Spring' (sig. G4v). In this George could well be seen as coming close to Perdita in *The Winter's Tale*, who is strongly associated with flowers. This is, then, a play which in one way or another seems to recall all of Shakespeare's last plays to tell its story of saints.

William Rowley's *A Shoemaker, A Gentleman*, probably acted around 1617–1618 although not printed until 1638,[32] is another play which mingles Shakespearean echoes with stories of saints. In this case the debt is to *Cymbeline*: there are three disguised princes, a princess who apparently marries beneath her, and a fight featuring Romans and Britons, as well as an excursus to Wales and several references to eagles.[33] Nor are this and *The Seven Champions of England* the only saint plays to show apparent signs of the influence of *Cymbeline* in particular: Shirley's play *Saint Patrick for Ireland* does so too. To some extent the source of Shirley's play is clearly Father B.B.'s 1625 translation of Joscelin, *The life of the glorious bishop S. Patricke*,[34] this being a safe and indeed a conservative choice in comparison with the other readily available text, Richard Stanihurst's *De vita S. Patricii*, which had been dedicated to the Duke of Parma and which, as Salvador Ryan points out, 'implicitly identified Patrick's mission with that of the Spanish campaign aimed at wiping out heresy that was currently active in the Low Countries'.[35] Shirley and Joscelin have much in common, although inevitably given that a second part was originally projected (Prologue 25–8), Shirley's play tells only a fraction of the story that the *Life* does: we hear nothing of Patrick's childhood or of his sisters, we glean only indirectly that he has previously been Milcho's slave (sig. E5v), and the play also stops well before the *Life* does.[36] However, Joscelin's *Life* is not the only source for Shirley's play: Hugh MacMullan notes,

> Gifford was the first to suggest that Shirley had Belarius' cave in mind when he wrote the scene of Dichu's cave in Act V.... A line for line comparison shows that *St. Patrick for Ireland* is much closer in thought to *Cymbeline* than it is to any of the plays which Forsythe mentions.[37]

(Calib in *The Seven Champions* also has a cave, though that may owe as much to Prospero as to Belarius). As MacMullan suggests, there certainly does seem to be an intertextual link between Belarius' cave and Dichu's, in which Dichu's two sons, who are both believed dead, discover him (sig. I1r).

Saint Patrick for Ireland shows traces not only of *Cymbeline* but of *Hamlet*. The scene in which the king offers poisoned wine to Patrick, at a party which includes the queen, who is moved to pity him, is reminiscent of the end of *Hamlet*, and so too are the Prologue's lines,

> We should be very happy, if at last,
> We could find out the humour of your taste,
> That we might fit, and feast it, so that you
> Were constant to your selves, and kept that true.[38]

This seems to echo Polonius' celebrated advice to Laertes, 'To thine own self be true' (1.3.78). It should not surprise us to find *Hamlet* remembered in Ireland, because it is in some intriguing ways a play with an Irish sensibility. Martin Holmes suggests that the name of the drowned Ophelia may encode an Irish reference, since it is sometimes used as an alternative form of the Irish district of Offaly[39] (Fynes Moryson calls it 'Ophalia'),[40] while Sir D. Plunket Barton notes that Ophelia's mad song "Bonny Sweet Robin" is an Irish tune.[41] Shirley's play postdates *Hamlet*, but the original version of Joscelin's *Life* does not, and intriguingly, there are also points of resemblance between it and *Hamlet*: the poisoning of the wine is present there, as is a story of a king's daughter named Dublinia (she subsequently gives her name to Dublin) who is drowned and her body laid next to that of a relative, in this case her dead brother; the saint resurrects both (pp. 39–40). Indeed, one of the things Patrick does most frequently in the *Life* is resurrect the dead, and *Hamlet* is a play in which a ghost returns to the world of the living from the country of the dead, bringing the two, as in Procopius' story of the rowing boats, into the same physical plane. Another thing Joscelin's Patrick often does is interfere in the succession, causing the collateral line to inherit: in one instance, a tyrant displeases him and 'the Saint denounced prophetically to him, That none of his posterity should succeed him, but that his Lordship should be transferred to his younger brother' (p. 70), as happens when Old Hamlet dies and Claudius succeeds him. When good people die, angels bear their souls away (see for instance p. 82), as Horatio prays will happen to Hamlet (5.2.365), and the source tells how St Patrick was abducted by pirates and taken from England to Ireland; Hamlet too falls victim to piracy. If Shirley thought of *Hamlet* in an Irish context, perhaps that should alert us to the extent to which an interest in the Celtic fringe and its eschatological possibilities was already present in the play.

Most notably, Hamlet himself swears, 'Yes by Saint Patrick but there is, Horatio' (1.5.142). Mention of St Patrick may conceivably have been prompted by the recollection of Edmund Campion, sometimes claimed as a possible source for *Hamlet*, since Christopher Highley suggests that Campion was 'captivated' by the story of Patrick: 'When he fled Ireland as a fugitive from the Protestant authorities, he dressed in the livery of the Earl of Kildare under the assumed name of Patrick', a pseudonym which he also used on subsequent occasions.[42] However in this context there also seems, as many critics have pointed out, to be an allusion to the famous pilgrimage site known as St Patrick's Purgatory at Lough Derg in Ireland, one of the many subterranean locations rumoured to offer direct access to the underworld. On the English mediaeval stage, this idea of a direct route to the underworld had found expression in the old property of the hell-mouth; more generally, it is also manifested in numerous local legends about specific caves, such as the Devil's Arse in the Peak District,[43] the description of Malengin's cave in *The Faerie Queene*, of which 'some doe say, it goeth downe to hell'[44] and George Chapman's *A Memorable Masque*, where Capriccio thinks Plutus must be a devil because he is under the earth.[45] Particularly notable for a connection with both the supernatural and *Hamlet* are the northern caves described by Olaus Magnus, a Catholic Swede self-exiled in Rome, in his 1555 bestseller *Description of the Northern Peoples*. Julie Maxwell has recently suggested that in *Hamlet*, Shakespeare shows knowledge of Magnus's book, as well as of work by Magnus' elder brother Johannes.[46] The younger Magnus writes of how when mining is undertaken in the north, 'with countless perils and deaths an entrance is produced to the very entrails of the mountains (where Pluto dwells)' and declares that 'we gather that in the northern kingdoms … demons make great efforts to perform services for the inhabitants of those parts, most often, however, in stables and cowsheds and in the mines'.[47] At Lough Derg, the cave's lakeside location supplements this imagined connection between overworld and underworld with the additional idea that, as in the classical river of the underworld, water may supply direct access from the world of the living to that of the dead, and the power of water is certainly evoked in *Hamlet*: Hamlet returns from a sea voyage meant to prove fatal to him, and though drowned Ophelia may stay dead, out of her grave emerge first the vividly evoked memory of Yorick and subsequently the living Hamlet and Laertes, in what is definitely not a miracle but does have something of the uncanny about it.

Hamlet makes his remark about St Patrick in connection with his dead father, who is presently

> Doom'd for a certain term to walk the night,
> And for the day confin'd to fast in fires,
> Till the foul crimes done in my days of nature
> Are burn't and purg'd away.
>
>   (1.5.10–13.)

It is surely pertinent that in *The Golden Legend* Jacobus de Voragine assured his readers that 'it was revealed to Patrick that the pit was the opening to a purgatory, and that those who chose to go down into it could expiate their sins therein, and would be spared their purgatory after death',[48] or as Henry Jones has it in his 1647 account of the site *Saint Patricks purgatory*, Ranulphus 'telleth that who so suffereth the paines of that Purgatory, if it be enjoyned him for penance, he shall never suffer the paines of Hell, but he shall die finally without repentance of sinne'.[49] In his reference to Patrick, Hamlet thus imaginatively conjures up a scenario in which his father could be spared his present suffering, and in which the passage from this world to the next could be eased and made direct so that, for Sharon Emmerichs, Hamlet 'participates in a very Catholic attempt to release his father from a definitively purgatorial suffering'.[50] As so often in *Hamlet*, though, things are not quite so simple, for actually this is *not* a world in which it easy to get to heaven, as Claudius clearly reveals when having failed to secure the grace necessary for true repentance, he notes ruefully, 'My words fly up, my thoughts remain below. / Words without thoughts never to heaven go' (3.3.97–8). The Catholic St Patrick may have been able to offer a simple geographical route to the forgiveness of sins, but in the Protestant theology of Hamlet's *alma mater* of Wittenberg it is far less simple than that: the spirit must be moved by grace, and Claudius's is not. *Hamlet* and *Saint Patrick for Ireland* may have elements in common, but they thus evince very different sensibilities on the subject of salvation.

Hamlet is not the only play whose later reuses seem to imply a different emphasis from the play itself. To a certain extent, the similarities between Rowley's *A Shoemaker, A Gentleman* and *Cymbeline* serve only to underline what Shakespeare does *not* say in *Cymbeline*. *A Shoemaker, A Gentleman* tells the stories of Sts Crispin, Crispian, Alban and Winifred, and it does so in a way which draws deliberate and pointed parallels between the persecuted Christians of Roman Britain and the persecuted Catholics of Jacobean Britain. Maximinius says of Alban, 'Hale him to the temple; or force him kneel / Unto our Roman god, or kill the heretic' (2.2.75–6), inaccurately but suggestively presenting ancient Roman beliefs as monotheistic, and so more able to be read as figuring 'Roman' in other senses too, and specifically as mapping onto Roman Catholicism. Maximinus also uses language openly suggestive of contemporary recusancy when he says,

> A second limb is from our body cut
> In Alban's relapse. It is that pedant prince,
> That seminary knight, Amphiabel,
> That poisons thus the current of our state.
>
> (2.2.82–6)

The term 'seminary knight' unmistakably invites us to transpose an apparently long-dead conflict into urgently modern terms and apply it directly to the contemporary situation. It is perhaps suggestive that Shakespeare elsewhere may, as I shall shortly explore, conceivably glance at Winifred and certainly mentions Crispin and Crispian in *Henry V* but never refers to Alban. As I explored in chapter 4, Richard Wilson has suggested that in *All's Well that Ends Well*, Helena's projected pilgrimage to Santiago de Compostela can never take place because '*All's Well* turns away from the Pyrenees to disavow the ultramontanes', since 'Spain is out of bounds to Shakespeare's characters because the most important fact of Counter-Reformation Europe was the sectarian wall that cut the pilgrim ways connecting Britain to Iberia and the shrine of Saint James'.[51] By the same token, I think it is possible that Shakespeare avoids St Alban because the college at Valladolid, which was founded by Robert Persons, was named the College of St Alban. In this respect, too, he will not go to Spain, and the side effect of that is that he confines himself instead to the Celtic fringe, where he can distance the potentially dangerous idea of Catholicism both physically and also temporally, since the idea of saints being found only in the west clearly evokes the process centuries earlier by which the established inhabitants of Britain had retreated before the Anglo-Saxon invaders to the so-called Celtic fringe. (This might perhaps be another reason why Shakespeare has no interest in Alban, whose martyrdom at St Albans brings him far too close to London.)

At first sight, to press for the idea of a contemporary resonance might seem inappropriate, since *Cymbeline* goes to considerable pains to present itself as a story whose resonances are far removed from the real world. It stresses its own affiliations with romance and folk tale when the First Gentleman says of the disappearance of the king's young sons, 'Howsoe'er 'tis strange, / Or that the negligence may well be laugh'd at, / Yet is it true, sir', and when the queen tells Imogen, 'No, be assured you shall not find me, daughter, / After the slander of most stepmothers, / Evil-ey'd unto you';[52] as Andrew King observes,

> Princes abducted in infancy and raised in a forest, ignorant of their royal identity; a 'squire of low degree' banished from the court; a slandered lady in flight, disguised as a boy; a murderous step-mother and her boorish son – *Cymbeline* can easily feel like a storehouse (or more appropriately tiring-house) of old and familiar narrative and thematic 'props' of earlier romance drama.[53]

At one point we actually catch a glimpse of the extraordinary in the act of being recuperated into the easily comprehensible and familiar form of a tale:

> *Lord.*   This was strange chance:
> A narrow lane, an old man, and two boys.
> *Posthumus.* Nay, do not wonder at it: you are made
> Rather to wonder at the things you hear
> Than to work any. Will you rhyme upon't,
> And vent it for a mock'ry? Here is one:
> Two boys, an old man twice a boy, a lane,
> Preserv'd the Britons, was the Romans' bane.
>   (5.3.51–8)

I want to suggest, though, that one particular legend might have been of interest to Shakespeare in *Cymbeline* and that it was a legend which had specific and potentially topical contemporary resonances. One of the saints featured in *A Shoemaker, A Gentleman* is St Winifred, a mediaeval Welsh princess who was beheaded by an unsuccessful suitor and restored to life by her uncle St Beuno. The supposedly miraculous pilgrimage site of St Winifred's Well not only continued to figure prominently in the popular consciousness long after the Reformation[54] but might also have had particular associations for Shakespeare: Phebe Jensen notes that 'Bodleian manuscript Eng.poet.b.5, transcribed in the mid-1650s and associated with the household of the Catholic yeoman Thomas Fairfax of Warwickshire, contains thirty-two poems by Robert Southwell, two poems on Campion ... [and] two poems to St. Winifred',[55] which, along with the fact that the Gunpowder plotters made a pilgrimage to St Winifred's Well shortly before the plot itself, suggests that St Winifred may have been particularly venerated in Shakespeare's native Warwickshire. By the same token, of course, this also implies that Winifred's political associations were dangerous and needed careful handling in something of the same way as Alban's did. Perhaps, though, we should notice that in both *Cymbeline* and *A Shoemaker, A Gentleman* there is an episode set in Wales in which an attempted rape by a loathed suitor is thwarted by a wronged and virtuous woman and that someone thought to have been beheaded subsequently comes back to life (St Winifred herself, Posthumus); one might even be tempted to compare Winifred's subsequent marriage to Christ as a nun with Imogen's marriage to Posthumus, which is explicitly spiritualised by Posthumus when he says, 'Hang there like fruit, my soul, / Till the tree die' (5.5.263–4). In *Antony and Cleopatra*, a series of proleptic echoes invites us to remember that the reign of Augustus saw the birth of Christ; in *Cymbeline* too we hear of Augustus, Antony and Cleopatra, and perhaps here too we should remember the potential Christian context of events.

Going West

In Rowley's play, an angel actually arises out of St Winifred's Well and promises that miracles will occur there, as indeed they subsequently do (1.3.103), so that water functions here quite literally as a gateway to the other world, emblematising the theology of *The Book of Common Prayer* where the service for baptism declares, 'None can enter into the kingdom of God, except he be regenerate and born anew of water and the Holy Ghost' in order that he 'may so pass the waves of this troublesome world, that finally [he] may come to the land of everlasting life'. All Shakespeare's last plays contain images of shipwreck which ultimately reveal the salvific power of water and which bring together the idea of metaphorical and literal journeys to death and salvation. In these rich, strange plays, so full of metrical and linguistic experiment, the ways in which these two ideas are linked create an insistent sense of a watery world, and of a watery western fringe in particular. *The Tempest* starts with a shipwreck, or at least with what appears to be one, since we are later told that neither vessel nor crew has sustained any actual hurt, and the motif is also strongly present in *The Winter's Tale* and *Pericles*. (It is even there in *The Two Noble Kinsmen*, for even though there is no actual shipwreck here, the Gaoler's Daughter imagines one.)[56] *Cymbeline* may appear the exception by being completely land-bound, but in this strange play, where characters believe in fairies, where '`'`Tis thought the old man, and his sons, were angels' (V.iii.85), and where we are explicitly shown that we need to read obliquely as the Soothsayer expounds Leo-natus as a lion's whelp and *mollis aer* as woman (5.5.444–53), language may alert us to some submerged seas on which the characters are in some sense tempest-tossed even while on land.

Imogen's own surroundings are watery from the outset, as we see when Iachimo describes her chamber: 'the chimney-piece' showed 'Chaste Dian, bathing' (2.4.81–2) and the tapestry the meeting of Antony and Cleopatra and how 'Cydnus swell'd above the banks, or for / The press of boats, or pride' (2.4.70–72). But the lapping of water really starts to be heard about halfway through the play, when the Queen reminds Cymbeline of

> The natural bravery of your isle, which stands
> As Neptune's park, rubb'd and pal'd in
> With rocks unscaleable and roaring waters,
> With sands that will not bear your enemies' boats,
> But suck them up to th'topmast.
> (3.1.19–23)

Cloten takes up the note of defiance by saying, 'You shall find us in our salt-water girdle' (3.1.80–81), and the island which lies within that girdle is revealed as a strange, otherworldly place when Imogen says, 'I'th'world's volume / Our Britain seems as of it, but not in't: / In a great pool, a swan's nest' (3.4.139–41).[57] From then on, the characters are constantly thinking of water. Belarius says,

> O melancholy,
> Who ever yet could sound thy bottom, find
> The ooze, to show what coast thy sluggish care
> Might easil'est harbour in?
> (4.2.203–6)

Imogen calls the supposed body of Posthumus 'this most bravest vessel of the world' from which Pisanio, as she thinks, has 'Struck the main-top!' (4.2.319–20), and Lucius thinks in the same terms when he asks her, 'What's thy interest / In this sad wreck?' (4.2.365–6). Later, Posthumus himself thinks of the sea when he says 'now our cowards / Like fragments in hard voyages became / The life o'th'need' (5.3.43–5); when they are reunited, Imogen says to Posthumus, 'Think that you are upon a rock, and now / Throw me again' (5.5.261–2), while Cymbeline evokes the waters of baptism as he prays, 'My tears that fall / Prove holy water on thee' as he becomes 'a mother to the birth of three' (5.5.268–70). Guiderius says of Cloten that 'he did provoke me / With language that would make me spurn the sea, / If it could so roar at me' (5.5.293–5), and in a very strange and often amended passage Cymbeline declares,

> Posthumus anchors upon Imogen;
> And she (like harmless lightning) throws her eye
> On him: her brothers, me: her master hitting
> Each object with a joy.
>
> (5.5.384–7)

The phrase 'her master' clearly implies that Cymbeline is at least temporarily troping his daughter as a ship, but whatever the precise details the generally nautical flavour of the metaphor is unmistakable.

In the context of sea voyages, it is worth noting that while much attention has been paid to the fact that Milford Haven was famously a site of invasion, where Henry VII landed on his way to the Battle of Bosworth, the play insists that it is also a potential point of departure: Lucius tells Cymbeline, 'I desire of you / A conduct over land, to Milford-Haven' (3.5.7–8) and Imogen in turn tells Lucius, 'I have a kinsman who / Is bound for Italy; he embark'd at Milford' (3.7.33–4). The idea of departures is underlined when Guiderius says, 'Nay, Cadwal, we must lay his head to the east, / My father hath a reason for't' (4.2.255–6), although traditional Christian practice was to lay the head to the west, as seen in the burials of saints.[58] (One might note that the names of the Scilly Isles, which lie off the westernmost part of mainland Britain, include St Martin's, St Mary's and St Agnes.) This is a play that is very interested in where people go when they die. Jupiter adjures the ghosts of Posthumus' parents and brothers to

> No more, you petty spirits of region low,
>   Offend our hearing: hush! How dare you ghosts
> Accuse the thunderer, whose bolt (you know)
>   Sky-planted, batters all rebelling coasts?
> Poor shadows of Elysium, hence, and rest
>   Upon your never-withering banks of flowers.
>
> (5.4.93–8)

Sicilius declares, 'The marble pavement closes, he is enter'd / His radiant roof' (5.4.120–21) and Posthumus contemplating death says, 'There are none want eyes to direct them the way I am going, but such as wink, and will not use them' (5.4.188–9). In the context of Posthumus' 'To darkness fleet souls that fly backwards' (5.3.25), Guiderius' instruction that Fidele's head should be to the east looks very like the preparation for a spiritual journey; if the head is to the east, the supposed Fidele's feet must be pointing to the west, as if that is the direction for the dead to travel. This is an idea that would have been particularly compelling if Shakespeare was aware that the Romans buried their dead at the sides of roads, as William Birnie seems to have been in his 1606 *The blame of kirk-buriall* when he notes that 'wee finde some Roman lawes, as by Emperour Hadrian, all cittie buriall was forbid.... And this aunctient policie wee perceiue practised in the ouldest of our owne countrey Kirkes',[59] for *Cymbeline* is technically a Roman play and Cymbeline himself reminisces, 'Thy Caesar knighted me; my youth I spent / Much under him' (3.2.70–71), which has presumably Romanised him. (Indeed as Miles Russell observes, and as Shakespeare may just conceivably have known given the unusual quantities in which they have survived and given that his friend Michael Drayton talks about having seen a coin of of Cunobelinus and notes, 'It is justifiable by Caesar, that they us'd to shaue all except their head & vpper lip, & ware very long haire; but in their old Coynes I see no such thing warranted',[60] coins of the historical Cunobelinus show an image so Romanised that it may well have been copied from a portrait of Augustus or Tiberius).[61] Moreover, *Cymbeline* is a play whose character names evoke the Aeneas story and which actually quotes a Virgilian tag, so we should perhaps remember that in the *Aeneid*, Aeneas enters the underworld through the crater of lake Avernus, near Naples, where physical geography intersects seamlessly with spiritual, as in Ortelius' map of *Aeneae Troiani Navigatio* where Avernus sits visibly on the map, a place like any other and reachable by travellers. Jane Pettegree sees *Cymbeline* as 'making Christendom an "absent" topography, a promised land towards which the prophetic conclusion points but which the play itself does not ultimately stage',[62] but perhaps it does gesture at some of the possible routes towards that topography, and if so, its gaze is consistently westwards.

Where that journey to the west would take one is most clearly imagined in *The Tempest*, which never names its setting but whose benevolent, book-loving magus looks so much as if he is inspired by John Dee's western dreams, and which ends by conjuring up the idea of a sea voyage to salvation when Prospero asks the audience to pray for him and to

> release me from my bands
> With the help of your good hands.
> Gentle breath of yours my sails
> Must fill.
>
> (Epilogue 9–12)

The Tempest clearly evokes not only the Mediterranean where it should logically be set and the Bermuda which it both resembles but which it disclaims to be, but also Ireland and, beyond that, the America to which both Ireland and Wales had supposedly proved springboards. In the case of Wales this had been through the mythical Prince Madoc, a figure in whom Dee believed implicitly and who also figures in William Strachey's *History of Travaile into Virginia Britannia* and in Drayton.[63] In at least one version of his story, Prince Madoc set sail from Milford Haven (though he is more usually said to have sailed first from North Wales and later from Lundy) and supposedly made two voyages to the New World 'sailing west, and leaving the coast of Ireland so far north, that he came to a land unknowen'.[64] In the case of Ireland it was through St Brendan, who, leaving Ireland, which Joscelin's *Life* repeatedly terms 'The Iland of Saints', and passing via the Paradise of Birds, was said to have sailed to America in quest of what Caxton's version of *The Golden Legend* names the 'Paradyse Terrestre', meeting on the way a former 'monke of Saynt Patrykes abbey in Yrelonde [who] was wardeyn of the place whereas men enter into Saynt Patrykes Purgatory'.[65] Although the phrase 'to go west' is not securely documented as a metaphor for dying until the twentieth century, OED does have a tentative first use of around 1532, and in the story of St Brendan there does certainly seem to be a suggestion that the journey west may take one beyond the confines of this world.

Again, though, as with his truncated evocation of St Patrick's Purgatory, Shakespeare does not fully commit to the vision of the other world at which he hints in *The Tempest*, holding back from a complete realisation of the vision just as the masque is not allowed to reach its conclusion. One of *The Tempest*'s many ironies is that the closest it comes to a saint is that 'thing of darkness'[66] and alleged son of the devil Caliban, for it is he who has the celestial vision which makes him cry to dream again (3.2.140–43). It is also he who, it seems, will be left alone on the island at the end of the play in the best tradition of the hermit. In *The Tempest*, we push to the farthest edge, the world beyond the west, but even as we reach it, the possibility that it might be paradise dissolves in front of our eyes: Gonzalo's vision of Utopia collapses into itself even as he attempts to articulate it as 'The latter end of his commonwealth forgets the beginning' (2.1.158), as elusive and unreal as the location of El Dorado or the land of the Amazons, forever just over the next hill and then the one after that. Here, finally, is the ultimate expression of the edginess of Shakespeare's westwards route to Paradise: you may just catch its shadow, but you will either never fully reach it or do so only to find it something other than itself, like the Eden of Calvin which had lost its delight. Shirley, Smith, Rowley and the company who played for Sir John Yorke may show us something which we might not otherwise have seen about Shakespeare's representation of the western fringes, but what they show us is much cruder than anything he ever does. Theirs is a brightly coloured world in which miracles happen and faith blazes hot and strong, but his is the shadowy twilight of the Celtic west where faith flickers, sainthood is never fully achieved and no society is perfect, but which nevertheless has not quite lost the sense that it might just be the edge of another world.

Notes

[1]   William Biddulph, *The trauels of certaine Englishmen into Africa, Asia, Troy, Bithynia, Thracia, and to the Blacke Sea* ... (London: T. Haveland for W. Aspley, 1609), pp. 39–20 and 78.

[2]   Biddulph, *The trauels of certaine Englishmen*, p. 79.

[3]   Alessandro Scafi, *Mapping Paradise: A History of Heaven on Earth* (London: The British Library, 2006), pp. 266, 268, 271 and 300–301.

[4]   Sir Thomas More, *Utopia*, translated by Paul Turner (Harmondsworth: Penguin, 1965), p. 39.

[5]   Christopher Marlowe, *Doctor Faustus, A text,* in *Christopher Marlowe: The Complete Plays*, edited by Mark Thornton Burnett (London: J.M. Dent, 1999), 1.3.78. Even when he later says that Hell is located 'Within the bowels of these elements' (2.1.121) he adds that 'Hell hath no limits, nor us circumscribed in one self place' (2.1.123–4).

[6]   C.A. Patrides, 'Renaissance and Modern Views on Hell', *The Harvard Theological Review* 57.3 (July, 1964), pp. 217–36, p. 231.

[7]   Henry Chettle, *The Tragedy of Hoffman* (London: J.N. for Hugh Perry, 1631), sig. B1v.

[8]   Thomas Hughes, *Certaine deu[is]es and shewes presented to her Maiestie by the gentlemen of Grayes-Inne at her Highnesse court in Greenewich, the twenty eighth day of Februarie in the thirtieth yeare of her Maiesties most happy raigne* (London: Robert Robinson, 1587), sig. G1r.

[9]   Thomas Kyd, *The tragedye of Solyman and Perseda* (London: Edward Allde for Edward White, 1592), sig. D4v.

[10]   Sharon Emmerichs, 'Shakespeare and the Landscape of Death: Crossing the Boundaries of Life and the Afterlife', Shakespeare 8.2 (June 2012), p. 175.

[11]   Scafi, *Mapping Paradise*, p. 285.

[12]   Clayton G. MacKenzie, 'Paradise and Paradise Lost in Richard II', *Shakespeare Quarterly* 37.3 (autumn, 1986), p. 318.

[13]   William Shakespeare, *Richard II*, edited by Stanley Wells (Harmondsworth: Penguin, 1969), 2.1.42.

[14]   MacKenzie, 'Paradise and Paradise Lost in Richard II', p. 52.

[15]   See for instance my essay 'The King's Melting Body: Richard II', in *A Companion to Shakespeare's Works*, vol. 2: *The Histories*, edited by Richard Dutton and Jean E. Howard (Oxford: Blackwell, 2003), pp. 395–411; and Helen Ostovich, '"Here in this garden": The Iconography of the Virgin Queen in Shakespeare's Richard II', in *Marian Moments in Early Modern Drama*, edited by Regina Buccola and Lisa Hopkins (Burlington: Ashgate, 2007), pp. 21–34.

[16]   Robert Greene, *Friar Bacon and Friar Bungay*, in *Five Elizabethan Comedies*, edited by A.K. McIlwraith (London: Oxford University Press, 1934), 5.3.66–7.

[17]   Josephine Waters Bennett, 'Britain among the Fortunate Isles', *Studies in Philology* 53.2 (April 1956), p. 123.

[18]   Sophia Kingshill and Jennifer Westwood, *The Fabled Coast: Legends and Traditions from around the Shores of Britain and Ireland* (London: Random House, 2012), p. 221.

[19]   Jane Pettegree, *Foreign and Native on the English Stage, 1588–1611* (Basinsgstoke: Palgrave, 2011), p. 100.

[20]   Samuel Daniel, *The first part of the historie of England* (London: Nicholas Okes, 1612), sig. B3r and p. 23.

[21]   David Hohnen, *Hamlet's Castle and Shakespeare's Elsinore* (Copenhagen: Christian Ejlers, 2000), pp. 23–4.

[22]   William Shakespeare, *Hamlet*, edited by Harold Jenkins (London: Methuen, 1980), pp. 531 and 533.

[23]   Scafi, *Mapping Paradise*, p. 46.

[24]   William Shakespeare [and George Wilkins], *Pericles*, edited by Suzanne Gossett (London: Arden Shakespeare, 2004), 1.0.5–6. All further quotations from the play will be taken from this edition and reference will be given in the text.

[25]   Lorraine Helms, 'The Saint in the Brothel: Or, Eloquence Rewarded', *Shakespeare Quarterly* 41.3 (autumn, 1990), p. 326.

[26]   Julia Reinhard Lupton, *Afterlives of the Saints: Hagiography, Typology and Renaissance Literature* (Stanford: Stanford University Press, 1996), p. 210. See also John Wasson, 'The Secular Saint Plays of the Elizabethan Era', in *The Saint Play in Medieval Europe*, edited by Clifford Davidson (Kalamazoo: Medieval Institute Publications, 1986), pp. 254–5; Ruth Vanita, 'Mariological Memory in The Winter's Tale and Henry VIII', *Studies in English Literature, 1500–1900* 40.2 (Spring 2000), p. 315; and Ruben Espinosa, *Masculinity and Marian Efficacy in Shakespeare's England* (Burlington: Ashgate, 2011), pp. 167–71.

[27]   William Barlow, *An answer to a Catholike English-man (so by himselfe entitvled) who, without a name, passed his censure vpon the apology made by the Right High and Mightie Prince Iames by the grace of God King of Great Brittaine, Framce, and Ireland & c. for the oath of allegiance* (London: Thomas Haueland for Matthew Law, 1609), p. 110.

[28]   Richard Wilson, *Secret Shakespeare: Studies in theatre, religion and resistance* (Manchester: Manchester University Press, 2004), pp. 270–71.

[29]   W.J. Lawrence, 'John Kirke, the Caroline Actor-Dramatist', *Studies in Philology* 21 (1924), p. 587.

[30]   John Freehafer, 'Shakespeare's *Tempest* and *The Seven Champions*', *Studies in Philology* 66.1 (1969), pp. 97, 87, 92–3, and 98–9.

[31]   John Kirke, *The Seven Champions of Christendom* (London: J. Okes for James Becket, 1638), sigs G2r and G3v. All further quotations from the play will be taken from this printing and reference will be given in the text.

[32]   See Trudi L. Darby, 'The Date of William Rowley's *A Shoemaker, A Gentleman*', *Notes and Queries* 53.1 (March, 2006), pp. 83–4.

[33]   William Rowley, *A Shoemaker, A Gentleman*, edited by Trudi L. Darby (London: Nick Hern Books, 2002), 3.4. passim.

[34]   Joscelin, *The life of the glorious bishop S. Patricke ...*, translated by Fr. B.B. (St Omers: [G Seutin?] for John Heigham, 1625).

[35]   Salvador Ryan, 'Steadfast Saints or Malleable Models? Seventeenth-Century Irish Hagiography Revisited', *Catholic Historical Review* 91.2 (2005), p. 253. Bernadette Cunningham and Raymond Gillespie note that Joscelin's too was originally a text with an agenda, having been composed 'as part of the Anglo-Norman attempt to appropriate the cult of Patrick', but that had long since been lost sight of (Bernadette Cunninhgam

and Raymond Gillespie, '"The most adaptable of saints": The cult of St Patrick in the seventeenth century', *Archivium Hibernicum* 49 [1995], p. 83).

36   The two share the names Leogarius, Conallus, Milcho, Dichu, Victor, Ethne, Fedella and Emeria, and Shirley also takes from the *Life* the idea that the King has posted soldiers at the havens to stop Patrick from landing (sig. A3r), the prophecy of Patrick arriving with shaven crown and staff (sig. A4r), and the idea that he has power over rocks and mountains and that he came to Ireland because he saw a vision of Irish infants in their mothers' wombs pleading with him to evangelise the island (sig. B2v). In both, Dichu, who initially opposes Patrick, is rendered miraculously unable to move (sig. B3r) and subsequently supports him; in both Dichu's two sons are taken hostage, though Shirley diverts from his source here to introduce a rather feeble romance plot in which they are in love with the king's two daughters while his two sons both pursue Emeria, culminating in the elder of the two disguising himself as a god and ravishing her, only to have her murder him when she penetrates his disguise and subsequently vow herself to a holy life. The name the rapist son adopts when in disguise, Ceanerachius, is clearly derived from the source's Ceancrochie (p. 33). Also shared between Shirley and his source is the story of the attempt to burn Patrick which he miraculously survives with the assistance of his guardian angel Victor (sig. G2r) and the information that Ireland is known as 'the Iland of the Saints' (sig. G2r, *Life* p. vi). We also learn that, as in the source, Victor has previously revealed to him the location of a treasure (sig. I2r), and hear, as in the source, about the indigenous magicians' fear and dislike of him.

37   Hugh MacMullan, 'The Sources of Shirley's *St. Patrick for Ireland*', *PMLA* 48.3 (September 1933), p. 813.

38   James Shirley, *St Patrick for Ireland* (London: J. Raworth for R. Whitaker, 1640), sigs D5v – E1r and Prologue 5-8. All further quotations from the play will be taken from this printing and reference will be given in the text.

39   Martin Holmes, *The Guns of Elsinore* (London: Chatto & Windus, 1964), p. 43.

40   John P. Harrington, ed., *The English Traveller in Ireland* (Dublin: Wolfhound Press, 1991), p. 94.

41   Sir D. Plunket Barton, *Links Between Ireland and Shakespeare* (Dublin and London: Maunsel & Co., 1919), p. 212.

42   Christopher Highley, *Catholics Writing the Nation in Early Modern Britain and Ireland* (Oxford: Oxford University Press, 2008), p. 127. On Campion as a possible source for Hamlet, see for instance Peter Milward, S.J., *The Catholicism of Shakespeare's Plays* (London: Saint Austin Press, 1997).

43   Ben Jonson, *The Gypsies Metamorphosed*, in *Ben Jonson*, edited by C.H. Herford and Percy and Evelyn Simpson (Oxford: The Clarendon Press, 1950), vol. 7, p. 601.

44   Edmund Spenser, *The Faerie Queene* (London: Richard Field for William Ponsonbie, 1596), V. ix, p. 297.

45   George Chapman, *The memorable maske of the two honorable Houses or Inns of court* (London: G. Eld for George Norton, 1613), p. 6.

46   Julie Maxwell, 'Counter-Reformation Versions of Saxo: A New Source for Hamlet?', *Renaissance Quarterly* 57.2 (summer 2004): 518–60.

47   Olaus Magnus, *Description of the Northern Peoples* [1555], translated by Peter Fisher and Humphrey Higgens (London: The Hakluyt Society, 1996), vol. 2, pp. 291 and 299.

⁴⁸   Jacobus de Voragine, *The Golden Legend*, translated by Granger Ryan and Helmut Ripperger (New York: Arno Press, 1969), pp. 192–3.

⁴⁹   Henry Jones, *Saint Patricks purgatory* (London: Richard Rosyton, 1647), p. 49.

⁵⁰   Emmerichs, 'Shakespeare and the Landscape of Death', p. 179.

⁵¹   Richard Wilson, 'To great St Jaques bound: *All's Well That Ends Well* in Shakespeare's Europe', in *Shakespeare et l'Europe de la Renaissance*, edited by Yves Peyré and Pierre Kapitaniak (Paris: Actes du Congrès de la Société Française Shakespeare, 2004), http://www.societefrancaiseshakespeare.org/document.php?id=847.

⁵²   William Shakespeare, *Cymbeline*, edited by J.M. Nosworthy [1955] (London: Cengage, 2007), 1.1.65–7 and 1.2.1–3.

⁵³   Andrew King, '"Howso'er 'tis strange … Yet it is true": The British History, Fiction and Performance in *Cymbeline*', in *Shakespeare and Wales: From the Marches to the Assembly*, edited by Willy Maley and Philip Schwyzer (Burlington: Ashgate, 2010), p. 157.

⁵⁴   See Alison Shell, 'Divine Muses, Catholic Poets and Pilgrims to St Winifred's Well: Literary Communities in Francis Chetwinde's "New Hellicon" (1642)', in *Writing and Religion in England, 1558–1689: Studies in Community-Making and Cultural Memory*, edited by Roger D. Sell and Anthony W. Johnson (Burlington: Ashgate, 2009), pp. 273–88. Shell discusses Francis Chetwinde's 1642 poem 'The New Hellicon' and argues, 'In the mythological schema of the poem, St Winifred stands in for Mnemosyne, mother of the Muses and patroness of the fountain named after her, whose springs counteracted Lethe's waters of oblivion' (p. 288).

⁵⁵   Phebe Jensen, *Religion and Revelry in Shakespeare's Festive World* (Cambridge: Cambridge University Press, 2008), p. 58.

⁵⁶   William Shakespeare and John Fletcher, *The Two Noble Kinsmen*, edited by Lois Potter (London: Thomas Nelson and Sons, 1997), 3.4.5–9. All further quotations from the play will be taken from this edition and reference will be given in the text. Although the play is co-authored, Douglas Bruster has argued that 'the dramatic idiolect of the Jailer's Daughter is remarkable because it appears to transcend the peculiarities of authorial style – to retain a stylistic integrity, that is, despite the two playwrights' own compositional idiolects'. (Douglas Bruster, 'The Jailer's Daughter and the Politics of Madwomen's Language', *Shakespeare Quarterly* 46.3 [autumn 1995], pp. 278–9).

⁵⁷   In one of the few engagements with this passage, Jane Pettegree suggests seeing the image of the swan's nest as representing strands of different literary traditions (Jane Pettegree, *Foreign and Native on the English Stage*, pp. 156–7).

⁵⁸   Arnold Angenendt, 'Relics and Their Veneration', in *Treasures of Heaven: Saints, Relics, and Devotion in Medieval Europe*, edited by Martina Bagnoli, Holger A. Klein, C. Griffith Mann, and James Robinson (London: The British Museum Press, 2011), p. 21.

⁵⁹   William Birnie, *The blame of kirk-buriall, tending to perswade cemiteriall ciuilitie* … (Edinburgh: Robert Charteris, 1606), sig. E1v.

⁶⁰   Michael Drayton, *Poly-Olbion* (London: Humphrey Lownes for M. Lownes, J. Browne, J. Helme, and J. Busbie 1612), pp. 125 and 127. John Clapham, says that Cunobelinus was the first king to have his own image stamped on his coins, so he too had presumably seen one or more. *The historie of Great Britannie declaring the successe of times and affaires in that iland, from the Romans first entrance, vntill the raigne of Egbert, the West-Saxon prince; who reduced the severall principalities of the Saxons and English,*

into a monarchie, and changed the name of Britanie into England (London: Valentine Simmes, 1606), pp. 25–6.

61   Miles Russell, *Bloodline: The Celtic Kings of Roman Britain* (Stroud: Amberley Publishing, 2010), p. 80.

62   Pettegree, *Foreign and Native on the English Stage*, p. 156.

63   William Strachey, *The Historie of Travaile into Virginia Britannia* (London: Hakluyt Society, 1849), pp. 5–6; Drayton, *Poly-Olbion*, p. 140.

64   Gwyn A. Williams, *Madoc: The Legend of the Welsh Discovery of America* (Oxford: Oxford University Press, 1979), pp. 45, 49–52, and 72.

65   W.R.J. Barron and Glyn S. Burgess, *The Voyage of Saint Brendan* (Exeter: Exeter University of Exeter Press, 2002), pp. 329 and 340.

66   William Shakespeare, *The Tempest*, edited by Virginia Mason Vaughan and Alden T. Vaughan (London: Thomas Nelson, 1999), 5.1.275. All further quotations from the play will be taken from this edition and reference will be given in the text.

Chapter 7
Jewels and the Edge of the Skin

In the last chapter, I glanced at the idea that below the surface of the earth there might lie other worlds of hell and purgatory, which might be accessed from caves and rifts in ways which gave this world an edge with another. While the existence of physical entrances to the underworld could only ever be guessed at, the Renaissance was well aware that penetrating the earth's crust by mining it yielded jewels, and that these were valuable and desirable. They might, however, also have a sinister side. In *An Englis[h] expositor[:] teaching the in[ter]pretation of the harde[st] words [vsed] in our language,* John Bullokar notes that the word carbuncle 'hath two significations, namely a precious stone, and a dangerous sore'.[1] Generally speaking Renaissance texts keep these two meanings separate: in ways which are inevitably conditioned by the nature of their subject matter, Renaissance authors tend to be interested in exploring *either* the idea of carbuncle as jewel *or* the idea of carbuncle as tumour without ever registering the possibility of the alternative meeting for the word. Nevertheless the ambiguity is there: a jewel, a thing of beauty intended for the adornment of the body, is also in some sense potentially a disfiguring mark, a scar on the body marking the site of a trauma, a thing not put *onto* the body but growing *out* of it. In *A Cyborg Manifesto*, Donna Haraway asks, 'Why should our bodies end at the skin?';[2] in this chapter, I shall argue that as far as Renaissance jewels are concerned, bodies do not in fact end at the skin, for jewels were understood as a hinge between body and mind as much as between body and dress in ways which position the skin too as an edge which activates fears about permeability, boundary blurring and the monstrous. Tanya Pollard argues for a general cultural shift in the late Tudor period which saw earlier ideas of skin as permeable being replaced by 'fantasies of skin as an impenetrable barrier',[3] but a focus on jewels reveals the falsity of those fancies.

The period's growing interest in anatomy was often troped by the figure of the flayed Marsyas displaying his own skin, and while anatomy offered new knowledge, it also troubled existing certainties. In particular it destabilised the idea of the skin as bounding and defining the body. In this respect, a jewel might in effect function as an anchor, pinning the skin in place and soothingly deflecting onto itself the idea of a movable and permeable edge, but a prevalent idea that jewels could affect the body depended on a view of the skin itself as ultimately permeable, a contact zone rather than a barrier, in ways which might troublingly destabilise the idea of the self. One of the rare instances of evoking both senses of carbuncle comes in *The Comedy of Errors*, where Dromio of Syracuse, having defined the kitchen maid Nell as 'spherical, like a globe', says that 'America, the Indies' are located in her nose, because it is 'all o'er embellished with rubies, carbuncles, sapphires, declining their rich aspect to the hot breath of Spain'.[4] To varying extent, the horror of the gross, the extreme and the unnatural which is implicit here can be seen as potentially lurking in all Renaissance descriptions of jewellery. In this chapter, I want to explore this phenomenon as it is manifested in the work of a variety of dramatists, starting with Marlowe and then moving through Webster to Shakespeare before glancing finally at John Ford. In all these cases, I shall suggest jewels feature on the body not only as adornments but also as scars, marking sites of disruption and trauma and figuring the skin as an eerie site of two-way traffic.

Giving Birth to Gemstones

The Renaissance was a period fascinated by jewels. In some ways, though, all jewellery inherently spoke of pain and loss as much as of beauty. In Andrew Marvell's 'To his Coy Mistress', the wooer muses on how if there were only enough time,

> Thou by the Indian Ganges' side
> Shouldst rubies find; I by the tide
> Of Humber would complain.[5]

India was famous as a site of jewels – in *Henry VI, Part 3*, King Henry muses, 'My crown is in my heart, not on my head; / Not decked with diamonds and Indian stones'[6] – but the idea of simply 'finding' them is no more credible than the pastoral abundance envisioned elsewhere by Marvell in 'The Garden' and is just as clearly a fantasy as that poem's prelapsarian vision. In fact 'the Golconda diamond mines in Hyderabad were opened up in the seventeenth century',[7] and Marvell would have been well aware that rubies must be mined, with considerable difficulty, rather than be simply 'found'. Pierre de la Primaudaye comments on the labour involved in Renaissance mining, observing that

> AS God declareth a great and maruellous prouidence in all his creatures (as we haue discoursed in treating vpon them) so also doth he manifest it vnto vs in the creation of mettals, and especially of gold and siluer, which are esteemed for the most precious. For we see how he hath hidden them in the most deepe places of the earth, and hath couered them with great and high mountaines: so that to dig & draw them out of their profound caues, men must therein so trauell, as if they had enterprised to ouerturne and to transport these lofty hils from one place to another, and to search and pierce through the earth from one side to another.[8]

There is also a faint sense in De la Primaudaye that it is not only the miners who are being incommoded and pained. We would look in vain for any proto-ecological sensibility in Renaissance attitudes to mining (or for any ethical concerns such as those which we now feel about blood diamonds), but there was an idea of stones as living entities of sorts, for De la Primaudaye speaks of stones as being conditioned by humours in much the same way as Renaissance medicine supposed the human body to be:

some precious stones which are white, haue beene generated by an humour hauing the colour of water, which maketh them more cleere and more transparent then others: and so the variety which is in the colours of all stones, bee they greene, blew, red, purple, yealow, or of many mingled colours, one must iudge the humours whereof they did proceede at first to haue beene such: and that other precious stones which are not transparent proceed from troubled, blacke and obscure humours.[9]

De la Primaudaye's implicitly anthropomorphising image tropes the gems as constituted by much the same processes as were thought to operate in the human body, and leaves open the possibility that their extraction from the earth might also make mines potential sites of scarring and loss.

Similar ideas of suffering and of traumatic birth also accrued to pearls, although these come from water rather than land. B.J. Sokol remarks on the increasing acceptance in the early modern period of the fact that pearls were produced as part of oysters' response to irritants, and observers like Sir Richard Hawkins were beginning to wonder whether older ideas involving dew as a catalyst were not 'some old philosopher's conceit, for it can not be made probable how the dew should come into the oyster'.[10] Sokol does though cite the wildly anthropomorphising perspective on pearl formation offered in Philemon Holland's 1601 translation of Pliny's *Natural History* (which G.F. Kunz argues that Shakespeare may have seen):[11]

> This shell-fish which is the mother of Pearle, differeth not much in the manner of breeding and generation, from the oysters: for when the season of the yeere requireth that they should engender, they seeme to yawne and gape, and so doe open wide; and then (by report) they conceive a certaine moist dew as seede, wherewith they swell and grow bigge; and when time commeth, labour to be delivered hereof: and the fruit of these shellfishes are the pearles, better or worse, great or small, according to the qualitie and quantitie of the dew which they received. For if the dew were pure and cleare which went into them, then are the pearles white, faire, and orient: if grosse and troubled, the pearles likewise are dimme, foule, and duskish; pale (I say) they are, if the weather were close, darke, and threatening raine in the time of their conception.[12]

Pearls, in this account, are conceived and brought forth almost like human babies, subject to the same process of an internal engendering precipitated by an external force, born of a 'mother' after a 'labour', and liable to display the characteristics of both 'parents'. Similar associations can be seen in Thomas Lodge's *A Margarite of America*, where a pearl is worn by the heroine in honour of her name, Margarite (which means pearl). Positioned provocatively close to her body – 'O curious Gem how I enuie each while, / To see thee play vpon my Ladies paps' – it is implicitly associated with the language of conception and fructification:

> And now thou plaist thee in that Garden gentill,
> Twixt golden fruite and neere her heart receiuest

> Thy rest, and all her secret thoughts conceiuest
> Vnder a vaile faire, white, diuine, and subtill.[13]

Following the logic of Pliny, the whiteness of the pearl is read as reflecting the conditions of its conception in the shape of the purity of Margarite's own thoughts.

If jewels were like people, it was also common to figure people as jewels, as in Shakespeare and Fletcher's *Henry VIII* where Norfolk says of the king that Catherine 'like a jewel has hung twenty years / About his neck, yet never lost her lustre' and the Lord Chamberlain says of Anne Boleyn that 'from this lady may proceed a gem / To lighten all this isle'.[14] In Lodge's *A Margarite of America* the pearl worn by the heroine is in fact imagined as effectively interchangeable with the narrator:

> Oh if I might from out your essence take you,
> And turne my selfe to shape what ere I would,
> How gladly would I be my Ladies Iewell?
>   (sig. C2v)

Similarly in *Tamburlaine the Great, Part 1*, we are told of the hero that

> 'twixt his manly pitch
> A pearl more worth than all the world is placed,
> Wherein by curious sovereignty of art
> Are fixed his piercing instruments of sight.[15]

It is fitting that Tamburlaine, himself a freak of nature and a character whom Tanya Pollard sees as particularly invested in the fantasy of the skin as impermeable,[16] should be associated with the monstrous birth of the pearl in this cyborg-like image of his head itself being made of pearl. Alternatively the gem can be an extension or emanation of the person, as in *Richard III* where Elizabeth's tears are figured as pearls:

> The liquid drops of tears that you have shed
> Shall come again, transformed to orient pearl,
> Advantaging their love with interest.[17]

Here the association of jewels with loss and pain is particularly clear as the pearls become the reified tokens of the bereaved queen's grief.

The suggestion of a parallelism and a potential reciprocity between jewels and people was reinforced by the idea that jewels could act directly on bodies, effectively by a sort of sympathetic magic. This is an idea evocatively captured by Oscar Wilde in *The Picture of Dorian Gray*, when we read how Dorian's aesthetic sensibilities led him to collect jewels:

> He discovered wonderful stories, also, about jewels.... According to the great alchemist, Pierre de Boniface, the diamond rendered a man invisible, and the agate of India made him eloquent. The cornelian appeased anger, and the

hyacinth provoked sleep, and the amethyst drove away the fumes of wine. The garnet cast out demons, and the hydropicus deprived the moon of her colour. The selenite waxed and waned with the moon, and the meloceus, that devours thieves, could be affected only by the blood of kids.[18]

Wilde lifted this pretty much wholesale from William Jones's *History and Mystery of Precious Stones*, which gives a doubtful reference in Nostradamus as the source of the supposed comments by Boniface,[19] but similar ideas can be readily found elsewhere, sometimes with the proviso that 'contact with the wearer was essential; occasionally open backs on pendants and rings allowed the stone to touch the skin'.[20] Some stones could in effect do magic directly; not for nothing does Cornelius in *Doctor Faustus* claim,

> He that is grounded in astrology,
> Enriched with tongues, well seen [in] minerals,
> Hath all the principles magic doth require.[21]

Albertus Magnus advised his readers, 'If thou wilt prouoke sorowe, feare, terrible fantasyes, & debate. Take the stone, which is called Onyx, which is of black coloure',[22] and he suggested, 'If thou wilt knowe whyther thy wyfe is chaste, or no. Take the stone, which is called Magnes in English, the lode stone, it is of sadde bl[e]w coloure, and it is founde in the sea of Inde sometime in partes of Almaine.... Laye thys stone vnder the head of a wyfe & yf she be chast, she wil embrace her husbande, if she be not chaste, she wil fall anone forth of the bedde' (sig. C1r). Since it is hard to see what natural explanation could account for this, we are forced to fall back on a supernatural one.

Other stones could be used for what we might now be tempted to class as effectively medicinal purposes. Magnus informed his readers, 'If thou wilt haue good vnder standing of thynges that may be felte, and that thou maye not be made dronked. Take the stone, whi[c]he is called Amaristus, and it is of purple colour, and the beste is found in Inde, and it is good agaynst drunkennes, and geueth good vnderstandynge in thynges that maye be vnderstande' (sig. C6r), the underlying logic here being the etymology of the word amethyst, which derives from the Greek *amethustos*, meaning 'not drunk'. De la Primaudaye, however, qualifies the advice by observing that amethysts prevent drunkenness only if tied to the navel; he also declares that a diamond 'being tied to the flesh of the left arme ... doth hinder and withstand the feares of night', while rubies make one joyous and drinking sapphires cures melancholy.[23] (Though James Robinson notes another connotation, 'Sapphires were prized for their celestial connotations but also because they cooled the body and chastened the spirit. They are known to have been chosen for bishops' rings for that reason'.)[24] De la Primaudaye also declares that emeralds, if drunk, render poison inoperative, and Vitelli in Massinger's *The Renegado*, who is disguised as a merchant for much of the play, ascribes similar protective powers to a gold and diamond dish which he is hawking:

> True to the owners,
> Corinthian plate studded with diamonds
> Concealed oft deadly poison; this pure metal
> So innocent is and faithful to the mistress
> Or master that possesses it that, rather
> Than hold one drop that's venomous, of itself
> It flies in pieces and deludes the traitor.[25]

Heather L. Sale Holian notes that such ideas were particularly attractive to rulers, who might reasonably be considered at greater risk of being poisoned, and points specifically to 'King Philip II and Queen Elizabeth, who wore and were given jewelry, respectively, set with stones believed to have protective powers'.[26]

In some cases there was imagined to be an effectively reciprocal relationship between people and stones. A surprising number of gems were sometimes said to originate inside animal or maybe even human bodies: according to Stephen Bateman's 1582 translation of Bartholomaeus Anglicus, which lists a number of stones rarely or never heard of elsewhere and allocates each one its own chapter, asterite 'is found in the mawe of a pure maid, that is fifty yeres of age', noset 'is taken out of a Toads head', reyben 'is found in a Crabs head', and the final chapter refers briefly to 'the stone that groweth in ye Snaile, and … the stone that growes in the maw of an Oxe'.[27] At least some of these gems are credited with properties directly related to their supposed places of origin: allectoria, for instance, is a stone that is found 'in the mawes of capons', that is, castrated roosters, and its properties are similarly focused on testicles in that 'the stone exciteth ye seruice of Venus' (chapter 18), while bitumen, which is described as 'gendering' in the soft earth of marshy ground, has properties that reflect this sense of being born of mother Earth: it 'is not broke with water nor with yron, but onelye with menstruall bloud … it is good to helpe the passions of the mother' (chapter 20). Other stones might be operative on specific genders: crystal 'filleth breasts and teates full of milke, if ye milke faileth before because of colde' (chapter 31); geraticen 'is a blacke stone … if a man wash cleane his owne mouth, & beareth the stone therein: he may anone tel what other men thinke of him' (chapter 52); and iena or ienia 'is a precious stone that is founde in the eyen of a beast that is called Hiena, & if this stone be put vnder a mans tongue, they say, that he shall tell many things that shall befall' (chapter 56).

Not only jewels themselves but also the designs of their settings might be seen as meaningful and symbolic, and settings too were seen as being able to signify and recall damage and loss, this time of a specifically cultural nature. Joan Evans in *A History of Jewellery 1100–1870* starts her account of the Renaissance period by observing, 'The jewellery of the Renaissance was, like every kind of contemporary art, affected by that of classical antiquity', but she also notes, 'Classical jewellery was little known and never imitated; only engraved gems formed any real link between the Roman past and the Renaissance present'.[28] A sense of loss and of the irrecoverability of the classical past is thus inscribed at the heart of Renaissance narratives of jewels. Nor was this sense of loss and absence a phenomenon confined to explicitly classicising jewellery. Biblical-themed jewels were particularly popular: Evans notes,

> The portraits of Catherine Howard painted about 1521 show her wearing an oval gold pendant set with a sapphire, chased with the story of Tobit, and Princess Mary Tudor's inventory of 1542 lists brooches with the stories of the finding of Moses, Moses striking the rock, Susanna, Solomon, Abraham, David, Noah and Jacob's Dream, as well as subjects drawn from the New Testament. The only recognisably secular subjects in her pictorial jewels, indeed, are a brooch with the history of Pyramus and Thisbe and another with 'an Antike' and a French motto.

There was a particular vogue for IHS – 'Jesus' – pendants, of which Anna of Denmark had one.[29] All these pieces of jewellery, though, could also be read as reminders of man's fallen state and of human incompleteness in the absence of God, not to mention their potential for evoking the fraught landscape of religious schism and for thus speaking of the contested edge between spiritual and secular authority which I traced in chapter 2. Martina Bagnoli notes that in the mediaeval period, 'Christian lapidaries usually concentrated on the stones mentioned in the Bible, which were often compared to virtues',[30] but other meanings could also be invoked, potentially in ways which pointed up the different interpretative preferences of the two confessions. This can be seen for instance in the case of amethyst, whose reputation as a preventer of drunkenness could be subject to suggestive inflection: classical legend had it that a nymph named amethyst was turned to quartz by Diana to save her from Dionysos, who then in his remorse shed tears on the stone, which was turned purple because of his vinous nature. Dionysos was a figure often perceived as the antithesis of Christ, and this in conjunction with the twin associations of transformation and wine could give amethysts Eucharistic connotations.[31] Something of this may be evoked in Ford's *The Broken Heart*, where the mad Penthea's seemingly nonsensical lament that 'every drop / Of blood is turnèd to an amethyst, / Which married bachelors hang in their ears' may perhaps encode a religious sensibility.[32] I have argued elsewhere that the pervasive starvation and blood imagery of Ford's play may trope a spiritual inanition and a nostalgia for the real presence of the body and blood in the Mass as opposed to the sublimated metaphors of Protestantism,[33] so that as Penthea dies pining for the husband she cannot have and the food she will not eat and which does not nourish, the amethyst becomes the charged and emotive emblem of her loss and lack.

Other jewellery of the period would seem, to modern eyes at least, to have more simply ironic overtones – heart pendants were thought to signify constancy, and the six-times-married Henry VIII had thirty-nine of them[34] – while others spoke unequivocally of death: 'Queen Elizabeth wore a book containing a copy of the last prayer of Edward VI, in golden covers', and a particularly famous piece of the period was the Lennox jewel, commissioned in memory of Margaret Lennox's murdered husband. Joan Evans observes more generally that 'in the second half of the sixteenth century … a constant preoccupation with death became once more a fashionable devotional trend, and appears in jewellery designs'.[35] Change and loss of a different sort are encoded at both ends of the story of the jewel known as the Mirror of Great Britain, which Roy Strong observes was 'clearly designed to be a most important Crown jewel commemorating the historic union of the kingdoms in 1604'.[36] To make it, the historic Scots crown jewel known as the 'Great Harry' was broken up and one of its stones symbolically reused in this new British context, but the new jewel had to be pawned in 1625 and ultimately passed to the ownership of the French crown. The jewel thus spoke both of the loss of Scotland as a state securely separate from England and of the parlous finances of the new 'British' crown.

Graven with Diamonds: Jewels and the Scar of Gender

Jewels could also be used effectively as branding, in ways which not only spoke of wealth and privilege but also pointed up the constraints which family and class imposed on individual women's identities. Heather Sale Holian has clearly shown this process at work in portraits of female members of the Medici family: she observes that 'in portraits of their female family members, the Medici used jewelry to demonstrate family ties and new alliances, and, by implication, political obligations and expectations, dynastic strength and stability, and ultimately power', and notes particularly 'the established association of the diamond with the Medici dynasty.... The Medici adopted the single point-cut diamond, set within a gold ring, as a familial device already in the early fifteenth century'; thus 'diamond and ruby were frequently worn by Medici women of these years, at times with pearls, but most often to the exclusion of any other gemstone when familial claims were being conveyed'.[37] Many of these women came to bad ends in ways often commemorated in Renaissance drama. One such play was Webster's *The White Devil*, which had the doomed Isabella de' Medici as a central character, and *The Duchess of Malfi* too focused on a murdered Italian duchess, albeit not a Medici one. Samuel Schuman notes that in both these plays 'The jewel and the ring are both ambiguous objects, embodying an ambiguity which is thematically germane to Webster's tragedies': 'Each time rings and jewels appear in the first two acts of *The White Devil* the institution of marriage is mocked'. Schuman also observes, 'A "jewel" may be that which is most precious to a woman – her honor, more specifically her chastity.... In a related sense, "jewel" or "jewels" have been used to describe both the male and female genitals'.[38] Schuman is certainly right that the metaphor can apply to both men and women, as in *The Renegado* where Carazie describes being made a eunuch as 'but parting with / A precious stone or two' (3.4.52–3), but it is much more commonly used of women, as in *All's Well That Ends Well* where Diana says 'Mine honour's such a ring; / My chastity's the jewel of our house'.[39] This both reifies female chastity and makes it something which is to be owned, a possession of a particularly valuable and sought-after kind which confers status on the male owner rather than on the woman herself; as Valerie Traub observes, 'The equation of female body parts with precious gems

– the body metaphorically revealed, undressed and dismembered through the poet-lover's voyeuristic gaze – is a crucial strategy in the attempt both to construct a modern masculine subjectivity and to exert control over a situation in which the poet-lover's power is limited and secondary'.[40] A jewel in this sense can be seen as the scar which marks the imperfection of a woman's separation from her family and of her incompleteness as a fully separate and independent entity.

David Golz suggests that the association between jewels and the objectification of women was especially true of diamonds, and that it had a particular currency on the stage:

> The writers of romances used them to symbolize the idealized, unalloyed beauty of the chaste females who were the objects of their heroes' quests. Players on the London stage in the time of Shakespeare invoked them to mark the role of the eminently desirable woman.[41]

In *The Duchess of Malfi* the equation of women and diamonds is made explicit in the exchange between the Duchess and her brother: 'Diamonds are of most value / They say, that have pass'd through most jewellers' hands', to which he counters, 'Whores, by that rule, are precious'. A piece of jewellery also figures the self when the Duchess says to Antonio,

> One of your eyes is blood-shot – use my ring to't,
> They say 'tis very sovereign – 'twas my wedding ring,
> And I did vow never to part with it,
> But to my second husband.[42]

In offering this ring to Antonio she is in fact, as he immediately perceives, offering him herself as a wife. Given the prominence of language about jewels in the plays about them and of jewellery in their portraiture, it seems reasonable to suppose that these stage duchesses wore things which at least appeared to be jewels, even if they were not actually so. They would certainly have had to wear at least the rings to which they so often refer, and in that respect, and possibly in others, there would have been a visual as well as linguistic correlation between the jewels which marked these women's heritage and status and the disasters which befall them, with rings, so often specifically ones which identify them as being 'owned' by men, particularly implicated. The suggestion that the jewels might be equated with their sexuality would serve to reinforce the sense that, for them at least, jewels are the scars which show the site of the femininity which is their destruction, and mark too the point at which they are irrevocably and fatally connected to a social order rather than having an independent identity.

'Infinite Riches in a Little Room': Marlowe and the Price of Pearls

Another playwright very much interested in jewels was Marlowe, but in him they work rather differently from in Webster. In Marlowe's plays as in Webster jewels are a site of intersection between the values of the individual and the values of the world, and so mark an edge between the self and the social. Here, though, what we are invited to notice is not social constraints on women but the ways in which a focus on wealth and accumulation blinds the plays' characters to all else: dazzled by the light and surface of jewels, they see nothing of what they might connote or suggest. In *The Jew of Malta*, Barabas (himself the ultimate border-crosser) likes all jewels; at the start of the play, he praises

> Bags of fiery opals, sapphires, amethysts,
> Jacinths, hard topaz, grass-green emeralds,
> Beauteous rubies, sparkling diamonds,
> And seld-seen costly stones of so great price[43]

Although he briefly registers the aesthetic appeal of shiny stones, it is clear that what he most values in jewels is their status as highly portable sources of wealth: they enclose 'infinite riches in a little room' (1.1.37). This, however, is a phrase fraught with irony on multiple levels. Intradiegetically, the audience registers that Barabas is deaf to the biblical echo of the phrase, which troped the baby Jesus in the womb of Mary. Extradiegetically, the image subsequently became associated with Marlowe's own death after its use by Touchstone in *As You Like It*, 'It strikes a man more dead than a great reckoning in a little room',[44] with the little room here evoking the room in Eleanor Bull's house where Marlowe was stabbed and died. In both these respects, Barabas' words evoke lack – from the characteristic perspective of an early modern audience, lack of the salvific Christianity from which his adherence to Judaism excludes him, and from our own, loss in the shape of the death that was so soon to befall the play's author.

This is typical of the way jewels work in Marlowe. On the surface, they are signs and repositories of wealth; thus Barabas assures Abigail that she need have no fear about their finances because he has a hidden fortune in jewels, consisting of 'great pearls, / Rich costly jewels, and stones infinite' (1.2.248–9), and just one of the pearls, his messenger later tells Selim-Calymath, is

> so big,
> So precious, and withal so orient,
> As be it valuèd but indifferently,
> The price thereof will serve to entertain
> Selim and all his soldiers for a month.
>
> (5.3.27–30)

Along with this acute awareness of wealth, however, goes an absolute indifference to what else jewels might mean; it is as if, for Marlowe's characters, there is *only* the surface. Like Barabas, Tamburlaine too likes pearls, musing on how fine it would be

> To wear a crown enchased with pearl and gold,
> Whose virtues carry with it life and death.
>
> (2.5.60–61)

There is no sense here of the quasi-magical properties which jewels might have: it is the money and hence the power which pearls and gold emblematise which Tamburlaine thinks can give life or death, and the illnesses first of Zenocrate and then of Tamburlaine himself will ultimately show him that they cannot. The dominant note is of a purely monetary value which overlooks even the most obvious possibilities of other meanings: when Barabas figures his daughter Abigail as a diamond (3.1.57–8) he registers no awareness that this is something which bodes ill for her, since, as Alison Findlay shows, when women in Renaissance plays are referred to by men as jewels it is generally as part of a process of commodification which rarely ends well for them.[45] Above all, jewels in Marlowe's plays serve by their very changelessness to emphasise the change and decay to which humans are subject. (It is true that pearls are subject to deterioration and destruction, but Marlowe, unlike Shakespeare, never represents that happening.) In *Tamburlaine the Great, Part 1*, Mycetes declares, 'Well, well, Meander, thou art deeply read, / And having thee I have a jewel sure' (2.2.54–5). Mycetes will soon die, and Meander will disappear from the play. Later, Tamburlaine himself apostrophises Zenocrate as one who

> Rainest on the earth resolvèd pearl in showers
> And sprinklest sapphires on thy shining face.
> (5.1.142–4)

Early in Part 2, though, Zenocrate too will die and the golden coffin in which Tamburlaine will encase her remains will provide a bitter emblem of the permanence and durability which gems have but she does not. For Marlowe, then, the jewel is the scar which marks both the wearer's vulnerability to death and the wilful blindness of a value system which ruthlessly privileges the purely material.

Chrysolites, Coral and Turquoise: Shakespearean Inversion and Irony

Shakespeare too is fond of using jewels in his plays, but he does so to rather different effect from either Webster or Marlowe. For him they are, characteristically, primarily instruments of irony, for the effects which they actually have are generally the exact opposite of those they were customarily supposed to have. Shylock may echo Barabas in associating his daughter with jewels, but the association works in different ways. As the news of Jessica's elopement breaks, Salerio says to Shylock, 'There is more difference between thy flesh and blood and hers than between jet and ivory'.[46] Hearing from Tubal the details of her flight and her extravagance, Shylock himself picks up this language when he wails 'A diamond gone cost me two thousand ducats in Frankfurt! ... I would my daughter were dead at my foot, and the jewels in her ear!' (3.1.76–81). But there is worse still to come:

> *Tubal.* One of them showed me a ring that he had of your daughter for a monkey.

Shylock. Out upon her! Thou torturest me, Tubal. It was my turquoise; I had it
of Leah when I was a bachelor. I would not have given it for a wilderness of
monkeys.

(3.1.108–113)

Leah, we assume, was Shylock's wife and the mother of Jessica, and since we
neither see nor hear of her anywhere else in the play, we assume that she is
dead. The turquoise which is Shylock's souvenir of her was meant to protect the
wearer from both mental anxiety and physical harm: Pierre Boiastuau observes
in *Certaine secrete wonders of nature* that 'the Turquise (accordyng to the moste
Philosophers) is of no singular propertie, but to chase awaye thoughtes and
troubles of the braine',[47] while De la Primaudaye notes that 'the Turkesse being
worne in a ring doth keepe a man from hurt that falleth, yea though it be from his
horse'.[48] If a man did come to grief, though, any turquoise that he owns will grow
pale in token of his sorrow, as Ben Jonson notes in *Sejanus*: 'true as turquoise in
the dear lord's ring, / Look well or ill with him'.[49] It is, therefore, richly ironic that
it should be this reputedly protective and sensitive stone that brings Shylock to the
height of his distress, and that it should be for him the scar which marks what we
are clearly invited to read as his own still-painful bereavement and loss, as well as
the equally painful lack of Jessica's indifference to her family and heritage. It is
also typical of Shakespeare's characteristic subtlety and ambiguity that it should
be the turquoise, a stone reputed both to affect and be affected by its wearer, that
he should choose for this play which is so essentially about the mutual interaction
of communities and individuals.

   Other Shakespeare plays also feature stones (in the nineteenth century, T.F.
Thiselton Dyer noted the importance of rings in particular),[50] and again they
characteristically deploy them with ironic force: G.F. Kunz's remark that 'we find
no trace in Shakespeare's works of any belief in the many quaint and curious
supermanic or curative virtues of precious stones' I think misses the point, for
Shakespeare's uses of stones work best if the audience is aware both of what they
should achieve or be used for and the fact that in any individual instance they
are spectacularly failing to produce that particular effect.[51] In *The Tempest*, Ariel
sings,

> Full fathom five thy father lies,
> Of his bones are coral made;
> Those are pearls that were his eyes,
> Nothing of him that doth fade
> But doth suffer a sea-change
> Into something rich and strange.[52]

De la Primaudaye, noting that although it is not strictly a jewel coral 'is put into
the number of stones', declares that 'the properties which are attributed to Coral,
are maruailous'.[53] Specifically, Bateman's rendering of Bartholomeus Anglicus
informed its readers that coral 'putteth off lightning, whirle winde, tempest and
stormes from Shippes',[54] while Magnus declares,

> If thou wilt pacifie tempestes and go ouer fluddes. Take the stone, which is called Corallus, Corall … it hath ben proueth that it stemmeth anone bloude, and putteth away the folishnes of hym that beareth it, & geueth wysedom … And it is good agaynst tempestes, and perils of fluddes. (sigs C6v–C7r)

It is, therefore, fraught with irony that this stone which is supposed to ward off tempests should be evoked by Ariel in direct connection with a disaster apparently caused by a tempest, while its other property of giving wisdom is similarly conspicuous by its absence in that Ferdinand during this scene has been comprehensively deceived: he is mourning for someone who is not dead on what he believes to be a deserted island on which he has been accidentally shipwrecked but which is in fact inhabited by someone who has planned what has happened to him. Similarly B.J. Sokol remarks of 'those are pearls that were his eyes' that

> an implication arises that a vision-dimming or vision-destroying pearliness has overtaken Alonso's perceptual inlets: this aligns with the scientific meaning of 'a pearl in the eye' for Shakespeare's age, which was a cataract.[55]

There is certainly interest in eye diseases in another late play, *The Winter's Tale*, where Leontes is sure that Polixenes and Hermione wish 'all eyes / Blind with the pin and web, but theirs',[56] and there has indeed been some speculation that Shakespeare himself suffered from an eye disease towards the end of his life,[57] so such a meaning may well be in play. Again, though, it is one which would be working to ironic effect, since blindness will soon give way to clear and accurate perception on the part of all the characters. To pair these two references allows a particularly sharp and focused apprehension of Shakespeare's characteristic technique in his uses of jewel imagery: coral, which should enable clarity of perception, is associated with a state of deception, while pearls, metaphorically associated with blindness, are here mentioned as part of the prelude to complete and clear revelation. Moreover, while the first image clearly depends on the idea of the skin as an edge, acting as the contact zone between the coral on the outside and the mind on the inside, the second uses a different but related strategy to trouble the idea that the human is a stable and separate category: if eyes can be pearls, people are not radically distinct from jewels, but are connected to them in much the same way as if jewels are seen as capable of modifying their physiology or their perception.

My final example from Shakespeare comes from *Othello*. Here the hero, who later castigates himself as one who 'like the base Indian, threw a pearl away / Richer than all his tribe', declares that

> Had she been true,
> If heaven would make me such another world
> Of one entire and perfect chrysolite,
> I'd not have sold her for it.[58]

As Valerie Traub points out, 'the comparison of Desdemona to jewels is part of Othello's strategy for containing her erotic power. By imaginatively transforming

Desdemona into a jewel – hard, cold, static, silent, yet also adored and desired – Othello is able to maintain both his distance from and his idealization of her'.[59] However, something else also seems to be at stake in this passage. Chrysolites are identified by De la Primaudaye as some of the most precious of jewels:

> Now amongst precious stones, these beare away the prise, and are praised with especiall praise, the white diamond, for hardnesse, and soliditie: the greene emerauld for beawty, the red carbuncle, called the rubie, for liuely colour, the skie coloured saphir, for grace, the yealow chrysolite for splendor, the diuers coloured opall, for varietie, and the cleere pearle for whitnesse, and roundnesse.[60]

According to Bateman, 'Crisolitus is a little stone of Ethiopia ... like to the sea in colour'; 'it feareth feendes and ... comforteth the vnderstanding'.[61] Magnus too is again pertinent here:

> If thou wilt dryue away fantasies and folishnes. Take the stone, which is called Chrysolitus, and it is of the same vertue with Attemicus, as Aaron & Euax say, in the boke of the nature of herbes, & stones: this stone set in golde, & borne, dryueth away folishnes, & expelleth fantasies. It is affirmed to geue wysedome, and it is good against feare.
>
> (sig. D2v)

Despite the affinity which their common origin in Africa might be supposed to give them, Othello has availed himself of none of the properties of the chrysolite: he has shown little wisdom, and has succumbed to the unjustified fear that Desdemona is betraying him. Irony is heaped on irony by the fact that the stone which supposedly 'feareth' (i.e. frightens) fiends should be evoked by the one of the very few Shakespearean characters who seriously imagines that a devil might actually and materially be in the room with him, as we see when he looks down at Iago's feet to see if they are cloven. All the way through the play, it has been apparent that Othello is too inclined to put his trust in narratives and stories, whether his own or those of others;[62] his glance at Iago's feet is a final instance of this, suggesting that he had been unable to conceive of an evil which was not clearly and simply manifested in easily readable terms. Othello's imagined chrysolite thus becomes the scar that marks the absence of the precise qualities and the exact measure of the lack of epistemological sophistication which could have saved him from himself: the jewel and the mind could and should have been connected, but the process has tragically failed.

Much later in the period, in John Ford's last play, *The Lady's Trial*, the heroine, Spinella, takes her name from a jewel, and Ford is very interested in general in the language of jewels. In *The Fancies Chaste and Noble* the marquis discusses knowledge of jewels with those around him:

ROMANELLO   I hope Sir
    You cannot thinke I am a lapidarie –
    I skill in Jewels?

```
OCTAVIO            'Tis a proper quality
    For any Gentleman; your other friends
    May be are not so coy.
JULIO                            Who, they? They know not
    A Topaze from an Opall.
CAMILLO                  We are ignorant
    In gems which are not common. (5.3.45–51)
```

Julio and Camillo might, therefore, have been baffled by a spinel, from which Spinella derives her name, for it is an unusual gem, being usually red in colour (although blue is also not uncommon) but rather less precious than a ruby: a good woman may be above the price of rubies (Proverbs 31: 10), but a spinel is not quite a ruby, and this is reflected in the play by the readiness with which Spinella, like Desdemona, is wrongly believed guilty of adultery. In Ford's early poem *Fame's Memorial* we are told, in typically abstract and laconic Ford style, that 'Jewell's being had for Jewel's are not know'n';[63] in his play *The Broken Heart*, Penthea figures her youth, her fame and her brother all as jewels (3.5.49–69); in *Love's Sacrifice*, the Duke boasts that

I am a monarch of felicity,
Proud in a pair of jewels rich and beautiful:
A perfect friend, a wife above compare.[64]

Here, jewels function first as an emblem of an innate inability to appreciate what we have, and secondly to trope things and people that Penthea and the Duke will very shortly lose forever. Collectively, all these instances, together with the others I have cited, suggest that Julio and Camillo in *The Fancies, Chaste and Noble* are quite wrong to scorn the knowledge of jewels, for a little learning in that field might well have saved the characters in many plays a great deal of trouble.

From Marlowe to Ford by way of Shakespeare and Webster, then, jewels in English Renaissance drama function not only as adornment, but also as beautiful scars, marking sites of loss and lack which all in different ways have to do with the question of the relation between individual humans and the wider world. For Webster, the scar they mark is that of the imperfect separation of the personal from the social, alerting us to the ways in which women are connected to society. For Marlowe, they mark the site of what is lost by characters' determined indifference to the spiritual, the emotional, the aesthetic and their relentless focus on wealth and power. In Shakespeare, the ironic disjunction between the reputed properties of jewels and their actual effects in the plays works to suggest that even if it is in some ways disturbing to think of the skin as a contact zone, it is better that that process should function properly than that it should not. For all these authors, the skin is thus an edge, and one whose permeability needs to be recognised if human beings are to function properly within their societies.

Notes

[1]   I[ohn] B[ullokar], *An Englis[h] expositor[:] teaching the in[ter]pretation of the harde[st] words [vsed] in our language* (London: printed by John Legatt, 1621), sig. D2r.

[2]   Donna Haraway, 'A Cyborg Manifesto: Science, Technology, and Socialist-Feminism in the Late Twentieth Century' (1985), http://www.egs.edu/faculty/donna-haraway/articles/donna-haraway-a-cyborg-manifesto/

[3]   Tanya Pollard, 'Enclosing the Body: Tudor Conceptions of Skin', in *A Companion to Tudor Literature and Culture, 1485–1603*, edited by Kent Cartwright (Oxford: Wiley-Blackwell, 2010), p. 111.

[4]   William Shakespeare, *The Comedy of Errors*, edited by Stanley Wells (Harmondsworth: Penguin, 1972), 3.2.120 and 140–43.

[5]   Andrew Marvell, 'The Garden', in *The Metaphysical Poets*, edited by Helen Gardner (Harmondsworth: Penguin, 1957), pp. 250–51.

[6]   William Shakespeare, *Henry VI, Part 3*, edited by Michael Hattaway (Cambridge: Cambridge University Press, 1993), 3.1.62–3.

[7]   Joan Evans, *A History of Jewellery 1100–1870* [1953] (New York: Dover, 1970), p. 130.

[8]   Pierre de la Primaudaye, *The French academie Fully discoursed and finished in foure bookes* (1618), pp. 854–5.

[9]   De la Primaudaye, *The French academie Fully discoursed and finished in foure bookes* (London: John Legat for Thomas Adams, 1618), p. 848.

[10]   Cited in G.F. Kunz and C.H. Stevenson, *The Book of the Pearl: Its History, Art, Science and Industry* [1908] (Mineola: Dover, 2001), p. 38.

[11]   G.F. Kunz, *Shakespeare and Precious Stones* (Philadelphia: J.B. Lippincott Company, 1916), p. 46.

[12]   B.J. Sokol, *A Brave New World of Knowledge: Shakespeare's* The Tempest *and Early Modern Epistemology* (London: Associated University Presses, 2003), p. 33.

[13]   Thomas Lodge, *A Margarite of America* (London: John Busbie, 1596), sig. C2v.

[14]   William Shakespeare, *Henry VIII*, edited by A.R. Humphreys (Harmondsworth: Penguin, 1971), 2.2.30–1 and 2.3.78–9.

[15]   Christopher Marlowe, *Tamburlaine the Great, Part 1*, in *Christopher Marlowe: The Complete Plays*, edited by Mark Thornton Burnett (London: Everyman, 1999), 2.1.11–14.

[16]   Pollard, 'Enclosing the Body', pp. 118–9.

[17]   William Shakespeare, *Richard III*, edited by E.A.J. Honigmann (Harmondsworth: Penguin, 1968), 4.4.321–3.

[18]   Oscar Wilde, *The Picture of Dorian Gray* (Harmondsworth: Penguin, 1984), pp. 156–7.

[19]   William Jones, *History and Mystery of Precious Stones* (London: Richard Bentley and son, 1880), p. 14.

[20]   James Robinson, 'From Altar to Amulet: Relics, Portability, and Devotion', in *Treasures of Heaven: Saints, Relics, and Devotion in Medieval Europe*, edited by Martina Bagnoli, Holger A. Klein, C. Griffith Mann, and James Robinson (London: The British Museum Press, 2011), p. 114.

[21]   Christopher Marlowe, *Doctor Faustus*, A text, in *The Complete Plays*, edited by Mark Thornton Burnett (London: J. M. Dent, 1999), 1.1.140–42.

[22]   Albertus Magnus, *The boke of secretes of Albertus Magnus of the vertues of herbes, stones, and certayne beasts* (London: John King, 1560), sig. C1v.

[23]   De la Primaudaye, *The French academie*, pp. 848–50.

[24]   Robinson, 'From Altar to Amulet: Relics, Portability, and Devotion', p. 113.

[25]   Philip Massinger, *The Renegado*, edited by Michael Neill (London: Methuen, 2010), 1.3.121–27.

[26]   Heather L. Sale Holian, 'Family Jewels: The Gendered Marking of Medici Women in Court Portraits of the Late Renaissance', *Mediterranean Studies* (2008), p. 149n2.

[27]   Bartholomaeus Anglicus, *Batman vppon Bartholome his booke De proprietaribus rerum*, translated by Stephen Bateman (London: Thomas East, 1582), Book 16, chapters 18, 71, 86 and 194.

[28]   Evans, *A History of Jewellery 1100–1870*, p. 81.

[29]   Evans, *A History of Jewellery 1100–1870*, pp. 94 and 97.

[30]   Martina Bagnoli, 'The Stuff of Heaven: Materials and Craftsmanship in Medieval Reliquaries', in *Treasures of Heaven: Saints, Relics, and Devotion in Medieval Europe*, edited by Martina Bagnoli, Holger A. Klein, C. Griffith Mann, and James Robinson (London: The British Museum Press, 2011), p. 138.

[31]   Robinson, 'From Altar to Amulet: Relics, Portability, and Devotion', p. 114.

[32]   John Ford, *The Broken Heart*, edited by T.J.B. Spencer (Manchester: Manchester University Press, 1980), 4.2.129–31.

[33]   Lisa Hopkins, *John Ford's Political Theatre* (Manchester: Manchester University Press, 1994), especially chapter 3.

[34]   Evans, *A History of Jewellery 1100–1870*, p. 98.

[35]   Evans, *A History of Jewellery 1100–1870*, pp. 101, 116, and 142.

[36]   Roy Strong, 'Three Royal Jewels: The Three Brothers, the Mirror of Great Britain and the Feather', *The Burlington Magazine* 108.760 (July, 1996), p. 351.

[37]   Sale Holian, 'Family Jewels', pp. 149 and 152.

[38]   Samuel Schuman, 'The Ring and the Jewel in Webster's Tragedies', *Texas Studies in Language and Literature* 14 (1972), pp. 253, 60 and 254.

[39]   William Shakespeare, *All's Well That Ends Well*, edited by G.K. Hunter (London: Cengage Learning, 2007), 4.2.45–6.

[40]   Valerie Traub, 'Jewels, Statues, and Corpses: Containment of Female Erotic Power in Shakespeare's Plays', in *Shakespeare and Gender: A History*, edited by Deborah E. Barker and Ivo Kamps (London: Verso, 1995), p. 131.

[41]   David Golz, 'Diamonds, Maidens, Widow Dido, and Cock-a-diddle dow', *Comparative Drama* 43.2 (summer 2008), p. 168.

[42]   John Webster, *The Duchess of Malfi*, edited by John Russell Brown (Manchester: Manchester University Press, 1974), 1.1.299–301 and 1.1.404–7.

[43]   William Shakespeare, *As You Like It*, edited by Agnes Latham (London: Methuen, 1975), 3.3.9–12.

[44]   Alison Findlay, *Women in Shakespeare: A Dictionary* (London: Continuum, 2010), pp. 212–14.

[45]   William Shakespeare, *The Merchant of Venice*, edited by M. Moelwyn Merchant (Harmondsworth: Penguin, 1967), 3.1.35–6. All further quotations from the play will be taken from this edition and reference will be given in the text.

46   Pierre Boiastuau, *Certaine secrete wonders of nature* … (London: Henry Bynneman, 1569), p. 41.

47   De la Primaudaye, *The French academie*, p. 852.

48   Ben Jonson, *Sejanus*, edited by Philip Ayres (Manchester: Manchester University Press, 1990), 1.1.37–8.

49   T.F. Thiselton Dyer, *Folk-lore of Shakespeare* (1883), http://www.sacred-texts.com/sks/flos/flos17.htm.

50   Kunz, *Shakespeare and Precious Stones*, p. 34.

51   William Shakespeare, *The Tempest*, edited by Virginia Mason Vaughan and Alden T. Vaughan (London: Thomas Nelson and Sons, 1999), 1.2.397–402.

52   De la Primaudaye, *The French academie*, pp. 853–4.

53   Anglicus, *Batman vppon Bartholome*, Book 16, chapter 33.

54   Sokol, *A Brave New World of Knowledge*, p. 45.

55   William Shakespeare, *The Winter's Tale*, edited by J.H. Pafford (London: Methuen, 1963), 1.2.290–91.

56   See for instance Rossella Lorenzi, 'Shakespeare's eye betrays rare cancer', http://www.abc.net.au/science/articles/2006/03/02/1582326.htm.

57   William Shakespeare, *Othello*, edited by E.A.J. Honigmann (London: Thomas Nelson and Sons, 1997), 5.2.139–142 and 5.2.345–6.

58   Traub, 'Jewels, Statues, and Corpses', p. 131.

59   De la Primaudaye, *The French academie*, p. 848.

60   Anglicus, *Batman vppon Bartholome*, Book 16, chapter 29.

61   For a fuller exploration of this, see my 'The representation of narrative: what happens in *Othello*', *Journal X* 1:2 (spring, 1997), pp. 159–174.

62   John Ford, *Fames Memoriall*, in *The Nondramatic Works of John Ford*, edited by L.E. Stock, Gilles D. Monsarrat, Judith M. Kennedy and Dennis Danielson (Binghampton: Medieval and Renaissance Texts and Studies, 1991), p. 130.

63   John Ford, *Love's Sacrifice*, edited by A.T. Moore (Manchester: Manchester University Press, 2002), 1.1.131–3.

Chapter 8
The Edge of the World

In this chapter, I want to discuss two sorts of places which on the English Renaissance stage appear to be associated with the divine, ruins and high places. Both of these, I shall suggest, have at least the potential to represent edges between this world and the next by offering possible points of contact with the numinous. A cliff is of course an obvious edge, and sometimes (as in the case of the White Cliffs of Dover) may also connote the edge of a national and territorial identity. Ruins are often seen in the period as an edge with a rather different adjacency, since a recurrent trope of figuring ruined bodies as ruined buildings, and vice versa, emblematises the edge which connects the self to society; moreover, the fact that so many ruins were either of Roman buildings or of dissolved monasteries means that ruins, like jewels, can be scars, marking the loss of the past and a leaching or shifting of material or confessional identities.

The Ruined Building and the Edge of Death

First, ruins, in which I include megalithic monuments because it was almost invariably as ruins of once-larger structures that these were construed. (Inigo Jones, for instance, understood Stonehenge as Roman and as following 'an *Architectonicall Scheam*' devised by Vitruvius.)[1] In *England's Ruins: Poetic Purpose and the National Landscape*, Anne Janowitz declares,

> The national images of both England and of Great Britain are built on Roman ruins.... In his translation of Du Bellay's *Antiquitez de Rome*, Spenser maps out the criteria for the *topos* of poetic permanence, and enacts the building of an English sonnet sequence upon Roman ruin.[2]

I want to argue that it is not only Spenser who uses the foundations of Roman ruins as building blocks for his own work, but that it is a widespread and crucially important phenomenon in English Renaissance writing: as Huw Griffiths observes,

> The literary, historical and mythical material that English writers of the sixteenth and seventeenth centuries draw on in their development of a sense of nation is littered with ruins, both real and symbolic. Amongst these ruins are the ransacked citadel of Troy, the plundered remains of the Roman Empire, the fallen Tower of Babel and the empty shells of the English and Welsh medieval abbeys.... Ruins in this period are, almost necessarily, ironic. They disclose failure in the place of achievement.[3]

Rodrigo Cacho Casal concurs, arguing that in general 'The Renaissance regarded the city of Rome as one of the privileged archives of the past. Its ruined buildings were also, however, a reminder that many achievements of the classical period had been irremediably lost',[4] and Spenser would certainly have agreed with this; for him, the thought evoked by the ruins of Rome is 'Behold what wreake, what ruine, and what wast'.[5]

Nevertheless, even if ruins signified failure, people wanted to see them, both in real life and on the stage. We can see something of this craving for even vicarious experience of famous and significant buildings in the title of Samuel Lewkenor's 1600 *A discourse not altogether vnprofitable, nor vnpleasant for such as are desirous to know the situation and customes of forraine cities without trauelling to see them*. More adventurously, Marlowe's Faustus declares

> Now by the kingdoms of infernal rule,
> Of Styx, Acheron, and the fiery lake
> Of ever-burning Phlegethon, I swear
> That I do long to see the monuments
> And situation of bright splendent Rome.[6]

This was, I think, a wish that was widely shared, yet at the same time felt to be never fully possible: indeed Leonard Barkan argues, 'The Renaissance inherits the supposition that ancient flourishing Rome and desolate modern Rome do not exist in the same dimension'.[7] In this chapter, I want to examine some possible ways in which written descriptions and fictional and dramatic imaginings sought to fulfil the wish to see ruins. I also want to suggest that ruins functioned rather differently in drama from in poetry. Rodrigo Cacho Casal comments on 'the development of the poetry about ruins' and suggests that a verse such as Francisco de Quevedo's *Silva* – like Spenser's 'Ruines', a translation of Du Bellay – 'becomes a portrait of immortal achievements linked with the Latin and humanistic traditions'.[8] Drama, though, was often perceived as ephemeral rather than immortal, and the huge popularity of historical and classical plays meant that one of its primary functions was to stage the dead to the living, as when the Emperor in *Doctor Faustus* longs to see Alexander. I want to argue that ruins in plays offer a heightened example of this potentiality, and that therefore ruins – or at least some ruins – not only function as signifiers of loss or absence but also can specifically be places where the living meet the dead, that in this sense they constitute an edge between this world and the next and that this is an edge where the possibility of cross-border traffic, though to a certain extent shadowed by the sense of the taboo, is also in some respects appealing.

The boundary between life and death was in some respects a very uncertain one in Renaissance culture. In his report of the execution of Mary, Queen of Scots, Robert Wynkfielde assures his readers, 'Then hir dressinge of Lawne fell from hir head, which appeared as graye as if shee had byn thre score and ten yeares olde powled very short. Hir face much altred, hir lips stirred upp and downe almost a quarter of an hower after hir head was cut off'.[9] An account of an execution in

Rome translated by Tobie Matthew, son of the Bishop of Durham, offered similar assurances: 'And my selfe, with many others also, did see, that his head being already cut off, did produce the last syllable of the name of *Iesus*, with a strong kind of hisse, or whisper'.[10] One of the gunpowder plotters was apparently even more animated after death: R.T. Petersson notes that

> when Sir Everard Digby was executed 'Holding up the heart on his sword the executioner then uttered the customary phrase: "Here is the heart of a traitor!" A macabre report goes with these last moments. According to John Aubrey, Sir Everard answered the executioner with the words, "Thou liest!"'.[11]

A different but related example of posthumous survival of sorts was afforded by Sir Walter Ralegh, who was legally dead after being found guilty of treason in 1603, with the result that when he came back from Guiana, 'The Lords gave it as their opinion that Ralegh, being attainted of high treason at Winchester in 1603, could not be judged for any offence committed since'.[12] Uncertainty about the border between life and death is also easy to detect in drama, since *The Revenger's Tragedy*, *The Duchess of Malfi*, *Othello*, and arguably *King Lear* all feature moments when characters whom we have supposed to be dead unexpectedly speak again.

Although the border with death might be inherently traversable, Protestantism had made stern efforts to prevent access to the potential crossing points.[13] This may have been one reason why the association of ruins with the dead, and often particularly with the famous dead, constituted an important part of their fascination, in ways that cut across national boundaries. In Germany, Christopher S. Wood quotes a contemporary as noting that 'Emperor Maximilian, a prince most zealous for everything ancient, when he celebrated the Imperial Diet at Worms in 1495, had Siegfried's grave-mound opened and excavated', though no body was found.[14] There was also strong and pan-European interest in megaliths, particularly when these were understood as funerary monuments. In Denmark, Ole Worm, court physician of Christian IV, described 144 runic monuments in *Danicorum Monumentorum Libri Sex* (1643), in order to 'demonstrate to the learned world that the north also had a long history',[15] and Olaus Magnus, in his *Description of the Northern Peoples* (1555), comments extensively on standing stones, which he identifies as signs of battle and death. Assuming that big stones broken off from mountains 'were first extracted from the earth and set up by giants on flat ground or in higher places, some marked with writings, others engraved', he declares, 'It was a very ancient custom of the old Götar and Swedes to set upright stones, in the manner of old Egyptian pyramids, wherever they had undertaken and successfully accomplished their fiercer fights':

> When the stones are marked with letters and put in a long, straight line they mark the contests of champions; square stones show the fights of cavalry squadrons; rounded ones indicate the burials of near kinsmen; wedge-shaped memorials testify that battle-lines of horsemen and foot were happily victorious at that spot or nearby.[16]

In Flanders, the cartographer Abraham Ortelius, who with Mercator and two other friends had carved his name on a supposedly druidical rock, the *Pierre Levée* near Poitiers, in 1560, included only one essay in his *Theatrum Orbis Terrarum*, which was Humphrey Lhuyd's on the neolithic monuments of Anglesey and their supposed connection with the Druids.[17]

As Lhuyd's involvement indicates, writers in Britain were also interested in megaliths, which they generally read both as ruined and as associated with a ritual and usually funereal function. In *A View of the Present State of Ireland*, Spenser notes the prevalence of stone circles, cairns and megalithic monuments in Ireland too,[18] and Joscelin noted in his *The Life of the glorious bishop S. Patrick*, translated into English in 1624 and used as a source for Shirley's *St Patrick for Ireland*, that 'the glorious Saint by conuerting stones into milke, & milke into stones, conuerted a Magitian from the worshiping of stones, to the seruice of the true and liuing God'.[19] Nearer still to home, George Owen of Henllys in Pembrokeshire was very interested in standing stones and cromlechs, not least Pentre Ifan, of which he provided a drawing;[20] understanding it as almost certainly a burial site, he lists it as one of the wonders of Pembrokeshire and calls it second only to Stonehenge,[21] and I wonder whether it is wholly a coincidence that on the only occasion when Shakespeare visits Pembrokeshire, in *Cymbeline*, he seems to be thinking both of supernatural encounters and also, as I suggested in Chapter 6, of the burial practices of its former inhabitants, since Marisa R. Cull reads Guiderius' injunction to Arviragus to lay the supposed Fidele's head to the east as best understood by situating it in the context of the region's ancient history: 'Guiderius instructs Arviragus to turn Fidele's head facing east, a Celtic custom'.[22] Later, a living character encounters dead ones, as Posthumus sees the spirits of his dead parents and brothers.

In England as well as Wales, cromlechs and standing stones attracted attention, but although James Shapiro observes that Shakespeare's regular route from London to Stratford would have taken him past the Rollright stones,[23] interest tended to centre on Stonehenge. Anthony à Wood records in *Atheniae Oxonienses* that John Speed, the first anatomy lecturer at Oxford and the son of John Speed the cartographer, wrote a pastoral called *Stonehenge* which was acted at Oxford in 1635, though if it is indeed identical with *The Converted Robber*,[24] its interest lies in the rural nature and inaccessibility of Salisbury Plain rather than in the monument. In *Philadelphvs, or A Defence of Brutes, and the Brutans History* (1593), Richard Harvey too focuses on Stonehenge, and associates it, as Olaus did the Scandinavian megaliths, with death. Harvey declares that

> *Aurely* desiring to teach the *Brutans*, to beware of outlandish friendship, which had in his days so intrapped and infected them, caused *Merlin* by his Art Soueraigne, to fetch the great stones out of Ireland, which are now upon Salsbury plain, and set them neere the place where *Hengist* and the Saxons against their Oath did murder hundreds of the best *Brutans* with kniues secretly prouided for the purpose, and tooke *Vortiger* their king prisoner, and ransomed him at their pleasure, That when they should see those stones or heare of them,

they might remember the stony heartes of outlandish friendes, the hypocrisie of Saxons, the untrueth of strangers, and either appoint them true ouerseers, or els away with them out of the Land.

In this account, Stonehenge stands both as xenophobic reminder of the true nature of 'English' national identity and as burial ground, and Harvey later adds that '*Aurely & Vter*' were buried at Stonehenge too, and also '*Constantine* the third'.[25] Spenser gave a largely similar account of Stonehenge,[26] though there is a slight variation in Rowley's *The Birth of Merlin*, where Stonehenge is understood uniquely as the burial place of Merlin's mother, Joan, whose son promises her,

> When you die, I will erect a Monument upon the verdant Plains of Salisbury, no King shall have so high a sepulchre, with pendulous stones that I will hang by art, where neither Lime nor Morter shalbe us'd, a dark Enigma to the memory, for none shall have the power to number then, a place that I will hollow for your rest,
>
> > Where no Night-hag shall walk. nor Ware-wolf tread,
> >
> > Where Merlins Mother shall be sepulcher'd.[27]

Confirmation that Stonehenge was understood primarily as a burial place is also found in John Weever, John Foxe, John Speed and Holinshed,[28] and this idea would have seemed to receive confirmation during James I's visit to Wilton in 1620 when courtiers including Buckingham, William Harvey and Inigo Jones mounted an expedition to Stonehenge, where they dug and found animal skulls; it was also supported by etymology, since 'the name is a conjunction of two Old English words, *stan* (stone) and *hengen* (hanging), due to the resembl[a]nce of the framework of the sarsens, especially the trilithons, to gallows. Stukeley understood that the word was "plainly Saxon & signifys only the hanging stones"'.[29] Similarly John Leland wrote of Silbury Hill that 'Both here and at Avebury one mile away, as well as at several other places on the downs, there are the burials and camps of warriors',[30] and a 1575 sketch of Stonehenge signed 'R. F.' actually 'shows diggers attacking the earth with shovels on a little hillock in front of the monument ... before them are two crossed femurs and a skull',[31] giving us a sharply focused glimpse of how loudly such monuments spoke of death. Indeed sometimes the link was even more direct: Jacqueline Simpson observes that Richard Carew's 1602 *The Survey of Cornwall* accounted for the stone circle known as The Hurlers as having been revellers who were turned to stone,[32] and similar legends accrue to many other stone circles, though they are not always so easy to date. Stones could be associated with death or danger in other ways too: as Alastair Moffat notes, standing stones were used to fix one of the limits of the Debatable Land between England and Scotland,[33] a no-go zone into which only Reivers could safely enter and which saw a number of bloody conflicts.

Also in the North, Hadrian's Wall and its associated forts were at the time much more extensive than they are now: John Leland quotes a Newcastle clergyman named Dr Robert Davell as having spoken to him, probably in 1539, of 'the great Ruines of the Castel of *Cairvoran*',[34] where there is now nothing at all still to be seen, and an unidentified writer in 1574 also notes the existence of 'the ruynes of an old town called by the country Caer Vurron'. We have already seen in chapter 3 that herbs growing near the Wall were considered to be particularly potent, and both the wall and its associated forts were often understood as specifically religious: in 1599 the important local antiquary Reginald Bainbrigg noted of the remains of the fort at Birdoswald that 'the inhabitants did shew me the plaice where the churche stode'.[35] Sometimes, this was because the observer was himself a cleric, like the Newcastle clergyman Dr Davell, or like Christopher Ridley, author of a manuscript entitled 'The Pightes Wall: Sir Christ. Ridley to Mr Wm. Claxton circa 1572', who seems to have been curate of Haltwhistle. Ridley's view of the wall was particularly influential, for though his claim that it was known locally as 'the *Kepe Wall*' does not register in any other writers that I know of, it is a different matter when it comes to the passage in which says that

> in this wall was theyr a trunck of brass or whatever kynd of mettal which went from one place to another along the wall, & came into the Captaynes chamber where at they had watchers for the same, and yf there had bene stryfe or business betwyxt the enemies and that the watchman did blow a horn it at the end of the truncke that came into the chamber, and so from one to one.[36]

Via Camden, traces of this can be found in Spenser, who describes the wall as 'brasen',[37] and in William Warner's *Albions England*.[38] Another important clerical observer of the Wall was Leonard Lowther, rector of Bowness-on-Solway, whose influence is felt in Camden via Bainbrigg, to whom he supplied information.[39] Collectively, these men helped promulgate an understanding of Hadrian's Wall in which the sacred loomed almost as large as the profane principle of defence with which we are now likely to associate it.

After the English Reformation a certain set of more obviously religious ruins inevitably acquired meanings which were both politically charged and also affected by ideas of death, and this time specifically of encounters between the living and the dead. Henry VIII's Dissolution of the Monasteries caused monastic ruins to become a prime feature of the landscape in many parts of the country; Jennifer Wallace observes of the impact of digging plague pits coupled with that of the Dissolution of the Monasteries that

> suddenly there is a wealth of material for antiquaries to study. New ruins to inspect, new graves to open and contemplate, new objects to unearth. But the material is tainted by scepticism and sickness. To get at it, the antiquaries must breach the rules of everything that was previously thought holy. They need to march into the old monasteries and take what used to belong to the monks. They need to peer into graves and rifle through the remains of the dead.[40]

Such discoveries fed in turn into the emerging discipline of chorography, and their nature and that of the circumstances in which they were made both contributed to colouring it with a pervading melancholy. As Eamon Duffy notes, William Lambarde's *Perambulation of Kent* (1576) lamented the despoliation of the religious buildings of Canterbury, while John Stow's *Survey of London* (1598) had a similar emphasis, as too did Speed's atlas, as J.B. Harley points out:

> Like Camden, Speed's aim was 'to acquaint the world with the ancient state of Britain ... to restore Britain to Antiquity and Antiquity to Britain'.... So in Speed's atlas, theirs was a country where Romans, Saxons, and Danes had fought over its space, while the landscape held a series of signposts to the destroyed monastic era.[41]

Andrew Escobedo points out that the past looms similarly large in the antiquarian work of another Catholic: 'The first major examination of Saxon culture, Richard Verstegan's *Restitution of Decayed Intelligence in Antiquities* (1605), presented itself above all as a restoration of origins'.[42] In all these texts, ruins offer an edge and point of possible contact between life and death and potentially between the present and the past.

Monasteries were also of interest to dramatists, who, Kristine Steenbergh suggests, homed in on their in-between status: she argues, 'Monasteries are, in fact, so much a liminal phenomenon that the theatre often employs them as *fictional* retreats'.[43] Sometimes, however, they are real, and when they are real they offer above all places for the living to think of and sometimes even to commune with the dead. In *The Duchess of Malfi*, which was actually staged in the converted former monastery of Blackfriars, as Antonio approaches the rendezvous which is to prove fatal to him, he and Delio pass through a ruined abbey. Antonio declares,

> I do love these ancient ruins:
> We never tread upon them but we set
> Our foot upon some reverend history.
> And questionless, here in this open court,
> Which now lies naked to the injuries
> Of stormy weather, some men lie interr'd
> Lov'd the church so well, and gave so largely to't,
> They thought it should have canopy'd their bones
> Till doomsday; but all things have their end:
> Churches and cities, which have diseases like to men,
> Must have like death that we have.
>
> *Echo.*   *Like death that we have.*
> (5.3.9–19)

The echo speaks the thoughts of Antonio's dead wife, and in many productions is played by her. It seems surprising that there should be a ruined abbey in Italy, since it was a country which had never undergone a Reformation, and this is a distinctively post-Reformation landscape, which would in fact be much more at home in an England pitted with the 'bare ruined choirs'[44] that bore testimony to a now lost faith. However J.Y. Michel argues of revenge tragedy in general that the narratives of the plays belonging to this genre are so death-oriented that they are bound to reflect, in some way or other, Elizabethan funerary rituals. Actually, late sixteenth-century playgoers, actors and playwrights considered the stage as a set of funerary items and buildings.

Michel further suggests that

Tombs and shrines, as they appear in late Elizabethan literature, are not merely holy sanctuaries symbolizing the victory of a culture over time. They are also decaying architectures containing dangerous items.[45]

A landscape containing religious ruins was, as English writers were well aware, a radically traumatised one, and above all one which spoke of death, as in *The Duchess of Malfi* where a ruin provides the location for this exchange between the living Antonio and the dead Duchess.

One particular ruined religious building seems to have been of special interest, and that was the Norfolk shrine of Walsingham. A popular ballad of which Philip Howard was probably the author[46] lamented the fate of Walsingham after the shrine was destroyed during the Reformation, and as Gary Waller points out,

the ghost of Walsingham uncannily haunted the Elizabethan age in poems and folk songs, including the famous Walsingham Ballad (spectacularly set by Byrd, Bull and others), Ophelia's song in *Hamlet* 4.5, and the strange and extraordinarily haunting poem by Ralegh, "As you came from the Holy Land," and Robert Sidney's Sixth Song, "Yonder Comes a Sad Pilgrim."[47]

I wonder if the memory of Walsingham is also present in *The Tempest*. One stanza of 'A Lament for Walsingham' ran as follows:

Such are the wracks as now do show
    Of that holy land.
Level, level with the ground
    the towers do lie
Which with their golden glittering tops
    pierced once to the sky.[48]

The Tempest seems to echo this:

The cloud-capped towers, the gorgeous palaces,
The solemn temples, the great globe itself,
Yea, all which it inherit, shall dissolve,
And like this insubstantial pageant faded,
Leave not a rack behind.[49]

The idea of towers being toppled and the homophone rack / wrack are common to both passages, as is the idea of reaching to the sky. Although *The Tempest* stages no meetings between individual members of the living and the dead communities (although Prospero has apparently raised the dead in the past), it might well be seen as doing so on a larger scale in the extent to which it puts a Virgilian past in direct contact with a present whose immediacy is emphasised by the topicality of the allusion to the wreck of the Sea Venture. Indeed Prospero's speech could in itself be seen as a collapsing of this world and the world beyond, and the play also offers a number of supposed, though not actual, resurrections of characters presumed dead, as well as direct communion with the world of spirits in the shape of Prospero's conversations with Ariel and his other spirit helpers.

The memory of Walsingham is certainly present in *Hamlet*, where Ophelia seems to sing both the words and the tune of one of the Walsingham ballads.[50] Philip Schwyzer has recently suggested that *Hamlet* may be closely related to another story of old structures, and indeed to a story which speaks specifically of an encounter between the living and the dead and a troubling of the boundary between the two. Tracing to Saxo Grammaticus the early Scandinavian story of Asvith and Asmund, which tells of a living brother buried with a dead one in a barrow who ends up fighting his brother's ghost, Schwyzer asks,

> Is it a coincidence that Saxo Grammaticus's *Gesta Danorum* is also the earliest known source for the story of Amleth, or Hamlet? Saxo's history of the Danish prince who avenges his father by killing his usurping uncle already contains most of the elements of the plot made famous by Shakespeare, with the notable exception of the Ghost, whose source scholars have been compelled to seek elsewhere. Yet, as we have seen, there are undead beings elsewhere in Saxo's book, and the tale of Asmund and Asvith was certainly known to the Elizabethans. Thomas Nashe retold the macabre history of 'Asuitus and Asmundus' in *Pierce Pennilesse his Supplication to the Divell* (1592).... There is thus some likelihood, as Cay Dollerup has suggested, that Shakespeare derived part of his conception of the Ghost from Saxo's barrow story, or from Nashe's retelling of that ghoulish tale.[51]

Dollerup marshals a range of evidence to support this possibility,[52] and we know that barrows were cut into in England and sometimes found to contain bones and urns (indeed John Dee himself may have cut into the Sutton Hoo ship-barrow),[53] so that it would not be surprising for Shakespeare to register an interest in a story associated with one.

Hamlet is, I think, not the only Shakespearean tragedy interested in encounters between the living and the dead; I want to suggest that *King Lear* is too, though its interest is more indirectly articulated. Huw Griffiths suggests,

> In the literature of the sixteenth and seventeenth centuries, the figure of the ruin is deployed as means to discuss the public world. The image of the ruined wall or building connects the piece of writing to the world of historical change and of political shifts and aspirations. Buildings and architecture constitute the public realm of political achievement and political interaction.[54]

Philip Schwyzer develops this idea of a link between the built and the human, suggesting of *Titus Andronicus* that 'it is appropriate that Aaron should be discovered within a ruined monastery because he is, in a special sense, like a ruined monastery. His stage presence invites the same sort of double or bifurcated vision'. Schwyzer also reproduces Maarten van Heemskerck's 1553 *Self-portrait, with the Colosseum behind* and suggests that it invites us to perceive an analogy between artist and building.[55] A similar idea is found in *Cymbeline*, where Lucius says of the headless Cloten, 'The ruin speaks that sometime / It was a worthy building' (4.2.354–5), and in *The Duchess of Malfi*, where the Duchess asks 'who do I look like now?' and Cariola replies 'like some reverend monument / Whose ruins are even pitied' (4.2.30, 33–4). Spenser too implies a correspondence between people and places when he personifies Rome in his translation of Du Bellay: declaring that '*Rome* now of *Rome* is th'onely funerall', he muses,

> *Rome* is no more: but if the shade of *Rome*
> May of the bodie yeeld a seeming sight,
> It's like a corse drawn forth out of the tombe
> By Magicke skill out of eternall night.[56]

Finally, Rodrigo Cacho Casal suggests that 'in Platonic terms, the ancient stones are also like the bones of a dead body that once belonged to a remarkable creature, and through which it is still possible to have a dialogue with its soul',[57] and this is, I think, the association that mobilises the potential of ruins in the playhouse and helps them act as a gateway to the world of the past: in dead buildings, we can see dead people. By implication, Jan Kott applies something of the same idea to King Lear, saying first that in the 1830s 'attempts were made to set *King Lear* in a definite historical period. With the help of archaeologists, celtic burial places were reconstructed on the stage. Lear became an old druid'; later, as his discussion of *King Lear* unfolds, Kott goes on to observe that 'the biblical Job, too, is the ruin of a man'.[58]

King Lear – and *King Lear* – can indeed be seen in terms of ruins. Stonehenge itself, or at least its location, is evoked when Kent says to Oswald,

> Goose, if I had you upon Sarum plain,
> I'd drive ye cackling home to Camelot.[59]

Gloucester says, 'We have seen the best of our time: machinations, hollowness, treachery, and all ruinous disorders follow us disquietly to our graves' (1.2.109–11), and Lear himself thinks increasingly in terms of buildings and their states of repair, saying, 'I abjure all roofs' (2.4.206) and apostrophising, 'You houseless poverty' (3.4.26). Lear also figures himself as a building, saying as he hits his own head, 'Beat at this gate, that let thy folly in, / And thy dear judgment out!' (1.4.269–70) and exclaiming against the idea that he should apologise to Goneril:

> Ask her forgiveness?
> Do you but mark how this becomes the house:
> 'Dear daughter, I confess that I am old'.
>
> (2.4.149–50)

By 'the house', presumably, he means himself, just as he has earlier figured himself as a building when he adjures himself 'O Lear, Lear, Lear! / Beat at this gate, that let thy folly in, / And thy dear judgement out' (1.4.268–70). This intertwining of the idea of the human and the idea of the ruin can be seen as simultaneously lending grandeur to the human and pathos to the ruin.

I think one particular ruin, or partial ruin, might conceivably be important for the play, even though it is never actually mentioned. When Regan asks 'Wherefore to Dover?' (3.7.51), one answer, I think, is that Dover Castle was there, something of which Shakespeare was likely to have been well aware given that Hubert de Burgh was the castellan of Dover Castle and held it against Prince Louis's invasion, as dramatised in *King John*. Dover Castle was renowned both for its antiquity – its grounds contain a Roman lighthouse, and in 1591 Hugh Broughton asserted that 'I haue seene an Englysh booke, founde in Douer Castle, 400. yeeres olde, that affyrmeth *Melchisedek* to be the sonne of *Noah*'[60] – and its strength. It was also supposedly the burial place of Sir Gawain, as apparently confirmed by the fact that it contained an Arthur's hall, and in Thomas Hughes's *The Misfortunes of Arthur* 'The argument of the *Tragedie*' tells us that '*Arthur* at his landing was resisted on the stronds of *Douer*, where he put *Mordred* to fight', while Robert Chester in *The annals of great Brittaine* promised his readers, 'At Dover likewise you may see Sir Gawins skull and Cradocks mantle'.[61] This association is echoed in *King Lear* in the play's interest in Arthuriana, as in the Fool's sharply observed parody of the prophecies of Merlin as recorded by Geoffrey of Monmouth (3.2.80–96). Dover Castle might, then, have been a background presence in Shakespeare's mind.

Cliffs: The Edge of the Land

Perhaps even more famous than Dover Castle, though, were Dover Cliffs (including what is now called Shakespeare Cliff), and indeed William Lambarde in his *Perambulation of Kent* suggested that Dover took its name from the height and steepness of these: his description of Dover is headed,

> DOVER, called diversely in Latine, Doris, Durus, Doveria, and Dubris: in Saxon, Du[fn]a: all which seeme to be drawen from the Bryttish woordes, Dufir, Water, or Dufirha, high or steepe: the scituation being upon a high rocke over the water, which serveth to either.[62]

To these cliffs in particular an eschatological charge seems readily to have attached itself in early modern eyes. The twin ports of Dover and Calais lent themselves naturally to discourses of religious controversy, and not only in texts involving the steady stream of Huguenots who crossed the Channel. In *The opening of heauen gates, or The ready way to euerlasting life*, Arthur Dent scorns one argument on the subject of predestination as requiring a 'leape ... longer then the passage between Douer and Callice';[63] in *The honor of the married clergie, maintayned against the malicious challenges of C.E. Masse-priest*, Joseph Hall stoutly affirmed that under

Protestantism 'the World is growne wiser, and findes Heauen no lesse neere to *Douer-Cliffe*, then to the Seuen-Hills'.[64] Similarly in *Tetrastylon papisticum, that is, The foure principal pillers of papistrie ...* Andrew Willet enlivens a sustained attack on Catholicism with two bright little images: 'If heauen fell, we should catch larkes. And if a bridge were made between Douer and Caleis, we might go to Boleine a foote, as William Sommer once told King Henrie the eight'.[65]

Alexandra Walsham has recently argued that we need to pay more attention to the resonances of natural spaces in Renaissance England: she suggests that priests trained on the continent and returning to England and Wales 'collaborated with the laity not merely in reconsecrating private houses and chambers as new arenas for worship but also in sanctifying hitherto neutral locations in the natural world – gardens, orchards, woods and fields – as spaces in which Catholics could meditate, pray, and commune with their Maker',[66] perhaps in something of the same way as pilgrims to the Holy Land had traditionally collected natural objects such as twigs, earth, water and stones.[67] In the context of early modern England such places could in a sense be seen as anti-ruins, left alone because of what they were not rather than attracting attention because of what they had been, but they, like ruins, were at least free of post-Reformation building. In this sense Dover Cliffs, simultaneously representing both England and the end of England, could, it seems, speak almost as easily of other worlds as of other lands.

For Shakespeare, and for some other dramatists too, a particular resonance and aura of the numinous certainly appears to have attached to cliffs and high places in particular. Partly, this was a natural mode of thinking for the inhabitants of a landscape still structured by a mediaeval logic in which the tallest buildings were church spires and steeples which put the land in dialogue with the sky; partly, it was because cliffs and high places were associated with the last bastions of the land's original civilisations. In *The Misfortunes of Arthur*, Conan says

> Let Saxons now, let Normans, Danes, and Scottes
> Enjoye our medowes, fieldes, and pleasant plaines:
> Come, let vs flye to Mountaines, Cliffes and Rockes.
>   (4.3)

High places were also, though, potential places of the sacred; as Arnold Angenendt notes, 'A common religious idea is that a holy place is situated where the earth "opens upward"',[68] and Alessandro Scafi comments, 'Geography, Eucherius pointed out, had a spiritual dimension: the earth stood for mankind; the mountains signified the Lord, the Church, or the apostles; and the valleys pointed to the contrition of humble saints'.[69] Prospero seems to speak of this immanent sense of place in *The Tempest* when he apostrophises, 'Ye elves of hills, brooks, standing lakes and groves' (5.1.33), and later in the same speech he goes on to recall how 'graves at my command / Have waked their sleepers, ope'd and let 'em forth By my so potent art' (5.1.48–50). Here, the idea of particularly charged natural spaces is explicitly associated with that of encounters between the living and the dead.

To Gloucester in *King Lear*, Dover is clearly somewhere he goes to find a high place, and he seems to do that, like Moses in the Bible, specifically in order to be close to the supernatural. Kent was already a deeply liminal location in its own right: Jane Pettegree notes of John Twyne's *De Rebus Albionicis, Britannicus atque Anglicus* (1590) that 'incidents of dramatic change in the Kentish landscape are cited in support of the argument that geographical boundaries are not absolute, that once England formed a continuum with the rest of Europe: the sunken island that is now Goodwin Sands; the extension of marshland around Romney; alluvial silt filling up Sandwich Haven', and Pettegree also explores more generally how the county's double identity as home of both the See of Canterbury and of some famous champions of popular liberty made it a test case for the border between secular and spiritual power.[70] On multiple levels, then, positioning the scene of Gloucester's attempted suicide at or near Dover thus makes for a radically liminal location, and one in which it might indeed seem possible for mortals to contact or at least invoke inhabitants of another world or plane; certainly Gloucester seems to think so, for offering a reward to the supposed Poor Tom, he says, 'Here, friend, 's another jewel: fairies and Gods / Prosper it with thee!' (4.6.28–30). The Arden editor's note on this tells us that 'Kittredge suggests that this refers to the superstition that hidden treasure is guarded by fairies, and that they make it multiply miraculously in the possession of the discoverer', but the idea that location may also be a significant factor here is reinforced when Gloucester apostrophises his gods on what he takes to be the very top of the cliff (4.6.33–5). Finally, after Gloucester thinks he has fallen, Edgar reinforces the idea that the tops of cliffs may be places to meet the representatives of the supernatural when he says,

> As I stood here below methought his eyes
> Were two full moons; he had a thousand noses,
> Horns whelk'd and wav'd like the enridged sea:
> It was some fiend; therefore, thou happy father,
> Think that the clearest Gods, who make them honours
> Of men's impossibilities, have preserved thee.
> (4.6.69–74)

In *Hamlet*, Horatio makes a similar assumption of an affinity between supernatural entities and high places when he advises Hamlet not to follow the Ghost:

> What if it tempt you toward the flood, my lord,
> Or to the dreadful summit of the cliff
> That beetles o'er his base into the sea,
> And there assume some other horrible form
> Which might deprive your sovereignty of reason
> And draw you into madness?
> (1.4.69–74)

Shakespeare himself may well have been to Elsinore,[71] and if so he would know that Kronborg Castle, like most of Denmark, does not really beetle over anything, but the idea of a high place is clearly important to him for a meeting between a man and a ghost. Moreover, Keith Brown calls 'Elsinore ... the Dover of the Sound' between Denmark and Sweden,[72] and if Shakespeare himself did indeed visit Elsinore, then he almost certainly went via Dover, which would make for a good case for reading these two clifftop passages as imaginatively connected here in the same way as Dover and Denmark are in *A wonderfull, strange and miraculous astrologicall prognostication for this yeere 1591*, a text which Shakespeare might well be remembering in *King Lear* since it, like Edmund, promises to 'discours[e] breefelye of the Eclipses both of Sunne and Moone'. This presents an author supposedly 'sitting Gentlemen vpon Douer cliffes, to quaint my selfe with the art of Nauigation, and know the course of the Tides, as the Danske Crowes gather on the Sandes against a storme', and the glance at Denmark here is picked up in the section on the eclipse of the moon, which, Hamlet-like, pokes fun at the notorious drinking habits of the Danes by warning that 'it is to bee feared, that the Danes shall this yeere bee greatlye giuen to drincke'.[73] An associative connection between *Hamlet* and *Lear* would certainly not be surprising, for in both plays the boundary between life and death is unclear: in *King Lear*, we cannot be certain when either Cordelia or Lear actually dies, while in *Hamlet* the Ghost crosses and recrosses the border between the two, and two living men jump into a grave, and Hamlet himself also mentions another place which was considered to be a point of access between the territory of the living and the territory of the dead when he seems to glance at St Patrick's Purgatory.

The places of the gods on the English Renaissance stage can thus be seen to be diverse, but ruins and high places, either separately or in collocation, clearly figure prominently among them. Between them, these two potential edges of the world also bear on all the concerns I have considered in this book. Cliffs are potential symbols of the edge not only of literal but of national territory, emblematising the sense of a connection between land and person which I explored in Chapters 3, 4 and 5. The reciprocal figuring of ruins as bodies and bodies as ruins is an instance of the edge between the self and the social which I explored in Chapters 1, 6 and 7. The fact that so many ruins were of buildings which had originally been either Roman or Roman Catholic also spoke of the particularly troubled edge between the spiritual and the secular on which I focused in chapter 2. Both ruins and high places thus speaks particularly loudly of their adjacencies as well as of themselves, underlining the extent to which an edge is always already a site of bleed.

Notes

[1]   Aubrey Burl, *Stonehenge* (London: Constable & Robinson, 2006), p. 36.

[2]   Anne Janowitz, *England's Ruins: Poetic Purpose and the National Landscape* (Oxford: Basil Blackwell, 1990), p. 20. For discussion of a rather different appropriation of the Du Bellay, Francisco de Quevedo's 'Roma antigua y moderna', see Rodrigo Cacho Casal, 'The Memory of Ruins: Quevedo's *Silva* to "Roma antigua y moderna"', *Renaissance Quarterly* 62 (2009), pp. 1167–203.

3   Huw Griffiths, 'The Sonnet in Ruins: Time and the Nation in 1599', *Early Modern Culture* 6, http://emc.eserver.org/1-6/issue6.html.

4   Casal, 'The Memory of Ruins', p. 1167.

5   Edmund Spenser, *Ruines of Rome*, in *Poetical Works*, edited by J.C. Smith and E. de Selincourt (Oxford: Oxford University Press, 1912), p. 509.

6   Christopher Marlowe, *Doctor Faustus*, A Text, in *The Complete Plays*, edited by Mark Thornton Burnett (London: J.M. Dent, 1999), 3.1.44–48.

7   Leonard Barkan, *Unearthing the Past: Archaeology and Aesthetics in the Making of Renaissance Culture* (New Haven: Yale University Press, 1999), p. 25.

8   Casal, 'The Memory of Ruins', pp. 1170 and 1192.

9   Robert Wynkfielde, *account of the execution of Mary, Queen of Scots*, http://englishhistory.net/tudor/exmary.html.

10   Giuseppe Biondi, *A Relation of the Most Illustrious Lord, Signor Troilo Sauelli, a Baron of Rome; Who was there beheaded, in the Castle of Sant-Angelo, on the 18. of Aprill, 1592. With a Preface, conteyning diuers particulers, which are wholy necessary to be knowne, for the better vnderstanding of the Relation it selfe*, translated by Tobie Matthew (Saint-Omer: The English College, 1620), p. 254.

11   R.T. Petersson, *Sir Kenelm Digby, The Ornament of England, 1603–1665* (London: Jonathan Cape, 1956), p. 23.

12   Paul Hyland, *Ralegh's Last Journey* (London: HarperCollins, 2003), pp. x and 189.

13   For comment on the closure of the border with death in the wake of the Reformation see for instance Sharon Emmerichs, 'Shakespeare and the Landscape of Death: Crossing the Boundaries of Life and the Afterlife', *Shakespeare* 8.2 (June 2012), p. 177–9.

14   Christopher S. Wood, 'Maximilian I as Archeologist', *Renaissance Quarterly* 58.4 (winter 2005), pp. 1145, 1128, and 1168.

15   Jole Shackelford, 'Documenting the factual and the antifactual: Ole Worm and public knowledge', *Endeavour* 23.3 (1999), p. 68.

16   Olaus Magnus, *Description of the Northern Peoples* [1555], translated by Peter Fisher and Humphrey Higgens (London: Hakluyt Society, 1966), vol. 1, pp. 65–6 and 69.

17   Paul Binding, *Imagined Corners: Exploring the World's First Atlas* (London: Hodder Headline, 2003), p. 126.

18   Edmund Spenser, *A View of the Present State of Ireland*, edited by Risa Bear, Part 2, 11–12, http://darkwing.uoregon.edu/~rbear/veue1.html. For comment on Spenser's representation of Irish ruins see Philip Schwyzer, *Archaeologies of English Renaissance Literature* (Oxford: Oxford University Press, 2007), p. 39.

19   Joscelin, *The life of the glorious bishop S. Patricke …*, translated by Fr. B.B. (St Omers: [G Seutin?] for John Heigham, 1625), p. 80.

20   B.G. Charles, *George Owen of Henllys: A Welsh Elizabethan* (Aberystwyth: National Library of Wales Press, 1973), p. 183.

21   George Owen of Henllys, *The Description of Pembrokeshire*, edited by Dillwyn Miles (Llandysul: Gomer Press, 1994), pp. 194–5.

22   Marisa R. Cull, 'Contextualizing 1610: *Cymbeline*, *The Valiant Welshman*, and The Princes of Wales', in *Shakespeare and Wales: From the Marches to the Assembly*, edited by Willy Maley and Philip Schwyzer (Burlington: Ashgate, 2010), p. 140n39.

23   James Shapiro, *1599: A Year in the Life of William Shakespeare* (London: Faber and Faber, 2005), p. 266.

[24] Gertrude Marian Sibley declared it lost (*The Lost Plays and Masques, 1500–1642* [Ithaca: Cornell University Press, 1933], p. 154), but see Matthew Steggle's entry on 'Stonehenge' in *The Lost Plays Database*, http://www.lostplays.org/index.php/Stonehenge.

[25] Richard Harvey, *Philadelphvs, or A Defence of Brutes, and the Brutans History* (London: John Wolfe, 1593), pp. 85 and 96.

[26] Edmund Spenser, *The Faerie Queene*. London: Richard Field for William Ponsonbie, 1596, 2.10, p. 343.

[27] William Rowley, *The Birth of Merlin* (London: Thomas Johnson for Francis Kirkman and Henry Marsh, 1662), sig. G3r. On the uniqueness of this tradition to Rowley's play see Megan Lynn Isaac, 'Structure, Legitimacy, and Magic in *The Birth of Merlin*', *Early Theatre* 9.1 (2006), p. 114.

[28] John Weever, *Ancient funerall monuments within the vnited monarchie of Great Britaine, Ireland, and the islands adjacent with the dissolued monasteries therein contained* (London: Thomas Harper for Laurence Sadler, 1631), p. 6; John Foxe, *Actes and Monuments* (London: John Daye, 1583), p. 108; John Speed, *The theatre of the empire of Great Britaine* (London: William Hall for John Sudbury, 1612), where the second table in the appendices lists Aurelius as buried at Stonehenge; and Raphael Holinshed, *The first and second volumes of Chronicles comprising 1 The description and historie of England, 2 The description and historie of Ireland, 3 The description and historie of Scotland* (London: Henry Denham, 1587), pp. 85 and 88.

[29] Burl, *Stonehenge*, pp. 33 and 24–5.

[30] John Chandler, ed., *John Leland's Tudor Itinerary: Travels in Tudor England* (Stroud: Alan Sutton, 1993), p. 500.

[31] Alain Schnapp, *The Discovery of the Past: The Origins of Archaeology* [1993], translated by Ian Kinnes and Gillian Varndell (London: British Museum Press, 1996), p. 150.

[32] Jacqueline Simpson, 'God's visible judgements: the Christian dimension of landscape legends', *Landscape History* 8 (1986), p. 55.

[33] Alastair Moffat, *The Reivers* (Edinburgh: Birlinn 2008), pp. 193–6.

[34] Eric Birley, *Research on Hadrian's Wall* (Kendal: Titus Wilson and son, 1961), p. 2.

[35] Birley, *Research on Hadrian's Wall*, p. 196. On Bainbrigg see also Ben Edwards, 'Reginald Bainbrigg, *scholemaister*, and his stones', in *Archaeology of the Roman Empire: A tribute to the life and works of Professor Barri Jones*, edited by N.J. Higham (Oxford: Archaeopress, 2001), pp. 25–33.

[36] Birley, *Research on Hadrian's Wall*, pp. 2–3.

[37] Spenser, *The Faerie Queene*, 4.11.36.

[38] William Warner, *Albions England* [1612] (Hildesheim: Georg Olms Verlag, 1971), pp. 356–7.

[39] Birley, *Research on Hadrian's Wall*, p. 8.

[40] Jennifer Wallace, *Digging the Dirt: The Archaeological Imagination* (London: George Duckworth, 2004), p. 132.

[41] J.B. Harley, 'Meaning and ambiguity in Tudor cartography', in *English Map-Making 1500–1650*, edited by Sarah Tyacke (London: The British Library, 1983), p. 27.

[42] Andrew Escobedo, 'From Britannia to England: *Cymbeline* and the Beginning of Nations', *Shakespeare Quarterly* 59.1 (Spring 2008), p. 74.

[43] Kristine Steenbergh, 'Bare Ruined Choirs: The Monastery as Heterotopia in Early Modern Drama', in *The Reformation Unsettled: British Literature and the Question*

of National Identity, 1560–1660, edited by Jan Frans van Dijkhuizen and Richard Todd (Turnhout: Brepols, 2008), p. 171.

⁴⁴   William Shakespeare, 'Sonnet 73', in *Shakespeare's Sonnets*, edited by Stephen Booth (New Haven: Yale University Press, 1977), p. 64.

⁴⁵   J.Y. Michel, 'Monuments in Late Elizabethan Literature: A Conservatory of Vanishing Traditions', *Early Modern Literary Studies* 9.2 (September, 2003), http://extra. shu.ac.uk/emls/09-2/michmonu.html.

⁴⁶   Eamon Duffy, 'Bare ruined choirs: remembering Catholicism in Shakespeare's England', in *Theatre and religion: Lancastrian Shakespeare*, edited by Richard Dutton, Alison Findlay and Richard Wilson (Manchester: Manchester University Press, 2003), pp. 41–3 and 48–9.

⁴⁷   Gary Waller, 'An Erasmian Pilgrimage to Walsingham', *Peregrinations* 2.2, http:// peregrinations.kenyon.edu/vol2-2/current.html. A Walsingham song is also alluded to in the anonymous play *The Weakest Goeth to the Wall* (possibly by Anthony Munday?).

⁴⁸   Quoted in Schwyzer, *Archaeologies of English Renaissance Literature*, p. 86.

⁴⁹   William Shakespeare, *The Tempest*, edited by Virginia Mason Vaughan and Alden T. Vaughan (London: Thomas Nelson, 1999), 4.1.152–6.

⁵⁰   William Shakespeare, *Hamlet*, edited by Harold Jenkins (London: Methuen, 1980), 531–2.

⁵¹   Schwyzer, *Archaeologies of English Renaissance Literature*, pp. 12–13.

⁵²   Cay Dollerup, *Denmark, Hamlet, and Shakespeare: A Study of Englishmen's Knowledge of Denmark towards the End of the Sixteenth Century with Special Reference to Hamlet* (Salzburg: Institut für Englische Sprache und Literatur, 1975), pp. 60–61.

⁵³   Barry M. Marsden, *The Early Barrow Diggers* (Stroud: Tempus, 1999), p. 8.

⁵⁴   Griffiths, 'The Sonnet in Ruins'.

⁵⁵   Schwyzer, *Archaeologies of English Renaissance Literature*, pp. 101 and 105.

⁵⁶   Spenser, *Ruines of Rome*, p. 509.

⁵⁷   Casal, 'The Memory of Ruins', p. 1170.

⁵⁸   Jan Kott, *Shakespeare Our Contemporary*, translated by Boleslaw Taborski (London: Methuen, 1965), pp. 101 and 125.

⁵⁹   William Shakespeare, *King Lear*, edited by Kenneth Muir (London: Methuen, 1972), 2.2.80–81.

⁶⁰   Hugh Broughton, *A treatise of Melchisedek prouing him to be Sem* …. (London: Richard Watkins for Gabriel Simson and William White, 1591), sig. C2v.

⁶¹   Robert Chester, *The annals of great Brittaine* (London: Matthew Lownes, 1611), p. 35.

⁶²   William Lambarde, *A Perambulation of Kent*, introduced by Robert Church (Bath: Adams & Dart, 1970), p. 131.

⁶³   Arthur Dent, *The opening of heauen gates, or The ready way to euerlasting life Deliuered in a most familier dialogue, between reason and religion, touching predestination, Gods word, and mans free-will, to the vnderstanding of the weakest capacitie, and the confirming of the more strong* (London: G. Eld for John Wright, 1610), p. 112.

⁶⁴   Joseph Hall, *The honor of the married clergie, maintayned against the malicious challenges of C. E. Masse-priest* (London: W. Stansby for H. Fetherstone, 1620), p. 13.

⁶⁵   Andrew Willet, *Tetrastylon papisticum, that is, The foure principal pillers of papistrie the first conteyning their raylings, slanders, forgeries, vntruthes* … (London: Robert Robinson for Thomas Man, 1593), sig. B3r.

[66]   Alexandra Walsham, 'Holywell: Contesting sacred space in post-Reformation Wales', in *Sacred Space in Early Modern Europe* (Cambridge: Cambridge University Press, 2005), p. 221.

[67]   Derek Krueger, 'The Religion of Relics in Late Antiquity and Byzantium', in *Treasures of Heaven: Saints, Relics, and Devotion in Medieval Europe*, edited by Martina Bagnoli, Holger A. Klein, C. Griffith Mann, and James Robinson (London: The British Museum Press, 2011), p. 11.

[68]   Arnold Angenendt, 'Relics and Their Veneration', in *Treasures of Heaven: Saints, Relics, and Devotion in Medieval Europe*, edited by Martina Bagnoli, Holger A. Klein, C. Griffith Mann, and James Robinson (London: The British Museum Press, 2011), p. 20.

[69]   Alessandro Scafi, *Mapping Paradise: A History of Heaven on Earth* (London: The British Library, 2006), p. 100.

[70]   Jane Pettegree, *Foreign and Native on the English Stage, 1588–1611* (Basinsgstoke: Palgrave, 2011), p. 82.

[71]   See for instance David Hohnen, *Hamlet's Castle and Shakespeare's Elsinore* (Copenhagen: Christian Ejlers, 2000).

[72]   Keith Brown, 'Hamlet's Place on the Map', *Shakespeare Studies* 23 (1995), p. 161.

[73]   Adam Foulweather (Thomas Nash?), *A wonderfull, strange and miraculous astrologicall prognostication for this yeere 1591* (London: Thomas Scarlet, 1591), sigs A2v, A2r and B3r.

Conclusion

The kinds of edges I have discussed in this book have varied substantially in both nature and characteristics, and have involved discussion of a number of different authors. Some, such as walls and frontiers, have been universally recognised, securely plotted and, in the case of walls, are actually visible: others, such as the relationship between jewels and bodies and between secular and spiritual power, are far more conceptual and less susceptible of either definition or secure identification. One thing has though emerged as characterising all of them alike, and that is that all permit two-way traffic. The first two chapters examine respectively the most visible and the most invisible of borders and find surprising similarities between them. In the first chapter, the walls around civic and private territory, ostensibly quite different in nature and function, prove in fact each to suggest the other, and to acknowledge similarity even as they appear to mark difference. In the second, secular and spiritual realms are seen not to be antithetical but easily to mimic each other, and yet the border between these two, so much less visible and tangible than those marked by walls, ironically proves in some respects to be the more easily identified and policed; it is, however, dangerous for either side to lose sight of the adjacency of the other.

The next three chapters all focus on civic or national borders, which are usually well understood even if not always actually marked. In the sixteenth century story of Friar Bacon and Friar Bungay, told in prose by an anonymous writer and dramatised by Robert Greene, Friar Bacon dreams of walling all England with brass, and an anonymous Elizabethan fantasised about rebuilding Hadrian's Wall; in the last hundred years we have seen Berlin divided by a concrete wall and the *ouvrages* of the Maginot line peppering the rural peace of the Franco-German border with underground tunnels and retractable turrets which could rise up into the landscape to strafe attackers. The twentieth-century fortifications became real and the sixteenth-century ones remained dreams, but both testify to similar levels of anxiety, even if the causes were different. For the early modern period, as the urge to erect a physical marker shows, that anxiety centred on fears that borders did not really mark difference. In the first of the three chapters in this second section, the fear is that the inhabitants of either side of the border may intermarry, or at least interbreed, in ways which are both socially inappropriate and which will also reduce even further any existing differences between the two populations by building ties of kinship and sympathy; in the remaining two, the borders of France prove an uncannily good metaphorical fit for discussion about the borders of England, and also allow for the suggestion of an analogy between personal control and strongly marked national borders in a way which ultimately works to weaken the normally secure distinction between personal and national.

The last three chapters examine intersections between the material and the spiritual. The first of these proposes that for Shakespeare, particularly in the last plays but also in *Hamlet*, sanctity and the numinous are insistently associated with the geographically marginal, especially the Celtic fringe, which thus speaks of a permeability between this word and a loosely conceived other. The second argues for a similar possibility of exchange and mutual influence between the properties of jewels and the properties of human bodies, while the third reverts to the idea of direct interface between the spiritual and material worlds to suggest that ruins and high places mark points of access on the landscape as a whole just as jewels mark them on individual bodies.

Overall, then, this book has argued that the plays it considers show us a world which was both profoundly interested in the idea of edges and borders and also profoundly anxious that all edges and borders were in fact potentially illusory or unstable. Walls and jewels might both seem to possess a fixed, concrete physical identity, but both could also provide points of contact, transfer and trafficking as much as of demarcation, walls in the shape of the gates which pierced them and jewels through their supposedly quasi-magical interaction with the body and mind beneath the skin on which they rested. National borders could be equally permeable and might also suggest parallels between people and territories which, like the supposed effects of jewels on the body, posited individual identity as constituted and inflected by the material rather than as securely separate from it. Even the border between this world and the next might be one that could be crossed. To look at the ways in which these plays negotiate the idea of the edge thus helps us focus more closely and more sharply on some of the most urgently felt hopes and fears underlying and animating English Renaissance plays, in which edges and their adjacencies stand revealed as contour markers of early modern shapes of insecurity and fear.

Works Cited

Adelman, Janet. *Suffocating Mothers*. London: Routledge, 1992.

Aggas, Edward. *An answeare to the supplication Against him, who seeming to giue the King counsel to become a Catholike, indeuoureth to stirre vp his good subiectes vnto rebellion*. Translated by E.A. London: John Wolfe, 1591.

Anderson, Peter D. *Black Patie: The Life and Times of Patrick Stewart, Earl of Orkney, Lord of Shetland*. Edinburgh: John Donald, 1992.

Angenendt, Arnold. 'Relics and Their Veneration'. In *Treasures of Heaven: Saints, Relics, and Devotion in Medieval Europe*. Edited by Martina Bagnoli, Holger A. Klein, C. Griffith Mann, and James Robinson. London: The British Museum Press, 2011. pp. 19–28.

Anglicus, Bartholomaeus. *Batman vppon Bartholome his booke De proprietaribus rerum*. Translated by Stephen Bateman. London: Thomas East, 1582.

Anonymous. *The famous history of Fryer Bacon*. London: G. Purslowe for F. Grove, 1627.

———. *The first and second part of the troublesome raigne of Iohn King of England*. London, 1611.

———. *King Edward III*. Edited by Giorgio Melchiori. Cambridge: Cambridge University Press, 1998.

———. ('W. S.'.) *The Lamentable Tragedy of Locrine*. Edited by Jane Lytton Gooch. London and New York: Garland, 1981.

———. *Northerne poems congratulating the Kings majesties entrance to the crowne*. London: J. Windet for E. Weaver, 1604.

———. *A true relation of the French kinge his good successe ...* London: John Wolfe, 1592.

———. *A Warning for Fair Women*. Edited by Gemma Leggott. http://extra.shu.ac.uk/emls/iemls/resources.html.

Archer, John Michael. *Old Worlds: Egypt, Southwest Asia, India, and Russia in Early Modern English Writing*. Stanford: Stanford University Press, 2001.

Attwater, Donald. *The Penguin Dictionary of Saints*, 2nd edition. Harmondsworth: Penguin, 1983.

Axton, Marie. *The Queen's Two Bodies: Drama and the Elizabethan Succession*. London: Royal Historical Society, 1977.

Bagnoli, Martina. 'The Stuff of Heaven: Materials and Craftsmanship in Medieval Reliquaries'. In *Treasures of Heaven: Saints, Relics, and Devotion in Medieval Europe*. Edited by Martina Bagnoli, Holger A. Klein, C. Griffith Mann, and James Robinson. London: The British Museum Press, 2011. pp. 137–47.

Barkan, Leonard. '"Living Sculptures": Ovid, Michelangelo, and *The Winter's Tale*'. *ELH* 48.4 (winter 1981). pp. 639–67.

———. *Unearthing the Past: Archaeology and Aesthetics in the Making of Renaissance Culture*. New Haven: Yale University Press, 1999.

Barlow, William. *An answer to a Catholike English-man (so by himselfe entitvled) who, without a name, passed his censure vpon the apology made by the Right High and Mightie Prince Iames by the grace of God King of Great Brittaine, Framce, and Ireland & c. for the oath of allegiance*. London: Thomas Haueland for Matthew Law, 1609.

Barron, W.R.J., and Glyn S. Burgess. *The Voyage of Saint Brendan*. Exeter: Exeter University of Exeter Press, 2002.

Bate, Jonathan. *Soul of the Age: The Life, Mind and World of William Shakespeare*. London: Viking, 2008.

Bayrou, François. *Henri IV: Le roi libre*. Paris: Editions j'ai lu, 1997.

Beaumont baptismal register, PRO 106/8 1820–1845 inclusive.

Bennett, Josephine Waters. 'Britain among the Fortunate Isles'. *Studies in Philology* 53.2 (April 1956). pp. 114–40.

Berners, John. *Huon of Bordeaux*. London: Thomas Purfoot for Edward White, 1601.

Biddulph, William. *The trauels of certaine Englishmen into Africa, Asia, Troy, Bithynia, Thracia, and to the Blacke Sea ...* London: T. Haveland for W. Aspley, 1609.

Binding, Paul. *Imagined Corners: Exploring the World's First Atlas*. London: Headline Books, 2003.

Biondi, Giuseppe. *A Relation of the Most Illustrious Lord, Signor Troilo Sauelli, a Baron of Rome; Who was there beheaded, in the Castle of Sant-Angelo, on the 18. of Aprill, 1592. With a Preface, conteyning diuers particulers, which are wholy necessary to be knowne, for the better vnderstanding of the Relation it selfe*. Translated by Tobie Matthew. Saint-Omer: The English College, 1620.

Birley, Eric. *Research on Hadrian's Wall*. Kendal: Titus Wilson and son, 1961.

Birnie, William. *The blame of kirk-buriall, tending to perswade cemiteriall ciuilitie ...* Edinburgh: Robert Charteris, 1606.

Blackwood, Adam. *Martyre de la Royne d'Escosse ...* Paris: Jean Nafeild, 1587.

Boiastuau, Pierre. *Certaine secrete wonders of nature ...* London: Henry Bynneman, 1569.

Breasted, Barbara. '*Comus* and the Castlehaven Scandal'. *Milton Studies* 3 (1971). pp. 201–204.

Bridges, John. *A defence of the gouernment established in the Church of Englande for ecclesiasticall matters Contayining an aunswere vnto a treatuse called, The learned discourse of eccl. gouernment ... and in degence of her Maiestie, and of all other Christian princes supreme gouernment in ecclesiasticall causes*. London: John Windet and T. Orwin for Thomas Chard, 1587.

Briggs, K. M. *The Anatomy of Puck*. London: Routledge and Kegan Paul, 1959.

Broughton, Hugh. *A treatise of Melchisedek prouing him to be Sem ....* London: Richard Watkins for Gabriel Simson and William White, 1591.

Brown, Keith. 'Hamlet's Place on the Map', *Shakespeare Studies* 23 (1995). pp. 160–82.

Brownlow, Frank. 'Southwell and Shakespeare', in *KM 80: A birthday album for Kenneth Muir*. Liverpool: Liverpool University Press, 1987. pp. 27–30.

———. *Shakespeare, Harsnett, and the Devils of Denham*. Newark: University of Delaware Press, 1993.

Bruster, Douglas. 'The Jailer's Daughter and the Politics of Madwomen's Language', *Shakespeare Quarterly* 46.3 (autumn 1995). pp. 277–300.

Buccola, Regina. *Fairies, Fractious Women, and the Old Faith: Fairy Lore in Early Modern British Drama and Culture*. Selinsgrove: Susquehanna University Press, 2006.

Bullokar, John. *An Englis[h] expositor[:] teaching the in[ter]pretation of the harde[st] words [vsed] in our language*. London: John Legatt, 1621.

Burl, Aubrey. *Stonehenge*. London: Constable & Robinson, 2006.

Butler, Chris. '"The howling of Irish wolves": *As You Like It* and the Celtic Essex Circle'. In *Celtic Shakespeare: The Bard and the Borderers*. Edited by Willy Maley and Rory Loughnane. Burlington: Ashgate, 2012.

Byrne, Muriel St Clare, ed., *The Lisle Letters*. Harmondsworth: Penguin, 1983.

Cacho Casal, Rodrigo. 'The Memory of Ruins: Quevedo's *Silva* to "Roma antigua y moderna"'. *Renaissance Quarterly* 62 (2009). pp. 1167–203.

Caesar, Julius. *The eyght bookes of Caius Iulius Caesar conteyning his martiall exploytes in the realme of Gallia and the countries bordering vppon the same translated oute of latin into English by Arthur Goldinge*. London: William Seres, 1565.

Cavell, Stanley. '"Who Does the Wolf Love?": *Coriolanus* and the Interpretation of Politics'. In *Shakespeare and the Question of Theory*. Edited by Patricia Parker and Geoffrey Hartman. London: Methuen, 1985. pp. 245–72.

Chandler, John, ed. *John Leland's Tudor Itinerary: Travels in Tudor England*. Stroud: Alan Sutton, 1993.

Chapman, George. *The memorable maske of the two honorable Houses or Inns of court*. London: G. Eld for George Norton, 1613.

Charles, B.G. *George Owen of Henllys: A Welsh Elizabethan*. Aberystwyth: National Library of Wales Press, 1973.

Chernaik, Warren. *The Myth of Rome in Shakespeare and his Contemporaries*. Cambridge: Cambridge University Press, 2011.

Chester, Robert. *The annals of great Brittaine*. London: Matthew Lownes, 1611.

Chettle, Henry. *The Tragedy of Hoffman*. London: J.N. for Hugh Perry, 1631.

Clapham, John. *The historie of Great Britannie declaring the successes of times and affaires in that iland, from the Romans first entrance, vntill the raigne of Egbert, the West-Saxon prince; who reduced the severall principalities of the Saxons and English, into a monarchie, and changed the name of Britannie into England*. London: Valentine Simmes, 1606.

Commynes, Philippe de. *The historie of Philip de Commines Knight, Lord of Argenton*. Translated by Thomas Danett. London Ar. Hatfield for J. Norton, 1596.

Conlan, J.P. 'Shakespeare's *Edward III*: A Consolation for English Recusants'. *Comparative Drama* 35.2 (summer 2001). pp. 177–202.

Connolly, Annaliese F. 'Guy of Warwick, Godfrey of Bouillon, and Elizabethan Repertory'. In *Early Modern England and Islamic Worlds*. Edited by Bernadette Andrea and Linda McJannet. Basingstoke: Palgrave Macmillan, 2011. pp. 139–58.

Cull, Marisa R. 'Contextualizing 1610: *Cymbeline*, *The Valiant Welshman*, and The Princes of Wales'. In *Shakespeare and Wales: From the Marches to the Assembly*. Edited by Willy Maley and Philip Schwyzer. Burlington: Ashgate, 2010. pp. 127–42.

Cunninhgam, Bernadette, and Raymond Gillespie. '"The most adaptable of saints": The cult of St Patrick in the seventeenth century'. *Archivium Hibernicum* 49 (1995). pp. 82–104.

Cutts, John P. 'British Museum Additional MS. 31342: William Lawes' writing for the theatre and the court'. *The Library*, 5th series, 7 (1952). pp. 225–34.

Daniel, Samuel. *The first part of the historie of England*. London: Nicholas Okes, 1612.

Danett, Thomas. *A continuation of the historie of France from the death of Charles the eight where Comines endeth, till the death of Henry the second*. London: Thomas East for Thomas Charde, 1600.

Darby, Trudi L. 'The Date of William Rowley's *A Shoemaker, A Gentleman*'. *Notes and Queries* 53.1 (March, 2006). pp. 83–4.

Davies, Norman. *Vanished Kingdoms: The History of Half-Forgotten Europe*. London: Allen Lane, 2011.

De Belloy, Pierre. *A Catholicke apologie against the libels, declarations, aduices, and consultations made, written, and published by those of the League …* London: G. Robinson for Edward Aggas, 1585.

Dent, Arthur. *The opening of heauen gates, or The ready way to euerlasting life Deliuered in a most familier dialogue, between reason and religion, touching predestination, Gods word, and mans free-will, to the vnderstanding of the weakest capacitie, and the confirming of the more strong*. London: G. Eld for John Wright, 1610.

Derrick, John. *The Image of Ireland*. London: J. Kingston for John Day, 1581.

Desai, R. W. 'Seneca, Nero, Claudius I, Democritus, Christ, St. Paul, and Luther in *Hamlet*'. In *Shakespeare's Intellectual Background*. Edited by Bhim S. Dahiya. New Delhi: Viva Books, 2008. pp. 89–103.

Diehl, Huston. '"Strike All that Look Upon With Marvel": Theatrical and Theological Wonder in *The Winter's Tale*'. In *Rematerializing Shakespeare: Authority and Representation on the Early Modern English Stage*. Edited by Bryan Reynolds and William N. West. Basingstoke: Palgrave, 2005. pp. 19–34.

Dolan, Frances. *Dangerous Familiars: Representations of Domestic Crime in England 1550–1700*. Ithaca: Cornell University Press, 1994.

Dollerup, Cay. *Denmark, Hamlet, and Shakespeare: A Study of Englishmen's Knowledge of Denmark towards the End of the Sixteenth Century with Special*

Reference to Hamlet. Salzburg: Institut für Englische Sprache und Literatur, 1975.

Dollimore, Jonathan. *Radical Tragedy*, 2nd edition. London: Harvester Wheatsheaf, 1989.

Drayton, Michael. *Poly-Olbion*. London: Humphrey Lownes for M. Lownes, J. Browne, J. Helme, and J. Busbie, 1612.

Duffy, Eamon. 'Bare ruined choirs: remembering Catholicism in Shakespeare's England'. In *Theatre and religion: Lancastrian Shakespeare*. Edited by Richard Dutton, Alison Findlay and Richard Wilson. Manchester: Manchester University Press, 2003. pp. 40–57.

Durant, David N. *Bess of Hardwick: Portrait of an Elizabethan Dynast* (1977). London: The Cromwell Press, 1988.

Edwards, Ben. 'Reginald Bainbrigg, *scholemaister*, and his stones'. In *Archaeology of the Roman Empire: A tribute to the life and works of Professor Barri Jones*. Edited by N.J. Higham. Oxford: Archaeopress, 2001. pp. 25–33.

Eisenberg, Elizabeth. *This Costly Countess: Bess of Hardwick*. Derby: J.H. Hall and sons, 1985.

Emmerichs, Sharon. 'Shakespeare and the Landscape of Death: Crossing the Boundaries of Life and the Afterlife'. *Shakespeare* 8.2 (June 2012). pp. 171–94.

Escobedo, Andrew. 'From Britannia to England: *Cymbeline* and the Beginning of Nations'. *Shakespeare Quarterly* 59.1 (Spring 2008). pp. 60–87.

Espinosa, Ruben. *Masculinity and Marian Efficacy in Shakespeare's England*. Burlington: Ashgate, 2011.

Evans, Joan. *A History of Jewellery 1100–1870* (1953). New York: Dover, 1970.

Findlay, Alison. *Women in Shakespeare: A Dictionary*. London: Continuum, 2010.

Ford, John. *The Broken Heart*. Edited by T.J.B. Spencer. Manchester: Manchester University Press, 1980.

———. *Fames Memoriall*. In *The Nondramatic Works of John Ford*. Edited by L.E. Stock, Gilles D. Monsarrat, Judith M. Kennedy and Dennis Danielson. Binghampton: Medieval and Renaissance Texts and Studies, 1991.

———. *The Fancies Chaste and Noble*. Edited by Lisa Hopkins. In *The Complete Works of John Ford*. Edited by Brian Vickers. Oxford: Oxford University Press, forthcoming. III.

———. *Love's Sacrifice*. Edited by A.T. Moore. Manchester: Manchester University Press, 2002.

———. *Perkin Warbeck*. Edited by Peter Ure. London: Methuen, 1968.

———. *'Tis Pity She's a Whore*. Edited by Derek Roper. Manchester: Manchester University Press, 1997.

Foulweather, Adam. (Thomas Nash). *A wonderfull, strange and miraculous astrologicall prognostication for this yeere 1591*. London: Thomas Scarlet, 1591.

Foxe, John. *Actes and Monuments*. London: John Daye, 1583.

Freehafer, John. 'Shakespeare's *Tempest* and *The Seven Champions*'. *Studies in Philology* 66.1 (1969). pp. 87–103.

Gasior, Mary Ann Weber. *Thomas Heywood's The Four Prentices of London: A Critical, Old-Spelling Edition.* New York: Garland, 1980.

Gillies, John. 'Marlowe, the *Timur* Myth, and the Motives of Geography'. In *Playing the Globe: Genre and Geography in English Renaissance Drama.* Edited by John Gillies and Virginia Mason Vaughan. Cranbury, N.J.: Associated University Presses, 1998. pp. 203–29.

Golz, David. 'Diamonds, Maidens, Widow Dido, and Cock-a-diddle dow'. *Comparative Drama* 43.2 (summer 2008). pp. 167–96.

Gordon, John. *Emotikon or A sermon of the vnion of Great Brittannie, in antiquitie of language, name, religion, and kingdome.* London: Elliot's Court Press, 1604.

———. *England and Scotlands happinesse in being reduced to vnitie of religion, vnder our invincible monarke King Iames.* London: V. S[immes] for William Aspley, 1604.

———. *A panegyrique of congratulation for the concord of the realmes of Great Britaine in vnitie of religion, and vnder one king.* London: R. Read for Geoffrey Chorlton, 1603.

Goulder, Michael. *St. Paul versus St. Peter: A Tale of Two Missions.* London: SCM Press, 1994.

Greene, Robert. *Friar Bacon and Friar Bungay.* In *Five Elizabethan Comedies.* Edited by A.K. McIlwraith. London: Oxford University Press, 1934.

———. *James the Fourth.* Edited by Norman Sanders. London: Methuen & co., 1970.

Griffiths, Huw. 'The Sonnet in Ruins: Time and the Nation in 1599'. *Early Modern Culture* 6. http://emc.eserver.org/1-6/issue6.html.

Hakluyt, Richard. *The principal nauigations, voyages, traffiques and discoueries of the English nation made by sea or ouer-land …* London: George Bishop, Ralph Newberie, and Robert Barker, 1599–1600.

Hall, Joseph. *The honor of the married clergie, maintayned against the malicious challenges of C. E. Masse-priest.* London: W. Stansby for H. Fetherstone, 1620.

Haraway, Donna. 'A Cyborg Manifesto: Science, Technology, and Socialist-Feminism in the Late Twentieth Century' (1985). http://www.egs.edu/faculty/donna-haraway/articles/donna-haraway-a-cyborg-manifesto/

Harbus, Antonina. *Helena of Britain in Medieval Legend.* Cambridge: D.S. Brewer, 2002.

Harley, J.B. 'Meaning and ambiguity in Tudor cartography'. In *English Map-Making 1500–1650.* Edited by Sarah Tyacke. London: The British Library, 1983. pp. 22–45.

Harrington, John P., ed. *The English Traveller in Ireland.* Dublin: Wolfhound Press, 1991.

Harvey, Richard. *Philadelphvs, or A Defence of Brutes, and the Brutans History.* London: John Wolfe, 1593.

Hastings, Francis. *A watch-word to all religious, and true hearted English-men.* London: Felix Kingston for Ralph Jackson, 1598.

Helms, Lorraine. 'The Saint in the Brothel: Or, Eloquence Rewarded'. *Shakespeare Quarterly* 41.3 (autumn, 1990). pp. 319–32.

Heywood, Thomas. *The Foure Prentises of London*. London: Nicholas Okes for J. Wright, 1615.

Highley, Christopher. *Catholics Writing the Nation in Early Modern Britain and Ireland*. Oxford: Oxford University Press, 2008.

Hillman, Richard. *Shakespeare, Marlowe and the Politics of France*. Basingstoke: Palgrave, 2002.

———. *French Reflections in the Shakespearean Tragic*. Manchester: Manchester University Press, 2012.

Hindle, Steve. 'Imagining Insurrection in Seventeenth-Century England: Representations of the Midland Rising of 1607'. *History Workshop Journal* 66 (2008). pp. 21–61.

Hingley, Richard. *The Recovery of Roman Britain 1586–1906: A Colony so Fertile*. Oxford: Oxford University Press, 2008.

Hohnen, David. *Hamlet's Castle and Shakespeare's Elsinore*. Copenhagen: Christian Ejlers, 2000.

Holian, Heather L. Sale. 'Family Jewels: The Gendered Marking of Medici Women in Court Portraits of the Late Renaissance'. *Mediterranean Studies* (2008). pp. 148–73.

Holinshed, Raphael. *The first and second volumes of Chronicles comprising 1 The description and historie of England, 2 The description and historie of Ireland, 3 The description and historie of Scotland*. London: Henry Denham, 1587.

Holmes, Martin. *The Guns of Elsinore*. London: Chatto & Windus, 1964.

Hopkins, Lisa. *A Christopher Marlowe Chronology*. Basingstoke: Palgrave, 2005.

———. *The Cultural Uses of the Caesars on the English Renaissance Stage*. Burlington: Ashgate, 2008.

———. *Drama and the Succession to the Crown, 1561–1633*. Burlington: Ashgate, 2011.

———. *John Ford's Political Theatre*. Manchester: Manchester University Press, 1994.

———. 'The King's Melting Body: *Richard II*'. In *A Companion to Shakespeare's Works*, vol. II: *The Histories*. Edited by Richard Dutton and Jean E. Howard. Oxford: Blackwell, 2003. pp. 395–411.

———. 'Marrying the Dead: *A Midsummer Night's Dream, Hamlet, Antony and Cleopatra, Cymbeline* and *The Tempest*'. In *Staged Transgression in Shakespeare's England*. Edited by Edel Semple and Rory Loughnane. Palgrave Macmillan, 2013.

———. 'Paris is Worth a Mass: *All's Well That Ends Well* and the Wars of Religion'. In *Shakespeare and the Culture of Christianity in Early Modern England*. Edited by Dennis Taylor. New York: Fordham University Press, 2003. pp. 369–81.

———. *Shakespeare on the Edge: Border-crossing in the Tragedies and the Henriad*. Burlington: Ashgate, 2005.

————. '*The Comedy of Errors* and the Date of Easter'. *Ben Jonson Journal* 7 (2000). pp. 55–64.

————. *The Shakespearean Marriage.* Basingstoke: Palgrave Macmillan, 1998.

————. 'Touching Touchets: *Perkin Warbeck* and the Buggery Statute'. *Renaissance Quarterly* 52:2 (summer, 1999). pp. 384–401.

Horstmann, C. *The Early South English Legendary* I, *Early English Texts and Studies*, old series 87. London, 1887.

Huffman, Clifford Chalmers. *Coriolanus in Context.* Lewisburg: Bucknell University Press, 1971.

Hughes, Thomas. *Certaine deu[is]es and shewes presented to her Maiestie by the gentlemen of Grayes-Inne at her Highnesse court in Greenewich, the twenty eighth day of Februarie in the thirtieth yeare of her Maiesties most happy raigne.* London: Robert Robinson, 1587.

Hyland, Paul. *Ralegh's Last Journey.* London: HarperCollins, 2003.

Isaac, Megan Lynn. 'Structure, Legitimacy, and Magic in *The Birth of Merlin*', *Early Theatre* 9.1 (2006). pp. 109–21.

Ive, Paul. *The Practise of Fortification* (1589). Amsterdam and New York: Da Capo Press, 1986.

Jackson, Ken, and Arthur F. Marotti, 'The Turn to Religion in Early Modern English Studies', *Criticism* 46.1 (2004). pp. 167–90.

Janowitz, Anne. *England's Ruins: Poetic Purpose and the National Landscape.* Oxford: Basil Blackwell, 1990.

Jensen, Phebe. *Religion and Revelry in Shakespeare's Festive World.* Cambridge: Cambridge University Press, 2008.

Jones, Henry. *Saint Patricks purgatory.* London: Richard Rosyton, 1647.

Jones, William. *History and Mystery of Precious Stones.* London: Richard Bentley and son, 1880.

Jonson, Ben. *The Gypsies Metamorphosed.* In *Ben Jonson.* Edited by C.H. Herford and Percy and Evelyn Simpson. Oxford: The Clarendon Press, 1950. VII.

————. *Sejanus.* Edited by Philip Ayres. Manchester: Manchester University Press, 1990.

Joscelin. *The life of the glorious bishop S. Patricke …* Translated by Fr B.B. St Omer: (G Seutin?) for John Heigham, 1625.

King, Andrew. '"Howso'er 'tis strange … Yet it is true": The British History, Fiction and Performance in *Cymbeline*'. In *Shakespeare and Wales: From the Marches to the Assembly.* Edited by Willy Maley and Philip Schwyzer. Burlington: Ashgate, 2010. pp. 157–76.

King, Ros. *Cymbeline: Constructions of Britain.* Aldershot: Ashgate, 2005.

Kingshill, Sophia, and Jennifer Westwood. *The Fabled Coast: Legends and Traditions from around the Shores of Britain and Ireland.* London: Random House, 2012.

Kirke, John. *The Seven Champions of Christendom.* London: J. Okes for James Becket, 1638.

Klause, John. 'New Sources for Shakespeare's *King John*: The Writings of Robert Southwell'. *Studies in Philology* 98.4 (Fall 2001). pp. 401–27.

Koebner, Richard. 'The Imperial Crown of this Realm: Henry VIII, Constantine the Great, and Polydore Vergil'. *Bulletin of the Institute of Historical Research* 25 (1953). pp. 29–52.

Kott, Jan. *Shakespeare Our Contemporary.* Translated by Boleslaw Taborski. London: Methuen, 1965.

Krueger, Derek. 'The Religion of Relics in Late Antiquity and Byzantium'. In *Treasures of Heaven: Saints, Relics, and Devotion in Medieval Europe.* Edited by Martina Bagnoli, Holger A. Klein, C. Griffith Mann, and James Robinson. London: The British Museum Press, 2011. pp. 5–17.

Kunz, G.F. *Shakespeare and Precious Stones.* Philadelphia: J.B. Lippincott Company, 1916.

Kunz, G.F., and C.H. Stevenson. *The Book of the Pearl: Its History, Art, Science and Industry.* (1908) Mineola: Dover, 2001.

Kuzner, James. 'Unbuilding the City: *Coriolanus* and the Birth of Republican Rome'. *Shakespeare Quarterly* 58.2 (2007). pp. 174–99.

Kyd, Thomas. *The tragedye of Solyman and Perseda.* London: Edward Allde for Edward White, 1592.

Lambarde, William. *A Perambulation of Kent.* Introduced by Robert Church. Bath: Adams & Dart, 1970.

Lawrence, W.J. 'John Kirke, the Caroline Actor-Dramatist', *Studies in Philology* 21 (1924). pp. 586–593.

Lithgow, William. *Scotlands Welcome* ... Edinburgh: John Wreittoun, 1633.

Lloyd, Lodowick. *The consent of time* ... London: George Bishop and Ralph Newberie, 1590.

Lodge, Thomas. *A Margarite of America.* London: John Busbie, 1596.

Londré, Felicia Hardison. 'Elizabethan Views of the "Other": French, Spanish, and Russians in *Love's Labour's Lost*'. In *Love's Labour's Lost: Critical Essays.* Edited by Felicia Hardison Londré. London: Routledge, 1997. pp. 325–41.

Lorenzi, Rossella. 'Shakespeare's eye betrays rare cancer'. http://www.abc.net.au/science/articles/2006/03/02/1582326.htm.

Lovell, Mary S. *Bess of Hardwick.* London: Little, Brown, 2005.

Lupton, Julia Reinhard. *Afterlives of the Saints: Hagiography, Typology and Renaissance Literature.* Stanford: Stanford University Press, 1996.

———. 'Paul Shakespeare: Exegetical Exercises'. In *Religion and Drama in Early Modern England: The Performance of Religion on the Renaissance Stage.* Edited by Jane Hwang Degenhardt and Elizabeth Williamson. Burlington: Ashgate, 2011. pp. 209–32.

MacDonald Fraser, George. *The Steel Bonnets.* London: HarperCollins, 1995.

Machiavelli, Niccolò. *The Prince.* Translated by George Bull. Harmondsworth: Penguin, 1961.

MacKenzie, Clayton G. 'Paradise and Paradise Lost in *Richard II*'. *Shakespeare Quarterly* 37.3 (autumn, 1986). pp. 318–39.

MacMullan, Hugh. 'The Sources of Shirley's *St. Patrick for Ireland*'. *PMLA* 48.3 (September 1933. pp. 806–814.

Magnus, Albertus. *The boke of secretes of Albertus Magnus of the vertues of herbes, stones, and certayne beasts*. London: John King, 1560.

Magnus, Olaus. *Description of the Northern Peoples* II (1555). Translated by Peter Fisher and Humphrey Higgens. 3 vols. London: The Hakluyt Society, 1996.

Maguire, Laurie. *Shakespeare's Names*. Oxford: Oxford University Press, 2007.

Mancall, Peter C. *Hakluyt's Promise: An Elizabethan's Obsession for an English America*. New Haven: Yale University Press, 2000.

Marcellinus, Ammianus. *The Roman historie*. Translated by Philemon Holland. London: Adam Islip, 1609.

Marcus, Leah S. *Puzzling Shakespeare: Local Reading and its Discontents*. Berkeley: University of California Press, 1988.

Marlowe, Christopher. *The Complete Plays*. Edited by Mark Thornton Burnett. London: J. M. Dent, 1999.

———. *Hero and Leander*. In *The Collected Poems of Christopher Marlowe*. Edited by Patrick Cheney and Brian J. Striar. Oxford: Oxford University Press, 2006.

Marsden, Barry M. *The Early Barrow Diggers*. Stroud: Tempus, 1999.

Massinger, Philip. *The Renegado*. Edited by Michael Neill (London: Methuen, 2010).

Maxwell, J.C. 'Helena's Pilgrimage'. *The Review of English Studies* 20 (May 1969). pp. 189–92.

Maxwell, Julie. 'Counter-Reformation Versions of Saxo: A New Source for *Hamlet*?'. *Renaissance Quarterly* 57.2 (summer 2004). pp. 518–60.

Mayer, Jean-Christophe. '"This Papist and his Poet": Shakespeare's Lancastrian kings and Robert Parsons's *Conference about the Next Succession*'. In *Theatre and religion: Lancastrian Shakespeare*. Edited by Richard Dutton, Alison Findlay and Richard Wilson. Manchester: Manchester University Press, 2003. pp. 116–29.

McMullan, Gordon. *The Politics of Unease in the Plays of John Fletcher*. Amherst: University of Massachusetts Press, 1994.

Michel, J.Y. 'Monuments in Late Elizabethan Literature: A Conservatory of Vanishing Traditions'. *Early Modern Literary Studies* 9.2 (September, 2003). http://extra.shu.ac.uk/emls/09-2/michmonu.html.

Middleton, Thomas. *A Chaste Maid in Cheapside*. Edited by Alan Brissenden. London: Ernest Benn, 1968.

Milton, John. *Comus*. In *The Portable Milton*. Edited by Douglas Bush. Harmondsworth: Penguin, 1977.

Milward, Peter, S.J. *The Catholicism of Shakespeare's Plays*. London: Saint Austin Press, 1997.

Moffat, Alastair. *The Reivers*. Edinburgh: Birlinn 2008.

Monmouth, Geoffrey of. *The History of the Kings of Britain*. Translated by Lewis Thorpe. Harmondsworth: Penguin, 1966.

More, Thomas. *Utopia*. Translated by Paul Turner. Harmondsworth: Penguin, 1965.

Mulligan, Winifred Joy. 'The British Constantine: an English historical myth', *Journal of Medieval and Renaissance Drama* 8 (1978). pp. 257–79.

Nicholl, Charles. *The Reckoning: The Murder of Christopher Marlowe*. London: Jonathan Cape, 1992.

Norris, John. *Newes from Brest. A diurnal of al that Sir John Norreis hath doone since his last arivall in Britaine: also of the taking in of the forte by Croyzon, and the names of such captaines gentlemen and others that were slaine and hurte in this service*. London: Peter Short for Thomas Millington, 1594.

Ostovich, Helen. '"Here in this garden": The Iconography of the Virgin Queen in Shakespeare's *Richard II*'. In *Marian Moments in Early Modern Drama*. Edited by Regina Buccola and Lisa Hopkins. Burlington: Ashgate, 2007. pp. 21–34.

Owen, George. *The Description of Pembrokeshire*. Edited by Dillwyn Miles. Llandysul: Gomer Press, 1994.

Parker, Barbara L. '"Cursèd Necromancy": Marlowe's *Faustus* as Anti-Catholic Satire'. *Marlowe Studies* 1 (2011). pp. 59–77.

Patrides, C.A. 'Renaissance and Modern Views on Hell', *The Harvard Theological Review* 57.3 (July, 1964). pp. 217–36.

Patterson, Annabel. *Shakespeare and the Popular Voice*. Oxford: Basil Blackwell, 1989.

Persons, Robert. *A manifestation of the great folly and bad spirit of certayne in England calling themselues secular priestes Who set forth dayly most infamous and contumelious libels against worthy men of their owne religion, and diuers of them their lawful superiors, of which libels sundry are heer examined and refuted*. Antwerp: A. Conincx, 1602.

Petersson, R. T. *Sir Kenelm Digby, The Ornament of England, 1603–1665*. London: Jonathan Cape, 1956.

Pettegree, Jane. *Foreign and Native on the English Stage, 1588–1611*. Basinsgstoke: Palgrave, 2011.

Pilarz, Scott R., S.J. *Robert Southwell, and the Mission of Literature, 1561–1595: Writing Reconciliation*. Burlington: Ashgate, 2004.

Plunket Barton, D. *Links Between Ireland and Shakespeare*. Dublin and London: Maunsel & Co., 1919.

Pollard, Tanya. 'Enclosing the Body: Tudor Conceptions of Skin'. In *A Companion to Tudor Literature and Culture, 1485–1603*. Edited by Kent Cartwright. Oxford: Wiley-Blackwell, 2010. pp. 111–23.

Primaudaye, Pierre de la. *The French academie Fully discoursed and finished in foure bookes*. London: John Legat for Thomas Adams, 1618.

Pringle, Denys. 'The Houses of the Stewart Earls in Orkney and Shetland'. *New Orkney Antiquarian Journal* 1 (1999). pp. 17–41.

Pucci, Michael S. 'Reforming Roman Emperors: John Foxe's Characterization of Constantine in the *Acts and Monuments*'. In *John Foxe: An Historical Perspective*. Edited by David Loades. Burlington: Ashgate, 1999. pp. 29–51.

Roberts, Jeanne Addison. *The Shakespearean Wild: Geography, Genus, and Gender*. Lincoln: University of Nebraska Press, 1991.

Robinson, James. 'From Altar to Amulet: Relics, Portability, and Devotion'. In *Treasures of Heaven: Saints, Relics, and Devotion in Medieval Europe*. Edited by Martina Bagnoli, Holger A. Klein, C. Griffith Mann, and James Robinson. London: The British Museum Press, 2011. pp. 111–16.

Roebuck, Thomas, and Laurie Maguire. '*Pericles* and the Language of National Origins'. In *This England, That Shakespeare: New Angles on Englishness and the Bard*. Edited by Willy Maley and Margaret Tudeau-Clayton. Burlington: Ashgate, 2010. pp. 23–48.

Rowland, T.H. *Medieval Castles, Towers, Peles and Bastles of Northumberland* (1987). Morpeth: Sandhill Press, 1994.

Rowley, William. *A Shoemaker, A Gentleman*. Edited by Trudi L. Darby. London: Nick Hern Books, 2002.

———. *The Birth of Merlin*. London: Thomas Johnson for Francis Kirkman and Henry Marsh, 1662.

Russell, Miles. *Bloodline: The Celtic Kings of Roman Britain*. Stroud: Amberley Publishing, 2010.

Rutter, Tom. *Work and Play on the Shakespearean Stage*. Cambridge: Cambridge University Press, 2008.

———. *The Cambridge Introduction to Christopher Marlowe*. Cambridge: Cambridge University Press, 2012.

Ryan, Salvador. 'Steadfast Saints or Malleable Models? Seventeenth-Century Irish Hagiography Revisited'. *Catholic Historical Review* 91.2 (2005). pp. 251–77.

Salter, Mike. *The Castles and Tower Houses of Cumbria*. Malvern: Folly Publications, 1998.

Scafi, Alessandro. *Mapping Paradise: A History of Heaven on Earth*. London: The British Library, 2006.

Schnapp, Alain. *The Discovery of the Past: The Origins of Archaeology*. Translated by Ian Kinnes and Gillian Varndell. London: British Museum Press, 1996.

Schuman, Samuel. 'The Ring and the Jewel in Webster's Tragedies'. *Texas Studies in Language and Literature* 14 (1972). pp. 253–68.

Schwyzer, Philip. *Archaeologies of English Renaissance Literature*. Oxford: Oxford University Press, 2007.

Scot, Reginald. *The Discovery of Witchcraft*. London: Henry Denham for William Brome, 1584.

Scott, Thomas, trans. *The Spaniards perpetuall designes to a vniuersall monarchie. Translated according to the French*. London: 1624.

Serres, Jean de. *A General Inventory of the History of France*. Translated by Edward Grimeston. London: George Eld, 1607.

Severin, Tim. *The Brendan Voyage*. London: Arrow, 1979.

Shackelford, Jole. 'Documenting the factual and the antifactual: Ole Worm and public knowledge'. *Endeavour* 23.3 (1999). pp. 65–71.

Shakespeare, William. *A Midsummer Night's Dream*. Edited by Harold F. Brooks. London: Methuen, 1979.

———. *All's Well That Ends Well*. Edited by G.K. Hunter. London: Cengage Learning, 2007.

————. *As You Like It*. Edited by Agnes Latham. London: Methuen, 1975.

————. *The Comedy of Errors*. Edited by Stanley Wells. Harmondsworth: Penguin, 1972.

————. *Coriolanus*. Edited by G.R. Hibbard. Harmondsworth: Penguin, 1967.

————. *Cymbeline*. Edited by J.M. Nosworthy. London: Cengage Learning, 2007.

————. *Hamlet*. Edited by Harold Jenkins. London: Methuen, 1982.

————. *Henry IV, Part 1*. Edited by P.H. Davison. Harmondsworth: Penguin, 1968.

————. *King Henry V*. Edited by T.W. Craik. London: Routledge, 1995.

————. *King Henry VI, Part 1*. Edited by Michael Hattaway. Cambridge: Cambridge University Press, 1990.

————. *Henry VI, Part 2*. Edited by Michael Hattaway. Cambridge: Cambridge University Press, 1991.

————. *Henry VI, Part 3*. Edited by Michael Hattaway. Cambridge: Cambridge University Press, 1993.

————. *Henry VIII*. Edited by A.R. Humphreys. Harmondsworth: Penguin, 1971.

————. *Julius Caesar*. Edited by Norman Sanders. Harmondsworth: Penguin, 1967.

————. *King John*. Edited by E.A.J. Honigmann. London: Routledge, 1967.

————. *King Lear*. Edited by Kenneth Muir. London: Methuen, 1972.

————. *Love's Labour's Lost*. Edited by John Kerrigan. Harmondsworth: Penguin, 1982.

————. *Measure for Measure*. Edited by J.M. Nosworthy. Harmondsworth: Penguin, 1969.

————. *The Merchant of Venice*. Edited by W. Moelwyn Merchant. Harmondsworth: Penguin, 1967.

————. *Othello*. Edited by E.A.J. Honigmann. London: Thomas Nelson and Sons, 1997.

————, and John Fletcher. *Pericles*. Edited by Suzanne Gossett. London: Arden Shakespeare, 2004.

————. *Richard II*. Edited by Stanley Wells. Harmondsworth: Penguin, 1969.

————. *Richard III*. Edited by E.A.J. Honigmann. Harmondsworth: Penguin, 1968.

————. *Shakespeare's Sonnets*. Edited by Stephen Booth. New Haven: Yale University Press, 1977.

————. *The Tempest*. Edited by Virginia Mason Vaughan and Alden T. Vaughan. London: Thomas Nelson & Sons, 1999.

————, and John Fletcher. *The Two Noble Kinsmen*. Edited by Lois Potter. London: Thomas Nelson and Sons, 1997.

————. *The Winter's Tale*. Edited by J.H. Pafford. London: Methuen, 1963.

Shapiro, James. *1599: A Year in the Life of William Shakespeare*. London: Faber and Faber, 2005.

Shell, Alison. 'Divine Muses, Catholic Poets and Pilgrims to St Winifred's Well: Literary Communities in Francis Chetwinde's "New Hellicon" (1642)'. In

Writing and Religion in England, 1558–1689: Studies in Community-Making and Cultural Memory. Edited by Roger D. Sell and Anthony W. Johnson. Burlington: Ashgate, 2009. pp. 273–88.

———. 'Why Didn't Shakespeare Write Religious Verse?'. In *Shakespeare, Marlowe, Jonson: New Directions in Biography*. Edited by Takashi Kozuka and J. R. Mulryne. Burlington: Ashgate, 2006. pp. 85–112.

Shenk, Linda. *Learned Queen: The Image of Elizabeth I in Politics and Poetry*. Basingstoke: Palgrave Macmillan, 2010.

Shepard, Alan. *Marlowe's Soldiers: Rhetorics of Masculinity in the Age of the Armada* Burlington: Ashgate, 2002.

Shirley, James. *St Patrick for Ireland*. London: J. Raworth for R. Whitaker, 1640.

Shrank, Cathy. 'Civility and the City in *Coriolanus*'. *Shakespeare Quarterly* 54.4 (Winter 2003). pp. 406–23.

Sibley, Gertrude Marian. *The Lost Plays and Masques, 1500–1642*. Ithaca: Cornell University Press, 1933.

Simpson, Jacqueline. 'God's visible judgements: the Christian dimension of landscape legends'. *Landscape History* 8 (1986). pp. 53–58.

Smith, Wentworth. *The Hector of Germany. Or The Palsgrave, prime Elector*. London: Thomas Creede for Josias Harrison, 1615.

Sokol, B.J. *A Brave New World of Knowledge: Shakespeare's* The Tempest *and Early Modern Epistemology*. London: Associated University Presses, 2003.

Southwell, Robert. *Marie Magdalens funeral teares*. London: John Wolfe for Gabriel Cawood, 1591.

Speed, John. *The theatre of the empire of Great Britaine*. London: William Hall for John Sudbury, 1612.

Spenser, Edmund. *A View of the Present State of Ireland*. Edited by Risa Bear. http://darkwing.uoregon.edu/~rbear/veue1.html.

———. *The faerie queene*. London: Richard Field for William Ponsonbie, 1596.

———. *Ruines of Rome*. In *Poetical Works*. Edited by J. C. Smith and E. de Selincourt. Oxford: Oxford University Press, 1912.

Staines, John D. *The Tragic Histories of Mary Queen of Scots, 1560–1900: Rhetoric, Passions, and Political Literature*. Burlington: Ashgate, 2009.

Steen, Sara Jayne, ed. 'The Crime of Marriage: Arbella Stuart and *The Duchess of Malfi*'. *Sixteenth Century Journal* 22.1 (1991). pp. 61–76.

———. ed. *The Letters of Lady Arbella Stuart*. Oxford: Oxford University Press, 1994.

Steenbergh, Kristine. 'Bare Ruined Choirs: The Monastery as Heterotopia in Early Modern Drama'. In *The Reformation Unsettled: British Literature and the Question of National Identity, 1560–1660*. Edited by Jan Frans van Dijkhuizen and Richard Todd. Turnhout: Brepols, 2008. pp. 165–79.

Steggle, Matthew. 'Stonehenge'. *The Lost Plays Database*. http://www.lostplays.org/index.php/Stonehenge

Strachey, William. *The Historie of Travaile into Virginia Britannia*. London: Hakluyt Society, 1849.

Strong, Roy. *The Renaissance Garden in England*. London: Thames and Hudson, 1979.

———. 'Three Royal Jewels: The Three Brothers, the Mirror of Great Britain and the Feather'. *The Burlington Magazine* 108, no. 760 (July, 1996). pp. 350–53.

Sweeney, Anne R. *Robert Southwell. Snow in Arcadia: Redrawing the English Lyric Landscape, 1586–95*. Manchester: Manchester University Press, 2006.

Taylor, Gary. 'Shakespeare's Mediterranean *Measure for Measure*. In *Shakespeare and the Mediterranean*. Edited by Tom Clayton, Susan Brock and Vicente Forés. Newark: University of Delaware Press, 2004. pp. 243–69.

Thiselton Dyer, T.F. *Folk-lore of Shakespeare* (1883). http://www.sacred-texts.com/sks/flos/flos17.htm.

Traub, Valerie. 'Jewels, Statues, and Corpses: Containment of Female Erotic Power in Shakespeare's Plays'. In *Shakespeare and Gender: A History*. Edited by Deborah E. Barker and Ivo Kamps. London: Verso, 1995. pp. 120–41.

Trousdale, Marion. '*Coriolanus* and the Playgoer in 1609'. In *The Arts of Performance in Elizabethan and Early Stuart Drama: Essays for G.K. Hunter*. Edited by Murray Biggs, Philip Edwards, Inga-Stina Ewbank and Eugene M. Waith. Edinburgh: Edinburgh University Press, 1991. pp. 124–34.

Vanita, Ruth. 'Mariological Memory in *The Winter's Tale* and *Henry VIII*'. *Studies in English Literature, 1500–1900* 40.2 (Spring 2000). pp. 311–37.

Voragine, Jacobus de. *The Golden Legend*. Translated by Granger Ryan and Helmut Ripperger. New York: Arno Press, 1969.

Wallace, Jennifer. *Digging the Dirt: The Archaeological Imagination*. London: George Duckworth, 2004.

Waller, Gary. 'An Erasmian Pilgrimage to Walsingham'. *Peregrinations* 2.2. http://peregrinations.kenyon.edu/vol2-2/current.html.

Walsham, Alexandra. 'Holywell: Contesting sacred space in post-Reformation Wales'. In *Sacred Space in Early Modern Europe*. Cambridge: Cambridge University Press, 2005. pp. 211–36.

Warner, William. *Albions England* [1612] (Hildesheim: Georg Olms Verlag, 1971)

Wasson, John. 'The Secular Saint Plays of the Elizabethan Era'. In *The Saint Play in Medieval Europe*. Edited by Clifford Davidson. Kalamazoo: Medieval Institute Publications, 1986. pp. 241–60.

Webster, John. *The Duchess of Malfi*. Edited by John Russell Brown. Manchester: Manchester University Press, 1974.

Weever, John. *Ancient funerall monuments within the vnited monarchie of Great Britaine, Ireland, and the islands adjacent with the dissolued monasteries therein contained*. London: Thomas Harper for Laurence Sadler, 1631.

Weis, René. *Shakespeare Revealed*. London: John Murray, 2007.

Wilcox, Helen. 'Shakespeare's Miracle Play: Religion in *All's Well That Ends Well*'. In *All's Well, That Ends Well: New Critical Essays*. Edited by Gary Waller. London: Routledge, 2007. pp. 140–54.

Wilde, Oscar. *The Picture of Dorian Gray*. Harmondsworth: Penguin, 1984.

Willet, Andrew. *Tetrastylon papisticum, that is, The foure principal pillers of papistrie the first conteyning their raylings, slanders, forgeries, vntruthes ...* London: Robert Robinson for Thomas Man, 1593.

Williams, Glyn A. *Madoc: The Legend of the Welsh Discovery of America.* Oxford: Oxford University Press, 1979.

Wilson, John. *The English Martyrology ...* St Omer: English College Press, 1608.

Wilson, Richard. *Will Power: Essays on Shakespearean Authority.* Hemel Hempstead: Harvester Wheatsheaf, 1993.

———. *Secret Shakespeare: Studies in theatre, religion and resistance.* Manchester: Manchester University Press, 2004.

———. 'To great St Jaques bound: *All's Well That Ends Well* in Shakespeare's Europe'. In *Shakespeare et l'Europe de la Renaissance.* Edited by Yves Peyré and Pierre Kapitaniak. Paris: Actes du Congrès de la Société Française Shakespeare, 2004, http://www.societefrancaiseshakespeare.org/document.php?id=847

Wood, Christopher S. 'Maximilian I as Archeologist', *Renaissance Quarterly* 58.4 (winter 2005). pp. 1128–74.

Wood, Michael. *In Search of Shakespeare.* London: BBC Worldwide, 2003.

Woodcock, Matthew. *Fairy in* The Faerie Queen: *Renaissance Elf-Fashioning and Elizabethan Myth-Making.* Burlington: Ashgate, 2004.

Wynkfielde, Robert. Account of the execution of Mary, Queen of Scots. http://englishhistory.net/tudor/exmary.html.

Index

www.ingramcontent.com/pod-product-compliance
Ingram Content Group UK Ltd.
Pitfield, Milton Keynes, MK11 3LW, UK
UKHW020351010325
455677UK00021B/406